THE KINGDOM OF GOD AN⟨...⟩ **S0-ATF-143**

# THE KINGDOM OF GOD AND HUMAN SOCIETY

Essays by members of the
Scripture, Theology and Society Group

Edited by Robin Barbour

T&T CLARK
EDINBURGH

T&T CLARK LTD
59 GEORGE STREET
EDINBURGH EH2 2LQ
SCOTLAND


Copyright © T&T Clark Ltd, 1993

First Published 1993


ISBN 0 567 29228 2


British Library Cataloguing-in-Publication Data
A catalogue record for this book is available from the British Library

Typeset by Trinity Typesetting, Edinburgh
Printed and bound in Great Britain by Redwood Books, Trowbridge, Wiltshire

# Contents

# List of Contributors

Robin Barbour, who is retired, is Chairman of the Scripture, Theology and Society Group. He was Professor of New Testament Studies in the University of Aberdeen.

Mark Chapman is Lecturer in Systematic Theology at Ripon College, Cuddesdon.

Ronald Clements was Samuel Davidson Professor of Old Testament Studies in King's College, University of London, until his retirement in 1992.

William Horbury is University Lecturer in Hebrew, Old Testament and Intertestamental Studies and Fellow of Corpus Christi College, Cambridge.

Walter Houston is Tutor in Biblical Studies at Northern College, Manchester.

Paul Joyce is Lecturer in Biblical Studies in the University of Birmingham and Home Secretary of the Society for Old Testament Study.

John McGuckin is Lecturer in the Department of Theology in the University of Leeds.

Robert Morgan is University Lecturer in New Testament and Fellow of Lineacre College, Oxford.

John Muddiman is Fellow of Mansfield College, Oxford.

Lesslie Newbigin, who is retired, has served as Presbyter and

Bishop in the Church of South India, has worked with the International Missionary Council and the World Council of Churches, and has been on the staff of the Selly Oak Colleges.

John Riches is Professor of Divinity and Biblical Studies in the University of Glasgow.

Christopher Rowland is Dean Ireland's Professor of the Exegesis of Holy Scripture and Fellow of Queen's College, Oxford.

Philip West is Head of Science at Leeds Girls' High School.

Frances Young is Edward Cadbury Professor of Theology in the University of Birmingham.

# Introduction

## I

People who want to see the Christian Gospel make an impact on society are accustomed to a wide range of reactions from their contemporaries. Some think Christian belief irrelevant to the twentieth century, and indeed the ancient world and the world of the twentieth century are profoundly different in many ways — a state of affairs which has evoked a great deal of reflection in recent years. Others have wanted the Christian ethic without its dogma, a position which was more popular two generations ago than it is today, although it still seems to flourish in the attitudes shown by many parents towards religious education in schools. Others are sure that there is indeed a relevance, but have considerable difficulty in spelling out what it might involve and how it should be understood; and there are many in the Church or on its fringes who appeal, sometimes with desperate urgency, for help in their dilemmas from the Bible, from the Christian tradition, and from those who are believed to be expert in both.

All too often in recent years we have seen reports issued by the Churches on controversial topics — abortion, the ethics of capitalism, homosexuality, nuclear warfare, relations between the sexes — which have contained an introductory section on the biblical evidence followed by an argument which appears largely to ignore that evidence. So the criticism is heard that what actually controls the views of many Christians today, and especially of the so-called 'liberal consensus', is no longer the Scriptures, or Scripture-and-Tradition, but a *Weltanschauung* derived in large measure from the European Enlightenment of the eighteenth and nineteenth centuries, and only indirectly or incidentally influenced by specifically Christian themes and convictions.

ix

Biblical scholars who seek to practise the historical, critical and other methods associated with the Enlightenment have lived with situations of this kind for a long time; and if they are also committed to the daily life of the Church as members, ministers or priests they have felt the pressure in their own lives. 'Jesus said' we say in the pulpit; but did he? And if not, what do we say? 'The Church says'; 'the Bible says' — but do they really say that? And what does it mean for today if they do?

Further, the methods and findings of biblical scholars have tended in recent years to become more complex, more esoteric, less easy to convey to those outside the charmed circle of the initiated. In the fifties of this century the so-called Biblical Theology movement purported to have brought to birth an easily understandable and powerful consensus about the nature of the Bible and its message for the modern world; complaints were often heard from the biblical theologians and others that the ordinary practitioners within the Church, ministers, priests and teachers, were failing their hungry flocks by not making this assimilable theology, this coherent new understanding of the Bible, more readily available from the preacher's pulpit and the teacher's chair. But even as the complaints were being made the theology was crumbling from within. The Bible, we now see, contains not one central theology but many theologies, not one view on most controversial topics but several; and these diverse theologies are mostly incapable of being applied in any simple or straightforward manner to the situations of today.

But the conviction persists among biblical scholars that the Scriptures still have a word, and a powerful one, to speak to the people of today, and that their scholarly work is, as much as ever it was, the work of the Church. So it came about in the mid-eighties that a number of biblical scholars in Britain, mostly of the younger generation, responded to the challenge by creating a group which would try to see how their own work could be related more closely to the needs and demands of the Churches, and would aim to discover what the difficulties in the way of realising this objective really are. The group has given itself an ambitious title: Scripture, Theology and Society; it has met annually for an intensive weekend's work based on papers and reflections from its members. Over the last few years it has explored many themes and stimulated some valuable discussion and writing.

One question which the group has set itself to consider is this: how does the teaching in the Bible about the Kingdom of God illuminate and enable action on contemporary social and political issues? It was in response to this that a member of the group, Professor James Dunn of the University of Durham, gathered a number of people in the north-east of England to examine ways in which God's Kingdom or rule in the world might be discerned in things which were happening in that area. The result was a volume edited by him and entitled *The Kingdom of God and North-East England* (London, 1986). The present volume, containing essays written by other members of the group, constitutes a response of another kind. It is an attempt to clarify some of the varied teaching in the Bible on what God's Kingdom or rule really means, so that as the third Christian millennium approaches we may begin to formulate a new biblical and theological understanding of God's rule in his world that will be adequate for the needs of a new age.


## II

It cannot escape notice that the question as formulated above, with its reference to 'the teaching in the Bible about the Kingdom of God', seems to assume what was denied in an earlier paragraph, namely that there are areas in which one can still refer to 'the biblical teaching' on a given subject, and that if so this is one of them. The use of the word 'teaching' may also contain some hidden, and undesirable, assumptions. We try to have as few preconceptions as possible; we can only find out whether the question is tenable in its present form by examining the relevant material. At least we can say that the Kingdom or rule of God in or over the world — and beyond it — is on any account of the situation quite central for Christian apologetic and proclamation. Deism is not on our agenda, for it cannot be denied that in the whole of the Bible — or in virtually all of it — God is one who acts, and acts by ruling or controlling, however much the *God who Acts* of biblical theology in the fifties (title of a monograph by G. E. Wright (London,

1952)) may have proved to be a chimera. The questions for us are (1) how was he conceived of as acting by the biblical authors? and (2) how can he be coherently conceived of as acting today? — in both cases with central reference to the analogies provided by the actions of a king or some other similar authority. The essays which follow form a series of attempts to give answers to the first question, with some sporadic and preliminary attention paid to the second. Answers to the second are something which we hope will follow in another volume or volumes.

It remains to add a few comments on this theme of the Kingdom of God. Those who are familiar with the main outlines of the history of biblical scholarship in the last century and a half know how central a theme it has been, especially in the study of the New Testament. For those who are not, it is perhaps enough here to say that discussion has revolved around a number of foci: is God's Kingdom to be thought of as a future state of affairs on earth, to be brought about by human effort in accordance with his will and the gift of his Spirit (the type of view often associated with the names of Ritschl, Rauschenbusch and others — see chapters 6, 7 and 9 below); or does it properly connote a future mighty act of God, a catastrophic change in the order of things, to which human beings can contribute little or nothing except an attitude of prayerful expectancy — here the name of Johannes Weiss is the most important, with those of Albert Schweitzer (chapter 8, below), Karl Barth and others? Is it an evolutionary or an apocalyptic, a this-worldly or an other-worldly concept? Or both? What are we to make of the obvious centrality of the phrase in Jesus' teaching and preaching in the first three Gospels, when set alongside the equally obvious fact that it is largely absent from the Fourth Gospel and the Pauline letters? Do the latter somehow supersede the former? All three — Synoptics, John, Paul — are in our New Testament. Again: how are we to understand Jesus' parables of the Kingdom? That debate is far from over, even if it is only touched on at a few points in the following pages. Granted that the phrase is, in its New Testament uses, often to be understood against an apocalyptic background, how did such apocalyptic hopes and expectations influence the political and social attitudes of the early centuries of our era? And how they should they do so today? The questions multiply; and they demand answers, both as historical questions and as questions which impinge on our contemporary problems.

Rather than attempting to provide systematic answers at this stage it seemed right to present the essays which follow as a report on work in progress. We hope to stimulate many to carry the investigations, and the whole enterprise, further. It is the King's business; his love for all his people, be it kingly or queenly, and his right of sovereignty, be it kingly or queenly too, humbly yet imperially exercised through and in all his people, alike demand an urgent response.

## III

It is perhaps right to add some brief reference to the contributions which follow.

Lesslie Newbigin gives an opening programmatic statement. He analyses Jesus' preaching and teaching about the Kingdom of God in the light of the centrality of the resurrection, and states a position which will be in part filled out and confirmed, in part questioned, in the essays which follow.

Ronald Clements, Walter Houston and Paul Joyce present aspects of the pictures of God's rule found in Old Testament attitudes to the poor, in the book of Isaiah, and in the Psalms: God's kingship is mediated, but also distorted, by human kingship; his rule of righteousness demands a righteous response. In an essay covering the Old Testament, the intertestamental literature and the New Testament, William Horbury stresses the close relationship between the Kingdom of God, the kingdom of Israel and the other kingdoms of this world.

There follow four contributions which discuss what the Kingdom of God has meant and means in recent research about Jesus. Robert Morgan traces the story from H. S. Reimarus in the eighteenth century to the present day. Mark Chapman pays particular attention to ethical and social questions in the same debates, and Philip West looks again at Albert Schweitzer's *The Quest of the Historical Jesus.*

Two papers about Jesus come next, one about his ministry

and one about his resurrection. John McGuckin looks at three aspects of the story of the ministry as it is told in the Synoptic Gospels which throw light on Jesus' understanding of God's rule or Kingdom. John Muddiman examines the relation of the resurrection to the coming of the Kingdom. Christopher Rowland then examines the politics of the gospels, and reflects, as does John Riches in his concluding contribution, on the ways in which eschatological and apocalpytic ideas found in the New Testament, which we can no longer take literally, nevertheless can have a vital place in forming our ethical and social attitudes. Frances Young reminds us that although explicit language about the Kingdom of God is rare in Paul it does occur and can point, along with other material in his letters, towards an attitude to the world, and to God's rule in it, which we can share today.

Readers will be able to detect some common themes. The Kingdom or rule of God is not to be seen in its fullness, but it can be discerned in today's world, and it is as vital as ever it was to discover how it can be discerned. A new way has to be found, and is being found, between the 'this worldliness' which asserts that God's rule can and must come in its plenitude on earth, and the 'other worldliness' which denies this. There are of course other common features. But there are also varieties, questions, dilemmas and problems ahead. One of the biggest questions still is: can we ever construct any kind of key or code or framework of biblical principles or axioms which will enable a host of differing issues (war, sex, genetic engineering, euthanasia, pollution, etc., etc.) to be dealt with in a systematic way or along broadly similar lines, or does the variety and the out-of-dateness of the biblical material necessarily imply that no general or generalizing codes or criteria can ever be applied as we seek to discern God's rule, and his will, in specific issues today? Are the biblical scholars now telling the Christian ethicists and writers on social issues that systematic expositions like those of the past can no longer be achieved or even attempted? Does our modern understanding of the poetic and metaphorical nature of much biblical language now make systematic theology itself, as traditionally understood, a thoroughly questionable exercise? And can we find any new light on the old questions about how to relate the Old and the New Testaments in our quest for guidance on burning issues?

The Scripture, Theology and Society Group tries to confront these and many other similar questions. If any of our readers have reflections to offer, or suggestions to make about work which could be taken up, let them send them to us.

Robin Barbour

# The Kingdom of God and Our Hopes for the Future

## by Lesslie Newbigin

The one thing we certainly know about the future is that we do not know. Our personal futures, and the futures of our nation, our civilisation, our world are hidden from us. But we cannot help trying to probe the unknown. We can try, on the basis of past and present experience, to forecast the future. Our ability to do so has recently been vastly increased by the development of computer science. 'Futurology' is a burgeoning science. Yet what is most striking is its record of failure. In spite of more and more sophisticated techniques for forecasting, the surprising and the unpredictable still play a major part in experience. Books such as Toffler's *Future Shock* were proved wrong almost before the print was dry. We must continue to do the best we can by way of extrapolation from past and present experience, but we must recognise that our ability to forecast is narrowly limited.

But human beings have always added another ingredient to their view of the future: hope. But what exactly is hope, if it is something different from rational expectation? Most of my ministry has been conducted in the Tamil language, and it was not long before I realised that there is really no word in that language for hope. When I discussed this with my (Hindu Brahmin) teacher I began to realise the ambivalence of this English word. From the point of view of my teacher, hope was merely wishful thinking. Things will be what they will be: why should we wish to be deceived by our desires? What is hope, other than a strong desire that the future will be what we wish it to be? Does the normal use of the word in English have any greater weight than that?

This led me to look again at the use of the word 'hope' in the New Testament. Hope is spoken of as one of the great abiding realities. It is described as 'a sure and steadfast anchor of the soul, a hope that enters into the inner shrine behind the curtain, where Jesus has gone as forerunner on our behalf' (Heb. 6.19). Here hope is clearly more than mere desire; it has a factual basis. It is founded upon what has been done, and therein revealed, in events which are a matter of record.

Hope so understood is also rational expectation. The difference between this and the 'rational expectation' of the scientific futurologists is not that reason operates in one case and something other than reason in the other. A great deal of confusion is caused by the habit of positing 'reason' and 'revelation' as alternative ways to the truth. There is no grasping of truth except by the exercise of reason. The difference is not in respect of the human faculty involved but in respect of the data regarded as a rational expectation about the future based upon what has happened in the past. The difference between this and (for example) the 'rational expectations' of an Alvin Toffler is a difference in regard to the view of what data are significant.

The hope of which the New Testament speaks is avowedly one which extends beyond this present life. It is based upon the fact that Jesus has 'entered into the inner shrine behind the curtain' — the curtain that hides from us everything that is beyond death. The Christian hope is born at the point where the resurrection of Jesus from the dead is acknowledged — not as an isolated phenomenon, but as the validation and fulfilment of that which had been made known of God through the history of Israel (Luke 24.27). The resurrection of Jesus was not an event blazoned publicly through the world to amaze and convince the unbelievers; it was a secret entrusted to those who had been chosen and prepared beforehand to understand it. It is the assurance to them, and through them to others, that this world does not have the last word; that things are not what they seem. It authorises a scepticism regarding the wisdom of this world. It makes possible a life of radical dissent. It makes it possible to believe that things are as they are, not because God wills it so, nor because he is unable to cope with the world's evil, but because he is merciful and patient. It makes it possible for 'rational expectations' to be founded on more than the sorry tale of human blindness and sin. It provides an Archimedean point beyond the world of normal experience from which it is possible to exercise leverage upon this world. It looks towards 'new heavens and a new earth' with a confidence in which it is possible to be both realistic and hopeful about this present world.

Two distortions have always threatened this Christian hope. It can be, and has constantly been, privatized. It has been understood as hope for the individual soul rather than hope for the world. This distortion goes very deep into the life of the Church. It is one symptom of a persistent distortion which interprets election as election to privilege; which thinks that those chosen as witnesses of the resurrection were chosen to be its beneficiaries rather than its trustees; which supposes that being a Christian confers a privileged status before God. This persistent and pervasive error has to be refuted again and again. The 'sure and steadfast hope' is hope for the world, not just hope for the individual soul. It is hope for, and eager expectation of, the gift of the holy city into which all the nations will bring their treasures.

The second way in which the apocalyptic hope of new heavens and a new earth is distorted is by conceiving it as authorising contempt for this world. It can be, and has been, thought to authorise a negative view of this world, its natural beauty, its rich cultural achievements, and its many joys and pleasures — a view more akin to Manicheeism than to the Bible. But this is a total distortion. Perhaps the point can best be made by considering the Christian hope first in relation to the person. Whatever our beliefs, we know that our life in this world must come to an end. It is possible to live without any belief in anything beyond death, possible therefore to think that one must experience as much as possible of the enjoyments this world affords while there is time. It is not clear that this leads to the best and happiest kind of human life. It is also possible to live in the sober recollection that life in this mortal body is not the end of the matter, and that we are to live in the hope and expectation of a fuller life in God's own good time. The effect of such belief is not to cause the believer to treat his present life, the care of his bodily health, the discharge of his human responsibilities and the exploration of the riches of creation with contempt. It may indeed lead to a certain modesty in one's expectations of happiness. It may lead to a recognition that there are limits, sometimes severe limits, to what can be achieved and enjoyed within one human life. But those who have lived in this faith testify that it has not involved an impoverishment of their life, but an enrichment.

The whole of the preceding discussion assumes that both the death and the resurrection of Jesus were events in history. It also assumes that these events, in their actual historical context of the whole story of Israel, are of decisive significance as data from which rational conclusions are to be drawn about the human situation and the human prospect. It is a widespread belief of contemporary western culture that these assumptions cannot be made, that — in particular — while the death of Jesus was an event in history, the resurrection was not, at least not in the same sense. It is agreed that as a matter of fact people came to believe that Jesus had risen from the dead, but it is taken for granted that the stories of resurrection are the result of this belief, not that the belief is the result of the events told in the story. These assumptions are a natural part of the fundamental character of this particular culture, which — in contrast to the cultures which have been predominant in history and are still widely dominant — assumes a sharp dichotomy between an inward and private world of personal experiences, personally chosen values and beliefs, and an outward and public world of accepted facts. The death of Jesus belongs to the latter world, the stories about the resurrection to the former.

To anyone who has worked as a foreign missionary, seeking to communicate the Gospel in a culture shaped by other assumptions, this is a familiar strategy for the handling of the gospel story, depriving it of its power to challenge cultural assumptions by domesticating it within the culture. One observes in the Indian world a precisely parallel domestication of the gospel story by making Jesus simply one of the many recurring manifestations of divinity in a world whose nature is interpreted on the analogy of the ever-circling wheel. With regard to this particular way of dealing with the story of the resurrection there is here only space for two brief remarks. Firstly, it is of course obvious that the story of the empty tomb and the risen Lord cannot be fitted into the assumptions which govern our culture. It can only make sense as the starting point for a wholly new way of understanding reality. That is indeed the whole point. The Christian tradition has recognised only one event comparable to what happened on the first Easter morning, namely the event of creation itself. The resurrection of Jesus is the beginning of a new creation. It is as incomprehensible as the coming into existence of a universe when there was nothing. But it is — or can be — the starting point of a way of understanding and coping with reality as a whole (including the reality of death) which is more rational than one which accepts the reigning assumptions of our contemporary culture. And, secondly, one must say a word about the idea that the Christian belief about the resurrection of Jesus was the result of the impact made upon the first disciples by the personality, ministry and mission of Jesus, a mission which ended in death. It must be said bluntly that this is a myth created by the supposed necessities of 'modern' thought as they appeared to nineteenth century liberals. The only available evidence which we have points to a quite different explanation. Unless we are simply to construct history out of imagination, we must accept that the belief of the first Christians that Jesus had overcome sin and death was a conclusion drawn from the resurrection, and accordingly reject the idea that the story of the resurrection was a consequence of their belief.

Christian believing, as I understand it, is the venture of faith (which is always the response — strong or feeble — to the prior initiative of God) that the long story of happenings which has its climax in the resurrection of the crucified Jesus provides the clue by following which one may be led into a progressively more adequate understanding of the real world and away from the illusions which are created by our undisciplined desires. These happenings are of course always interpreted happenings, and Christian believing starts from the interpretations of those who were the most immediate participants and witnesses. We therefore turn to the New Testament, and especially to the Gospels, not expecting to find the *ipsissima verba* of Jesus, but to find the most authoritative interpretations of the *verba* and *gesta Christi* by those who had the immediate task of interpreting them in their varieties of situations. But these different interpretations have a recognisable centre in the one story of the one man Jesus — his ministry, death and resurrection — and a sufficient coherence amply to justify their acknowledgment by the Church from very early times as 'canon'. So I turn to the evidence of the New Testament regarding the Christian hope for the world, a hope which is not merely desire but also rational expectation.

The teaching of Jesus about the Kingdom of God, as it is given in the Gospels, is not reducible to simple uniform affirmations. It is essential to take seriously the tensions between different words of Jesus on the subject, and not to try to reduce them to a single formula.

In the first place, and most obviously, Jesus speaks of the kingdom in both present and future tenses. Many sayings speak of the kingdom as already present (e.g. Matt. 11.12; 12.28; Luke 10.9; 17.21). Others speak of it unambiguously as future (e.g. Matt. 6.10; 13.47-50; 16.28; 20.21; 26.29; Luke 13.29).

In the second place, there are texts which speak of the kingdom as imminent, 'at the door' (e.g. Mark 1.15; 9.1). Many other passages, covering a substantial part of the total body of teaching, imply a considerable period of time before the coming of the kingdom. These might be grouped into three types:

(a) The passages which speak of the gathering in of the Gentiles as the necessary precondition for the coming of the kingdom. This is explicit, for example, in Matt. 24.14 and Mark 13.10-13. It is also implicit in the fact that Jesus both foretells the ingathering of the nations and at the same time confines the mission of the Twelve to the house of Israel (cf. Matt. 8.11f. with 10.5f.).

(b)  The large parts of the teaching which describe the way in which the disciples of Jesus are to live in the world. The material gathered together in the 'Sermon on the Mount', for example, implies that the disciples will have to go on living in a world where there are still quarrels and lawsuits, where there are still daring thieves and arrogant soldiers, where the just and the unjust still go on living side by side in the same world.

(c)  The words of Jesus at the Last Supper clearly imply the expectation of a continuing earthly life in which the disciples will eat and drink together as they had done with Jesus in the days of his flesh.

In the third place, there is a tension between the texts which suggest that the coming of the kingdom is to be preceded by recognisable signs and texts which affirm that the hour of its coming is unknown even to the Son, and known only to the Father (cf. Mark 13.28f. with 13.32f.).

Many attempts have been made to rationalise or remove these apparent contradictions, whether by discarding the texts which do not conform to the preferred interpretation, or by attempting to interpret one set of texts so as to bring them into harmony with those that seem to contradict them.

Thus, for example, the attempt has been made to take as determinative the texts which speak of the kingdom as an imminent future event. Jesus' teaching is understood as one more example of apocalyptic expectations which proved to be mistaken. Jesus was (in this view) wrong in his central announcement, and the Church has had to come to terms with this fact, abandoning the idea of a future coming in glory (at least for the foreseeable future) and settling down to living in the world on the assumption that things will go on without fundamental change. In spite of the fact that Jesus was mistaken in the main thrust of his message, nevertheless his teaching and example can still inspire us, as they inspired Albert Schweitzer to devote his life to the service of the sick in Africa.

Alternatively, the whole emphasis may be placed upon the sayings which speak of the kingdom as already present. 'Realised eschatology' is the clue to understanding. The result in practice is very much the same as that of the apocalyptic interpretation:

there is no significant future history after Jesus: we are in the kingdom now and we learn from Jesus how its citizens should behave. This conclusion seems to receive support (albeit negatively) from the fact that innumerable prophecies of the End, based on the alleged presence of the 'signs', have been falsified by events. The conclusion seems to many unavoidable: whatever may have been the expectation of Jesus, Christians living nineteen centuries later cannot in any realistic sense look forward to an end to history such as the New Testament seems to suggest.

The practical problem which remains is that purposeful action is only possible if one has some sense of its context, of the story of which one is a part, of where we have come from and where we are going. Purposeful action is action which looks to the future and therefore requires some vision of the future and its possibilities, some horizon of expectations. C. H. Dodd summarises the contemporary meaning of Jesus' teaching on the kingdom in the following words: 'The world becomes the scene of a divine drama in which the eternal issues are laid bare. It is the hour of decision. It is realised eschatology.' (*The Parables of the Kingdom* (1935) p. 198). But 'decision' is meaningless unless it is decision between alternative courses of action, and no course of action can be plotted except with the help of some map of the terrain, some concept of the goal. The same problem arises in respect of Bultmann's existentialist interpretation of the teaching of Jesus.

The New Testament writers all seem to think in terms of a real goal, a real end to history, a consummation to which we look forward and which is 'nearer to us now than when we first believed' (Rom. 13.11). This is true even of the Johannine texts which, in spite of their strong evidence of commitment to a 'realised eschatology', nevertheless speak emphatically of a future consummation (e.g. John 6.39f.; 12.48; 1 John 3.2). It is this which provides the horizon for purposeful action. And when this fades from view (as it has in fact faded in the history of the Church), two substitutes are available (apart from the purely naturalistic, cyclical view of human events which has perhaps been that of the majority of humankind).

One alternative is a view of the future shaped by an evolutionary, progress-oriented vision. Hope is then pinned to the vision of a perfect human society at some future date in history. We have become familiar with various forms of this intra-mundane eschatology in the past 200 years. It evokes little belief today except among Marxists living under non-Marxist governments. Its defects are obvious. It tends inevitably to marginalise the human persons now living, treating them as expendable in view of the glory to be revealed to their descendants. It distorts the relations between old and young in society. It tends to lead in the end to a widespread denial or diminution of the rights of individual human persons.

The other alternative, much more prevalent in contemporary churches, is a privatised eschatology which pins all hope to the vision of a life of personal blessedness after death. This has the effect of encouraging the old to withdraw from the responsibilities of public life, viewing it at best as a training ground for personal virtue. One notable expression of this in the Protestant world is the lack of interest in the communion of saints, the disappearance of prayers for the dead, and the assumption that those who have died have no continuing relationship with or concern for the on-going history of the human family of which they are a part.

This privatised eschatology fits well with the mood of a society which has lost faith in a meaningful future for the public life of the world — the world which we share with all our fellow human beings.

I believe that if we are willing to take into account all the differing emphases of the teaching of Jesus about the kingdom and not feel obliged to slacken its internal tensions by various rationalising strategies, we are given a perspective in which purposeful action is possible, a horizon towards which we can move hopefully. The following, I think, are elements in such a perspective.

1.    Jesus is Lord. The kingship of God has become a credible reality by what Jesus is, has done and has taught. To put it otherwise: the reality against which all purposes will be tested and by which all actions will be finally judged to have succeeded or failed is no longer unknown. It is known to us in the concrete human person, career and teaching of Jesus.

✦

2.   The heart of Jesus' teaching about the kingdom is not merely a call to decision in the abstract, but a call to act in certain ways which correspond to the nature of God's kingly rule. It is a call to do God's revealed will on earth as it is done in heaven.

3.   There is therefore a continuing history after Jesus in which the Church is to learn, step by step, what this will entail. This learning is inseparable from the mission of the Church to all the nations by which they are to be gathered into the kingdom and to bring 'all that the Father has' under the allegiance of Jesus (John 16.13-15). This on-going teaching will be the work of the Spirit who is the Spirit of the Father and the Spirit of Jesus.

4.   This on-going history is not, however, a smooth ascent which leads gradually to 'the kingdom of God on earth'. Such a vision of future history (*post Christum*) is precluded by the events of Jesus' career. The ministry and teaching of Jesus do not lead to a chain of events in which the will of God visibly prevails over the powers that oppose it. They lead to rejection, failure and death. That this death is in truth the victory of God is a secret revealed only to those chosen to be witnesses of it. They are in turn told in the plainest terms that their path into the future will be the same as his — the way of the cross. But they are assured that as they follow this way to the end, they will become the inheritors of the victory of the kingdom.

What vision of future history does this give us? Not, as I have said, the progressive realisation of 'the kingdom of God on earth'. There is no discernible path leading steadily upwards towards a society of perfect peace, justice and fellowship. The vision of the perfect society beckons us, and is promised as a gift from God. Of the trustworthiness of this promise, the resurrection of Jesus from the dead is the pledge. But the path into the future disappears from our view. Every human life comes to an end before the end of the whole human story — the story of which every life is a part. Every human project directed to the goal of a just and peaceful society becomes at some point distorted and corrupted by human sin and is eventually (mercifully) buried under the rubble of later history.

The road ahead disappears below the horizon. But the disciples of Jesus can still follow it with confidence, because Jesus has gone that way, has gone down into that chasm which hides the future from our view, and has been raised as the pledge and first-fruit of a new age beyond death and the dissolution of the cosmos. Jesus in fact is himself the way, and the disciples of Jesus can stick to it knowing that as they do so they are not lost — even though the future is unknown. The goal lies beyond but it is sure. We have the pledge of it in the resurrection of Jesus, and the first taste of it in the gifts of the Spirit.

5.    The pattern of cross and resurrection precludes any purely this-worldly eschatology. But this does not authorise or excuse what has been common in contemporary Christian thinking, namely the alliance of a (proper) otherworldliness with an (improper) privatisation of hope. The Christian hope is not merely hope for the soul, but hope for the world. If we say, as we must, that the horizon for purposeful action cannot be a putative earthly utopia at some date in the future, we have also to say that the horizon cannot be the death of the individual. The true horizon — if we follow the New Testament — is expressed in the words: 'He shall come again in glory to judge the living and the dead.' With that as the horizon, as the future to which I direct my energies, purposeful action becomes possible and hopeful. I know the one who will finally assess what I do. And this 'doing' is of course in the public field of politics, economics and culture as much as in the more private world of intimate personal relations. The sundering of these two, and the suggestion that action in one sphere is to be directed by the revelation in Christ but not in the other, is simply one of the illusions of contemporary western culture. The human being is one person whether at home or at work, and there is one judge of all his deeds. Whether at home or at work, I am part of one human family and of one world of nature. My story is part of the wider story and cannot be understood apart from it. The true horizon to which I must direct my energies can only be that which is the horizon for the story as a whole. It cannot be a private horizon.

6.   The tensions in the teaching of the New Testament about the kingdom are not, therefore, to be rationalised away. The kingdom is both present and future. It is present in that, through the total work of Jesus, we are given here and now the foretaste, the first-fruit, the *arrabon* of its grace and peace. It is future in that the story of which our lives are a part, the story of creation and of the human family, is not a meaningless and mindless pantomime but a movement directed towards a real goal, a real event in which it becomes clear that something has been accomplished which makes all the agony and conflict worthy of our participation as rational and moral beings. That goal, that accomplishment, which forms the proper horizon for purposeful action, is in one sense known and in another sense not known. It is known in that in Jesus we have seen the one in whom all human and cosmic history is in the end to find its coherence. Therefore where he is present, the end is at hand. Our true horizon beckons here and now. It is here, at the very door. But in another sense the goal is not known. It is, according to a saying which surely cannot have been invented by the Church, unknown even to Jesus. In all this tangled web of good and evil which makes up the human story, only the Father knows what possibilities for good remain, what further frontiers remain for the human family to cross, what further opportunities for new good remain. Only he knows when and how to bring the story of his creation to its completion.

For the practical business of discipleship the implications of this knowing and not knowing are clear. We know the one who is to come, but we do not know when and how he will come. Therefore 'you must be ready, for the Son of Man is coming at an hour you do not expect' (Luke 12.40).

# 2

# Poverty and the Kingdom of God — an Old Testament View

## by Ronald Clements

I. *The Poor in Ancient Israel*

When we look at the general social conditions that are reflected in the Old Testament it becomes clear that, in general terms, we should have to describe them as standing very close to the subsistence level. There were undoubtedly many people living in conditions of severe poverty, and, although it is only in times of exceptional hardship, such as that of military siege (cf. Lam. 2.11-12), that we read of people dying in large numbers of hunger, this cannot have been a particularly rare occurrence. Serious undernourishment and its attendant illnesses must have been commonplace and the effects of hunger were clearly the most evident consequences of the general level of very limited prosperity that most of the population enjoyed in Old Testament times. Other painful effects, such as the possibility that a poor person would possess only a single garment with which to keep warm (cf. Exod. 22.26; Amos 2.8) and might, if dispossessed of this, die of cold, are certainly envisaged. As to the general extent of a person's other possessions, the quality of the house or tent in which he or she lived and the amount of money or other capital that might be owned, we can only surmise that these were usually very meagre indeed. Certainly this was dramatically so when compared to the situation of those that we should term 'poor' in most modern western societies.

At the same time it is very noteworthy in the biblical situation that, over against the poor, there were some who were rich and whose enjoyment of their relative wealth was all the more obvious and exemplary because they cannot have been all that numerous. By comparable standards of wealth and poverty that we are familiar with, those that are held up to scrutiny in the writings of the Old Testament were unlikely to have been exceptional.

A number of factors flow from these very general observations that lend to the biblical literature a special interest in respect of what it has to say regarding wealth and poverty. It draws particular attention to the contrasting destinies which such distinctions could bring and to the power that could be exercised by the rich over the poor.

The lack of any great level of material wealth on the part of large numbers of people is also shown up in other aspects of the literature of the Old Testament. One of these is the fact that in its legislation laws protecting property and the right of property ownership are only developed to a very limited degree. The general directive 'You shall not steal' (Exod. 20.15) is forced to serve a wide variety of situations. Along with this we can note that, such were the vicissitudes of life, even those who were relatively wealthy would have been very conscious of the uncertain security that their prosperity brought to them. The rich could find that, all too suddenly, they had been reduced to poverty (cf. 1 Sam. 2.7-8). It must also have been the case that the threat of drought and a consequent famine, the onset of an insect plague, the ravages of frequent war, and the disastrous effect if the senior breadwinner should die prematurely, were all factors that could plunge those who had a modest subsistence level into a situation of fatal ruination. Even for the rich, poverty was never far away, certainly in the local sense and possibly in a temporal one also.

All of this suggests that we could easily look back upon the fact of poverty in Old Testament times simply as a reflection of the stage of development to which the science of agriculture had attained at this time. This, coupled with the general conditions of human existence, would be sufficient to explain why there were many 'poor' in biblical times. The poverty of ancient Israel reflects the productivity levels possible in the light of the general knowledge of agriculture available at the time. When we add to this the sharp contrasts that are to be found in both the soil and climate of the region it was inevitable that some should grow up to be poor and others rich.

Such, however, is clearly not the whole story, since these factors, which are so obvious to us, were not at all clear to the people of the time who relied on more religious concepts of blessing and welfare (Heb. *shalom* = 'peace, wellbeing'). They were, nonetheless, very well aware that, quite apart from such broad factors which they could not very readily have changed, there were others which belonged intrinsically to the social structures of their patterns of life. There were therefore certain classes of person who were assumed to be poor as a consequence of their social situation. They are repeatedly pointed to as typical and representative of those who stood in need of special consideration. Their poverty was to some degree 'institutionalised', since they are persons who found themselves in impoverished circumstances relative to others through no special fault of their own. Such persons are the widow, the orphan and the alien (cf. Lev. 19.10; 23.22; Job 29.12-13; Isa. 10.2). We could add to this list the position of the Levite in the book of Deuteronomy, whose lack of any territorial possession demanded that he too should be given special consideration (cf. Deut. 12.18-19; Lev. 25.35-46).

It is not difficult to see that, with these classes of person, a number of very obvious factors would have occasioned the impoverished circumstances in which they were placed. Widows, precisely because they were women, as well as orphans who were thought of as still not adult, would have lacked the physical strength to perform the heavy tasks that work on the land demanded. They were assumed to be unable to work the fields effectively, although just as important as this lack of physical strength (since in many communities women do much of the work in the fields) was a very uncertain situation regarding the ownership of land and property. Alongside these factors, and perhaps outweighing both of them, was the apparent fact that such women would have lacked the support of a strong and respected male group around them, and so would have found themselves to be easy prey to exploitation and being defrauded.

The circumstances that might have led to an alien from another community seeking to establish himself in Israel would have varied considerably. Former slaves, fugitives from oppressive labour service, and those accused of various crimes, could all have found themselves forced to seek refuge in an alien community where their presence would not have been readily welcomed. They too were likely to be targets of exploitation precisely because they could not easily protect their interests.

It is the presence of these groups in ancient Israelite society which has undoubtedly occasioned the greatest degree of attention as indicative of a class of those who were 'poor', and it is they who are most frequently mentioned as illustrative of the victims of poverty. This must be taken to indicate not merely that their condition was significantly worse than that of others, but that their situation was more or less looked upon as permanent. They were the 'poor' who were likely to remain in Israel, even when the general level of national prosperity was greatly increased (cf. Deut. 15.7-11, with the cautionary comment in v. 4).

It is certainly a significant feature of the Old Testament legislation, and of the prophetic protests against poverty, that the poor in general, and especially the three classes of impoverished citizens indicated, were very vulnerable to exploitation by more fortunately placed persons. As so often in history the 'rich' could take advantage of the poor. How they were able to do so is made explicit at a number of points. In the first place the poor could easily become the victims of legal manipulation. Through false charges and the use of perjured evidence the poor could easily be defrauded of justice. Bribery too appears to have been rife, as it has apparently been endemic to many human societies. By such manipulation of the processes of law unscrupulous moneylenders, landowners, or even better placed neighbours, could wrest from the poor what little they possessed. All of this took place because such persons did not have the power, and in some cases the entitlement, to establish effective representation of their cause in courts of law. Their cases went by default.

A second cause of exploitation appears to have been the practice of debt-slavery in which persons were compelled to sell either their own services or that of their family, or even both, in order to pay off debts (cf. Deut. 15.12-13). Such debts could become unmanageable precisely on account of the exorbitant rates of interest charged. In an economy where bad harvests were commonplace and the ravages of invading armies a further hazard it seems likely that even a reasonably industrious peasant farmer with a small holding of land could fall foul of such a system. Such a practice of usury meant that an ever-tightening grip of exploitation could be placed upon a citizen so that the situation quickly dropped beyond all normal routes of recovery. The gradual spread of the use of silver weights as a form of money-exchange also suggests that the economy of ancient Israel was never in a very stable condition. Values of land, cattle feed, and of food generally, could fluctuate wildly.

The passages in Isa. 5.8-9 and Mic. 2.1-5 further suggest that Israel suffered from the existence of two different, and to some degree competing, systems of land tenure. The older tribal tradition, reflected in the system of Jubilee, allowed for tribal holdings to be held in common and for a periodic reallocation of each family's holding. No permanent sale of the land could take place (cf. Lev. 25.29-34). In the walled (Canaanite) cities, however, land could be sold in perpetuity, and this may also be taken to suggest that the sale of land was a much more frequent and commonplace action. In this too, therefore, the opportunities for unscrupulous persons to take advantage of another's temporary difficulties must have been considerably increased.

Nor should we leave out of our reckoning the frequently noted warning against removing a neighbour's (border) landmark. The warnings are sufficient to show that such a form of stealing of land cannot have been all that unusual.

Taken together, this body of evidence from the Old Testament may be sufficient to show that there existed in ancient Israel a general concern for the alleviation of the consequences of poverty as an undesirable condition for any member of the people of God. More specifically there was a very widely recognised awareness that such poor persons, and especially widows, orphans and immigrant aliens, were vulnerable to even more damaging exploitation by more fortunate fellow-citizens.

## II. *Welfare Systems in Ancient Israel*

The fact that poverty was a recognised, and virtually permanent, condition for many in ancient Israel inevitably called forth concern from legislators and prophets alike, and demanded various kinds of welfare action in order to alleviate its worst consequences. In many ways the most prominent method of attempting to deal with the situation was the most obvious one. This was simply to appeal to other citizens to recognise the wretchedness of such a plight and to urge an attitude of charitableness and conscientious concern. 'Charity' in the form of a relatively indeterminate and spontaneous response to need was upheld as a form of divine service. Helping the poor was a sign of regard for God. In the book of Deuteronomy in particular there is a very distinctive emphasis placed upon the need to remember that one's own ancestors had been slaves in Egypt and had been savagely exploited there. So a kind of fellow feeling for the poor was inculcated which it was hoped would encourage a generous and unstinted willingness to think of helping the poor as a normal part of life. In a very interesting passage dealing with the release of those who had served a period as debt-slaves (Deut. 15.10), the biblical legislator affirms that the slave's owner should, when releasing him, furnish him generously out of his own flocks and herds so as to make it possible for such a freed person to make a new start. The very presence of such a rider to the law and the recognition of such a need show just how very difficult it was for the poor person ever to escape effectively from the trap into which he, or she, had fallen. Poverty clearly had the effect of removing most of its victims from participation in any normal pattern of social life and property ownership. Only with great difficulty and much public goodwill does it appear that such a person was likely to recover from the state into which he, or she, had fallen.

It could be thought that this appeal to public compassion and generosity was the best and most effective way of dealing with the problem of poverty. It might, alternatively, be looked upon as the weakest and least helpful of the solutions that could be considered. It was all up to the individual and his, or her, responsiveness to the situation. We do not have any very clear indications whether this appeal was satisfactorily heeded, or largely ignored. It seems probable that, at best, it was only able to deal with the worst cases. Who may actually have starved to death in ancient Israelite society, while others around had food to spare, we do not know. The prevalence of the appeal suggests that many did suffer in this way.

The Old Testament, however, does contain evidence of what we might describe as a 'social welfare' system, even though it was only in a very rudimentary state. We can note a number of pointers to such a system. Prominent among these was an awareness of the special plight, and extra vulnerability, of women who were widowed. This situation is highlighted in the case of Ruth and we can see different ways in which the problem is given attention in the book. Simplest among the remedies noted is that the widow should return to live with her kinsfolk, from whom she had become separated by her marriage outside the family (cf. Ruth 1.8-14). This is what Orpah does and what Ruth is advised to do.

Clearly a more satisfactory solution would be for the widow to remarry and thereby acquire fresh support from her husband and his kin-group to fend off the dangers of exploitation. This is eventually what Ruth manages to do, but the wiles she has to resort to in order to achieve this end show that it may not usually have been a very attractive solution. This presumably was due to a reluctance on the new husband's part and the considerations affecting such a choice were probably related to the lack of a wedding dowry and the liabilities such a woman might bring.

The practice of allowing gleaning at harvest time, which is also referred to in the book of Ruth (Ruth 2.1-23; cf. Lev. 23.22), shows how certain charitable conventions could become something of an institution in order to assist the poor. It is noteworthy that in Deuteronomy the presentation of tithes to the Levites is looked upon as a comparable form of institutionalised charity, although this cannot have been its true origin (Deut. 14.27, 29). It was essentially a way of giving back to God some of the living substance that he had first given.

The return of a widow to her parental family in order to find support among them illustrates the importance of the extended family as the chief support group for persons who were suddenly plunged into poverty. This points us to the great significance for any study of poverty in Old Testament times of the tensions that arose between the larger social unit represented by the 'father's house' and the much smaller unit that appears to have operated as the norm on the smallholdings of the cities. Tensions between tribal society and urban society, even allowing for a considerable mix between arable farming and sheep-farming, must all have contributed towards worsening the plight of the poor. As arable farming, and the urban life that went with it, flourished so it would seem that its appeal to offer greater wealth was combined with far greater risks for the poor.

There are clearly other residual elements of a kind of welfare system operating in ancient Israel which the Old Testament brings to our attention. Most to the forefront is the rather strange practice of levirate marriage, which was clearly designed to provide support and protection for a widow who had lost her husband before mature male heirs had been born and who could, by this practice, be incorporated into the dead husband's family.

The introduction of a system of land tenure which entitled a woman to inherit and farm a family estate can also clearly be seen as a means of dealing with the poverty that would otherwise befall a woman with no husband (Num. 27.1-11). What remains unclear in regard to such a right of a woman to inherit property is the extent to which it also, at the same time, provided any means of effective representation of such a woman in the processes of law. As we have noted, without a strong male voice in public legal proceedings, it seems that many citizens in ancient Israel were easily exploited. It would seem therefore that the right of a woman to inherit may sometimes have been a rather hollow one if the means were not at the same time granted to ensure that such a woman could protect her rights in a law court. This simply highlights the problem that is already shown up by the Deuteronomic law concerning the release of a person enslaved for a set period of years. On gaining freedom, in accordance with the requirements of the law and assuming that these were honoured, the release would often simply leave the freed person with little option but to return to slavery, unless he could obtain sufficient capital to eke out a living.

We may note that two other features relating to the ownership and use of land contain elements of what we can describe as a primitive welfare system. The first of these was the practice of observing a year of Jubilee when all land transactions would be cancelled and a return to a form of original ownership upheld (Lev. 25.8-28). There are many obscurities in understanding how this could actually have worked in practice. In any case there were obviously sufficient exceptions to its implementation (cf. Lev. 25.29-30) to indicate that it probably did little to lessen the impact of immediate and dire situations of impoverishment. The rise of debt-slavery in Israel, and its continuance well into post-exilic times, points to a situation in which such a system of observing a Jubilee in order to avoid permanent alienation from property ownership offered little real alleviation of the problem.

Much the same must undoubtedly be said of the protection of family entitlement to property as a permanent feature of the family inheritance. This would appear to have been a deeply felt concern and is illustrated by the story of Naboth's vineyard (1 Kings 21.1-16). It was obviously an attractive way of protecting the interests of the family as a whole, and the same may be said of granting certain specified privileges to the nearest kinsman when land came up for sale. This situation is well illustrated by the story of Jeremiah's purchase of a field in Anathoth (Jer. 32.1-15).

Overall, by protecting the ownership of land and seeking to ensure that every opportunity was offered for it to remain permanently within the control of one family, efforts were made to establish some kind of secure capital base on which a family could support itself. The rise and prevalence of debt-slavery shows that it worked in only a very partial fashion and signally failed to prevent a significant number of persons falling so heavily into debt that slavery for themselves and their families was the only path left to them if they were not to starve.

Judging from the book of Ruth the same would appear to have been true of women who were widowed, especially early in life. The entire purpose of the story appears to be to highlight the case of a young woman (Ruth) whose entry into the social structures of Israelite society was about as marginal as could be conceived. She is of alien origin, living in an alien land, and would normally be expected to seek protection among her own former kinsfolk. She, however, maintains to the fullest extent her obligations and loyalties to her kin-group achieved through marriage. In turn those of her kinsfolk are seen to fall down one after the other in showing a comparable degree of loyalty to her, until she forces their hand. The plot of the story therefore hinges on the limited and inadequate protection afforded by those conventions of welfare and assistance which Israelite society had adopted. It would appear that, in the end, the poor tended to remain poor in spite of practices designed to remedy their predicament. Again and again, if we are to judge from the strictures of the prophets, the appeal to show compassion towards the poor was the primary weapon with which it was hoped that some lessening of their unenviable plight was to be achieved.

### III. *Blessed are the Poor*

We come now to consider how the experience of poverty in Old Testament times came to be linked with that of the Kingdom of God. Essentially the contention is made that it is as an aspect of his kingly rule that God himself fulfils the role of a compassionate fellow-citizen and looks after the cause of the poor. The special vulnerability of aliens, widows and orphans is even uniquely singled out as a matter to which he pays particular attention. We may cite Ps. 146.9:

> The LORD watches over the aliens,
> he upholds the widow and the fatherless;
> but the way of the wicked he brings to ruin.

This is then followed in the next verse by the affirmation that the Lord reigns for ever. A very similar conjunction of the idea of the kingly rule of God with that of a unique care and provision for the needs of all creatures is maintained in Ps. 145.16-20. After affirming the eternal nature of God's kingdom in v. 13, the psalmist proceeds to combine this with the notion of a beneficent and all-pervasive order extending throughout creation. In this fashion the theme of world order, which would appear to have had its roots in wisdom concepts, appears in close connection with ideas of justice and righteousness. This connection between natural, moral and political realities formed part of a scheme of what has been termed cosmic righteousness and world order. It clearly had an important bearing on the political realm where the earthly king reigned as the vice-gerent and representative of God.

This bringing together of ideas relating to a divine compassion for the poor and a special responsibility for their welfare with ideas concerned with justice and righteousness maintained through the political order appears only to have been reached at a relatively late stage in ancient Israel. What we discover when we look at the broader spectrum of ideas concerning divine rule and the experience of poverty is that they were frequently to be found in considerable tension with each other. It can then be argued that it was precisely on the basis of the experience of this tension that this more ideal vision of a divine kingdom in which the welfare of the poor was given an especially prominent place took its origin.

We may draw attention to a number of salient features which may be held to be broadly true, even where many of the details remain confused. In the first place we may draw attention to the fact that it was especially the responsibility of the king to maintain a just and law-abiding social order. Nowhere is this more clearly brought out than in Ps. 101. We may take it as certain that this is a pre-exilic royal psalm, to be spoken by the king, in which the royal obligation to uphold justice and righteousness is forcibly and clearly expressed:

No man who practises deceit
    shall dwell in my house;
no man who utters lies
    shall continue in my presence (Ps. 101.7)

What is striking is that the king is not simply to maintain a system of justice (i.e. a community-wide system of law), but is to ensure that truth and integrity may flourish. Clearly such affirmations were not wholly devoid of being something of a propaganda exercise on the part of the monarchy, but they were undoubtedly far more than this. They expressed something deeply rooted in the ideology of kingship and its responsibility for putting an end to the brigandage, corruption and uncontrolled violence which must constantly have threatened much ancient society. The advent of kingship in the ancient Near East was very closely intertwined with the arrival of concepts of territorially based systems of law such as we find in the great law codes. The institution of kingship claimed to administer justice in the name of God, and undoubtedly sought to implement such a claim by setting up systems of legal administration and by introducing codes of legal practice for the use of judges and officials.

It is especially important to note that this claim that human kingship could serve as an agency for the upholding of a just social order was presented as having its foundations in the divine realm. Human kingship was seen as an extension of the divine order and human systems of justice were looked upon as a bringing down to earth of a divine justice. Nowhere is this more clearly evident than in the Babylonian sphere where, at the head of Hammurabi's law code, the god Shamash is portrayed as handing down to his earthly representative (Hammurabi) the tablets of law.

In similar vein the opening lines of the Babylonian Creation Story (*Enuma Elish*) present the period before the world began as a time when no knowledge of the mystery and authority of kingship was found on earth. Kingship itself, with all that this was taken to imply about a knowledge of the divine way of doing things, was not known until it was disclosed to humankind by the king of the gods.

It is this close interlocking of a human system of kingship, however strongly supported by claims concerning its divine origin, with the human administration of the state, and especially of its basis of law, which brought tensions in Old Testament times. However much kings boasted of their maintenance of justice and welfare for all their subjects, as exemplified in Ps.

101, it was very difficult in practice for them to back up such claims with real achievements. Rather the opposite appears often to have been the case and the impact of monarchy upon the social order was far from being generally beneficial. Instead of lessening the burden of poverty from the poor the opposite appears usually to have been the case. The poor were made poorer. Moreover it may be argued on the basis of the rather piecemeal evidence from the Old Testament that the effect that kingship had upon the poor in ancient Israel was rather to 'institutionalise' their plight. By this I am suggesting that the position of the poor, already weak and vulnerable, was made even more weak and vulnerable and became almost impossible to change.

The reasons why this came about were various, but are not too difficult to trace from what we learn from the Old Testament prophets and from what we read between the lines of the Pentateuchal laws. We can readily set in the forefront here the quite unequivocal declaration made by Samuel of the manner of kingship that Israel would find itself burdened with (1 Sam. 8.11-17). The theme is simply 'He will take . . .; he will take . . .; he will take . . . — and you will cry out!'. The concern of kings for other aspects of kingly estate, with elaborate palaces and an extravagant lifestyle, would ensure that kings took from both rich and poor alike. Regrettably this has been the way of kings throughout much of human history.

Just as relevant to an understanding of the biblical notion of justice, however, is the evidence of resistance and hostility which we find expressed in the Old Testament to the encroachment of kings upon the administration of justice. So often, even where the aims of the royal court may have been honourable and good, the achievements of the officials who administered the law were lamentable. Power was placed in the hands of men who were susceptible to corruption, and who blatantly favoured the rich at the expense of the poor. Such experiences would appear to lie behind the strictures of Amos (Amos 5.11-12; 6.4-7). In this way the very claim of the monarchy to offer a new, and better, system of justice than that upheld through the protection of the kin-group proved hollow and ruinous. No system of law intended to protect the weak and vulnerable could work effectively unless those who administered it were free from corruption.

From other passages of the Old Testament, however, there are further indications that the kingship, with its claims to mediate a realm of divine order and justice, failed to do so. These concern the administration of land, where passages such as Isa. 5.8-9 and Mic. 2.1-5 point us to recognise that the take-over of land administration by the urban centres, backed by the authority of the king, could result in a gross deprivation of the rights of the poorer citizens. The very system of legality and justice which the crown represented could become a system of injustice! As the power of the urban communities grew, so was the power of the rural communities impoverished and weakened.

It may also be suggested that, under the legal arrangements which operated in ancient Israel, the royal court stood to benefit from action taken against wealthy citizens. Fines imposed upon such persons fell to the royal exchequer and properties confiscated after a successful prosecution became a possession of the crown. Such at least is the picture that is presented through the salutary story of Naboth's vineyard (1 Kgs. 21.1-16).

What this picture presents us with is something of a conflict of ideologies. The idea of divine power and love necessarily pointed to a deep conviction that a compassionate God would use his power to watch over the cause of the poor and defenceless. The very arguments which urged a charitable regard for the poor on the part of fellow-Israelites did so in the conviction that this action mirrored the concern of God. Against this, however, was an ideology built upon the notion of a just social order in which the king, and the administration of which he was the head, occupied the central position. As was almost inevitable, given all that we know of all human social structures, the reality so often fell far short of the ideal. The kingship, claiming to mediate the kingly rule of God, became an agency of exploitation and oppression. Almost certainly in the post-exilic period, when the governmental administration of Judah was in the hands of officials operating under the oversight of foreign (Persian, Greek and later Roman) rulers, the situation worsened.

It is in this context that we must understand the special emphasis that appears in the late Psalms 145 and 146 upon the kingdom of God as an everlasting and wholly just realm of order and peace. Within it a particular stress is placed upon the divine compassion for the poor, and a special protection of their interests. Inevitably it contrasts the notion of divine kingship with that of a kingly rule administered through human beings. The one has come largely to be felt and seen as the opposite of the other. In origin, however, this was not the case. The roots of a notion of kingship in which the human political order was looked upon as a channel for the divine have undergone a radical transformation. The divine kingly order transcends that of the human, standing over and above it and, where necessary, even threatening to replace it. It leaves a picture of human society which is in a perpetual state of becoming. It points to a richer, more just and more compassionate divine order which it seeks to embody and establish. At the same time it remains fully aware of the unsatisfactoriness of what is actually experienced in the world and seeks continually to change and overcome this so that it may conform to the true divine pattern of justice and order.

## BIBLIOGRAPHY

C. Boerma, *The Rich, the Poor — and the Bible* (London, SCM, 1979)

D. E. Gowan, 'Wealth and poverty in the Old Testament', *Interpretation* 41 (1987), pp. 341-353.

B. Lang, 'The social organisation of peasant poverty in biblical Israel,' *Anthropological Approaches to the Old Testament* ed. B. Lang (London, SPCK, 1985) pp. 83-99.

N. W. Porteous, 'The care of the poor in the Old Testament,' *Living the Mystery. Collected Essays* (Oxford, B. H. Blackwell, 1967) pp. 143-155.

H. E. von Waldow, 'Social responsibility and social structure in early Israel', *CBQ* 32 (1970), pp. 182-204.

# 3

# The Kingdom of God in Isaiah: Divine Power and Human Response

## by Walter Houston

In every age the people who put their trust in the Lord of history have experienced tension, often agonising, between their hope as people of God and the rational expectations which they have felt able to entertain for the social world which they have inhabited. They have adopted various means of resolving the tension. Through much of Christian history, the world has been seen as a place of soul-making: it is a temporary home, our real destiny is in heaven, and consequently there is no reason to do much to overcome the world's imperfections, for it is destined in any case for destruction. Conversely, many in the modern liberal tradition have seen it as the Christian's responsibility to 'build the Kingdom of God on earth', which seems to leave no room for the work of God himself.

The solution, or rather the expression, of this tension traditionally given by Christians of the Reformed tradition to which I belong is more finely balanced. The full reality of the Christian hope, of the Kingdom of God in the full sense, is a matter of the world to come: however, even in this present age, the moral characteristics of life under the sovereignty of God — faith, love and righteousness — can be expressed in a practical way in human society. The world is corrupt, but not so corrupt that under the rule of the 'saints' it cannot exhibit justice. Therefore it makes sense for Christian people to struggle to transform the world in which they live so that it may conform more closely to the kind of world which God requires and is bringing into being.[1]

Now any view that claims to be Christian must be able to show how it stands in continuity with the Old and New Testaments. It must be rational and arise from real experience, but at the same time be intelligible as a reading of the biblical tradition. That does not mean that we have in the Bible a theological system or a set of axioms which have only to be applied to our experience. No-one who reads the Bible with unprejudiced eyes can imagine that we have. Rather, it offers us a multitude of stories and pictures and poems, works of the imagination which shape the imagination of the faithful readers and mould the way in which they view their experience and their situation and understand the world in which they live. It is in this informal way, via the faithful imagination, that the Bible guides the development of theological systems and axioms which govern belief and action.

I think it is worthwhile to look briefly at one major source in the Bible of the imaginative shaping of Christian hope, to see to what extent it supports the Reformed view that I sketched above and what it offers to fuel our imagination who need to hope, but dare not expect.

There can be no question about the central place held by the book of Isaiah in the development of Jewish and, especially, Christian doctrines of a future hope. No-one who ever goes to church in Advent can be unaware of how passages from Isaiah, usually described as Messianic, such as 9.2-7; 11.1-9; 40.1-11; 60 or 62, have shaped the Christian imagination. If Christians have applied them in great part to the past events of the life of Jesus of Nazareth, they have done so in the consciousness that they are interpreting those events as the consummation of the story of Israel which itself foreshadowed the consummation of world history.

---

[1]Nicholas Wolterstorff, in *Until Justice and Peace Embrace.* (Grand Rapids: Eerdmans 1983) argues persuasively (pp. 3ff.) that in its origins Calvinism was a 'world formative' type of Christianity: it wished to remake the world and not simply individual souls.

But it would be a mistake to think of this simply as a perverse Christian interpretation imposed on some isolated passages. The application to Jesus is of course distinctively Christian, some would say arbitrarily; but the implied character of the book of Isaiah as a book about the future God has in store for his people is firmly grounded in the text itself. Anyone who takes the trouble to read through the book must be struck by the number of passages which one might describe as portraits of the goal God is aiming for: a just, peaceful and prosperous human community. They are in the first chapter and the last and perhaps as many as a score in between, though not evenly spread. Here are references to the more obvious ones: 1.24-28; 2.2-4; 9.2-7; 11.1-9; 14.1f.; 16.4b-5; 25.6-8; 29.17-24; 30.19-26; 32.1-8, 15-20; 33.17-24; 35;49.14-23; 54.1-5, 11-17; 60; 61; 62; 65.17-25; 66.7-14, 18-24. Many of these passages, however, are closely connected with their context. It would be worth anyone's while who wishes to follow my argument closely to read through not only these passages but the whole book.

In many respects these passages are extremely varied. They differ first in the symbolism used. The greater number are centred on the idea of Zion as the holy hill or holy city, where God's presence is known: 1.24-28; 2.2-4; 25.6ff.; 33.20ff.; 49; 54; 60; 62; 65.17-25; 66.7ff. But some use a Messianic imagery, where the central figure is the righteous king. This is true of 9.2-7; 11.1-9; 16.4f.; 32.1-8; 33.17; 61.1-3.[2]

Some passages foresee that God's kingdom will ultimately embrace all nations without distinction, for example 2.2b-3; 25.6; possibly 66.18-21. Others place foreign nations in a subordinate position to Israel — 60.10a; 61.5f.; or call attention, like the last verse of the book, to the ultimately necessary exclusion of all who will not accept the kingship of the Lord.

Some readers may be wondering just what sense it makes to take the book of Isaiah as a whole as our field, since biblical scholarship has shown that the book comes from at least two prophets separated by at least a hundred and fifty years — as if

---

[2]For 61.1-3 see J. H. Eaton: *Festival Drama in Deutero-Isaiah* (London: SPCK, 1979), pp. 90f.

we were to try to explain Marlowe's *Faustus* and Goethe's *Faust* as a single work because someone had happened to publish them in one volume (as has actually been done).

The analogy is inaccurate. Certainly the book of Isaiah is composite. It contains the work of far more than two authors or speakers. But scholars are coming to recognise that there is nevertheless a unity in the book; it has been put together as a single work, and shows signs of conscious artistry in the way it has been put together out of a great number of individual pieces.[3] And for our present purposes the historical background of the individual pieces can often be ignored; not because they are not important in themselves, but because we are looking at an aspect of the book which transcends the immediate historical situation out of which it emerged. The visible reign of God is announced in response to individual historical situations of oppression or injustice. But it is never a narrowly political concept. It is expressed in broad and even cosmic terms, and clothed in a rich imagery much of which is derived from the festival worship of the Jerusalem temple which celebrates the yearly renewal of God's goodness.[4] It is not tied to the situation but expresses a continuing tradition which the people of God in every age can read as addressed to them, and understand in terms of the realities of their own age.[5]

It is a further encouragement to do so that most of the passages are quite unspecific about the timing of their

---

[3] See especially R. Lack: *La Symbolique du Livre d'Isaïe* (Rome: Biblical Institute Press, 1973); B. S. Childs: *An Introduction to the Old Testament as Scripture* (London: SCM Press, 1979), pp. 325ff.; R. Rendtorff: *The Old Testament: an Introduction* (ET London: SCM Press, 1985 (German 1983)), pp. 198ff.

[4] J. H. Eaton, 'The Isaiah tradition', in *Israel's Prophetic Tradition*, ed. R. Coggins and others (Cambridge: University Press, 1982), pp. 58ff.

[5] Childs, op. cit., p. 327; W. J. Houston: 'Today in your very hearing: some comments on the Christological use of the Old Testament' in *The Glory of Christ in the New Testament* ed. L. D. Hurst and N. T. Wright (Oxford: Clarendon Press, 1987), pp. 37ff. Robert Alter, in *The Art of Biblical Poetry* (New York: Basic Books, 1985), p. 141, sees this effect as grounded for prophecy in general in the use of poetry as such as a vehicle: 'the form of the speech exhibits the historical indeterminacy of the language of poetry, which helps explain why these discourses have touched the lives of millions of readers far removed in time, space and political predicament'.

expectations. 'In days to come' (2.2)[6] is a characteristic phrase. However, in chapters 40–55 the emphasis lies on what God is *now* doing to restore his people and glorify his name: an idea which is open in a different way to being read as addressed to the reader's own age. When in 56ff. we find expressions like 'my deliverance is *close at hand*' (56.1), or '*At its appointed time* I the LORD will bring this swiftly to pass' (60.22), this has often been seen, in a diachronic view of the text, as an adjustment by disappointed hearers of 'Deutero-Isaiah's' message to the apparent delay in fulfilment.[7] In the approach we are now adopting it has rather to be seen as the articulation of an inescapable aspect of the expectation: God is now acting, but the fulfilment of his purpose has yet to be accomplished. The dilemma will be familiar from the study of the Kingdom of God in the gospels. Hermeneutically, this aspect of the expectation may be read in two quite different ways. Either it may be said that the fulfilment of God's purpose is for some specific time in the future of the prophet, therefore perhaps the reader's own time: or that it lies in an ideal future not realisable in ordinary conditions in the world as we know it.

This raises the first of two major questions about the book of Isaiah that are significant for us. Have we not in Isaiah an exclusively this-worldly 'eschatology'? This is not a simple matter. On the one hand, the prophecies without exception look forward to the coming of God's kingdom here on earth. Their scene is not set in heaven, and there is no idea of the destruction of the old world to bring in the new, or of the rejection of earthly existence. On the other, they are full of language which suggests a radical transformation in the conditions of earthly existence by God's intervention.

The former of these two points may seem to be challenged by 65.17: 'See, I am creating new heavens and a new earth' (and compare 66.22). But what does this mean in its context? The phrase 'I am creating' is used three times in two verses here, and on the third occasion we have 'I am creating Jerusalem as

---

[6]Biblical quotations have been cited according to the Revised English Bible (Oxford and Cambridge University Presses, 1989) (=REB), occasionally modified.

[7]See e.g. R. P. Carroll: *When Prophecy Failed* (London: SCM Press, 1979), p. 153.

a delight and her people as a joy'. This makes it clear that this new creation does not involve the destruction of the old. Jerusalem and her people still exist, but they are transformed. In Hebrew, when God is said to 'create' (*bara*) it means that he does something utterly new, not necessarily that he *makes* something new (see Num. 16.30). So v. 17a could be rendered 'I shall renew heaven and earth'.[8] But even so, the passage as a whole concentrates on Jerusalem, where the transformation covers every area of life. No distinction is made between cosmic, physical, social and biological transformation: longevity (v. 20), freedom from foreign invasion (vv. 21-3; cf. Deut. 28.30), and a peace which extends to the animal world (v. 25; cf. 11.6-9). There are similar broad perspectives in many other visions of the future in Isaiah, as in chs. 25 and 60.

It is impossible to make sense of these poems by taking them literally within the framework of a modern scientific world-view. They express in vivid poetic imagery the expectation of a world where God visibly reigns. But it is equally impossible to say that their writers did not literally expect such things to happen: they place no limit on the power of the creator God.

This leads us to the second question: where everything, seemingly, is attributed to the power of God, does human obedience have any part to play in the realisation of the vision?[9] But first of all we must appreciate the full force of the question.

As Remi Lack has shown,[10] the book of Isaiah is held together by cycles of recurring ideas and imagery. The images of the holy city and of the king who reigns in righteousness, expressing the goal of God's action, are just two of these. The book is equally rich in recurring images of the negative situation which calls forth God's response, and of his dynamic intervention; but above all, of his eternal rule in history. Isaiah's tremendous vision of Yahweh of Hosts enthroned as

---

[8]So, e.g., C. Westermann: *Isaiah 40-66* (ET London: SCM Press, 1969), p. 408.

[9]Just this question, but of the historical Isaiah, is asked by J. J. M. Roberts in 'The divine King and the human community in Isaiah's vision of the future' in *The Quest for the Kingdom of God*, ed. H. B. Huffmon and others (Winona Lake. Ind: Eisenbrauns, 1983), pp. 127ff.; and he answers it in a very similar way.

[10]Op. cit. (n. 3).

king (ch. 6) dominates the entire book even though it is not directly referred to elsewhere. 'Holy, holy, holy is the LORD of hosts: the whole earth is full of his glory' cry the seraphim (6.3) and the prophets respond by exalting him as 'the Holy One of Israel', a title distinctive of the book of Isaiah;[11] and by proclaiming 'the glory of the LORD will be revealed' (40.5; compare 60.1; 66.18f.). The perceptive comment has been made on 6.3 that 'glory is the correlative of holiness. Glory is that in which holiness comes to expression.'[12] God's holiness is his character in himself, transcendent and inaccessible, while his glory is his immanent activity in the world, as it becomes visible to the eyes of faith.

The fundamental impression is of the irresistible power of Yahweh either to judge or to save, and this is frequently contrasted with the impotence of any other power to hinder him. 'The LORD of Hosts has a day of doom in store for all that is proud and lofty, for all that is high and lifted up' (2.12); the huffing and puffing of the kings of Aram and Israel are of no concern to him (7–8), but even mighty Assyria is no more than a stick in his hand, to be broken and thrown away when it has served its turn (10). A major theme of chs. 40–58 is the impotence of the pagan gods, and most of ch. 40 is concerned with the utter incomparability of God, before whom all mankind is like grass (vv. 6-8), and its princes as nothing (vv. 23f.).

If Isaiah's vision of 'the King, the LORD of hosts' is the symbolic centre of the book, its climax is surely 52.7-10, with the ringing cry of the herald as he comes over the mountains: 'Your God has become king.' If one were asked what the book of Isaiah 'is about', this would be the answer: the kingship of God now visible to the eye of faith and to be made visible to all in the new world that is about to dawn.

One word, more than any other, which encapsulates this idea in the book is 'righteousness' (*sedaqa*).[13] First and foremost

---

[11]1.4; 5.19, 24; 10.20; 12.6; 17.7; 29.23; 30.11, 12, 15; 31.1; 37.23; 41.14; 43.3, 14; 45:11; 47.4; 48.17; 49.7; 54.5; 60.14, and only three times elsewhere.

[12]G. A. Smith: *The Book of Isaiah* (The Expositor's Bible, London: Hodder and Stoughton, n. d.), vol. 1, p. 68.

[13]Cf. Lack, op. cit. (n. 3), pp. 238ff., for much of what follows.

in Isaiah this is an activity of God. Perhaps the most central
verse in the entire book is 5.16:

> But the LORD of Hosts is exalted by judgement,
> and by righteousness the Holy God reveals his holiness.

Here it is righteousness that is the visible expression of God's
holiness, more explicitly so than is his glory in 6.3. In the
context, the exaltation of Yahweh is contrasted with the
humiliation of the haughty looks (v. 15), of those who have
refused to recognise 'the work of the LORD' (v. 12). God's
'judgement' or 'justice' (*mishpaṭ*) and 'righteousness' is his
action in power to restore the proper order of things in which
his sovereignty and holiness is acknowledged. In 28.17, similarly,
God deals in 'justice' and 'righteousness' with those who have
relied on falsehood and self-deception to protect them, rather
than on him.

Naturally, the proper order of things, which God acts to
restore, covers also the proper relationships within human
society: in the first part of the book the pair 'judgement/justice
and righteousness' (*mishpaṭ, ṣedeq/ṣedaqa*) occur frequently as
a definition of the demand which God makes on his people at
the present, and of the characteristics of the restored community
of the future.[14] 1.22-8 contrasts the present state of the strumpet
city with her ideal former state as the faithful city, and again
with what God intends to do for her: 'once the home of justice
where righteousness dwelt', now the home of corruption and
oppression. After Yahweh's purifying vengeance she is called
once again 'Home of Righteousness, the Faithful City', the
words 'faithful city' echoing v. 21 and thus completing the
circle. Vv. 27ff. add that this will be accomplished *by* justice and
righteousness, but they also point out something implicit in
what has already been said: that purification means separation:
those *who return* will be redeemed, but those who continue
rebellious will be broken. We shall be coming back to this very
important point.

[14]Ib.; Rendtorff, op. cit. (n. 3), p. 199.

'Justice and righteousness' are likewise that for which God looks in vain from his people in the conclusion to the parable of the vineyard, 5.7; and this general judgement is made more particular in the denunciations that follow in the rest of the chapter: compare 1.17; 33.5. And on the other hand, it is the special characteristic of the future king that he rules in justice and righteousness: 9.7; 11.3-5; 16.5; 32.1.

But when we come to chs. 40-55 the ideas change somewhat. The words *ṣedeq* and *ṣedaqa* are still just as common, but instead of being linked with *mishpaṭ*, justice, they are linked often with *yesha'*, *yeshua'* or *teshua'* salvation or deliverance.[15] In this connection they are often translated 'victory', or 'saving power' (51.6 REB). The connection of ideas is possibly through the law court. To have judgement given for you is to be given 'righteousness', while 'salvation' in its original meaning is military victory granted by God: so metaphorically the words are synonymous, they both refer to God's victory, which is also his people's victory: their deliverance by him from oppression and exile, the establishment of his holy city in peace and plenty (49; 54), and beyond that his open triumph over the whole world (45.22-4). This part of the book is concerned with the deliverance of the people of God from foreign oppression: so 'righteousness' is here the *gift* of God's saving power, while in the earlier part of the book, which rather faces the question of injustice, oppression, idolatry and impious pride *within* God's people, justice and righteousness are frequently God's *demand*. Where the words express God's own victory, it is demonstrated *there* often in his power put forth to punish and purify his people (as in 5.16), *here* always in his deliverance of them from their oppressors.

But in the last big section of the book, chs. 56–66, there is a remarkable development. As Rendtorff has seen,[16] 56.1 neatly brings together the two main use of *ṣedaqa* which have become familiar to us in the two previous parts of the book:

---

[15]45.8; 46.13; 51.5, 6; cf. also 41.2, 10; 42.6, 21; 45.13, 21, 23f.; 54.14 and see Rendtorff, ib.

[16]Ib. pp. 199f.

These are the words of the LORD:
Maintain justice (*mispaṭ*), and do what is right (*ṣedaqa*);
for my deliverance (*yeshuaʿ*) is close at hand, and my victory
(*ṣedaqa*) will soon be revealed.

The proclamation of God's saving righteousness requires a
response. Nothing can hinder it, and yet it cannot be effective
unless people respond to God by acting appropriately. This is
necessarily so: for God's saving righteousness is not simply
shown in the removal of hindrances to his people's freedom,
but more positively in the establishment of peace and justice.
There is no way in which this can happen without people's
voluntary co-operation.[17] The idea is developed in chs. 58 and 59.
59.1f. has been seen as a convenient excuse for the failure of
God's salvation to make an appearance.[18] While this may be so,
it is also true that on a deeper level it brings out an unavoidable
aspect of the meaning of that salvation. 'Righteousness' is a
whole: God's true victory necessarily involves the human exercise
of righteousness. In 59.9, 14 a brilliant word-play which is more
than mere play makes this clear: 'justice' and 'righteousness'
are far removed from us because 'justice is rebuffed and
flouted'.

It is true that this is immediately followed by a report of
God's unilateral intervention to establish justice. But the result
of this is a separation in the ranks of his people as in 1.24ff.

According to their deeds he will repay:
for his adversaries, anger:
for his enemies, retribution! . . .
He will come as a redeemer to Zion
and to those in Jacob who repent of their rebellion
(59.18, 20)

This still implies that the human response — repentance — is
a necessary condition for experiencing the benefits of God's

---

[17]Cf. Roberts, op. cit. (n. 9), pp. 129ff. (referring to 1.28 and in particular to
32.1-8).
[18]Carroll, op. cit. (n. 7), p. 153.

righteousness. This seems to be the condition understood for the scenario of peace and prosperity in the following three chapters, and is explicit in 60.21: 'Your people, all of them righteous...' The last two chapters place great emphasis on the division between 'my servants' and their opponents, as does 1.27. Given the prominence of this theme at the beginning and the end of the book, it seems likely that it is intended as a key to the understanding of the whole. The avenging judgement, wherever it may appear, is intended for God's foes, the impenitent rebels of 66.24; the saving righteousness for the penitents of ch. 64.[19]

The book read as a whole therefore gains in moral coherence and credibility over its individual pieces, but at a heavy cost in two respects. Firstly, we lose the innocent universalism and unconditional nature of the vision. Hell is as permanent a possibility as paradise: the way the book ends ensures we do not forget that.

But that in turn, secondly, places a question mark against the irresistible sovereignty of God which so impresses one upon first reading. It has become clear that there is an important sense in which that sovereignty is not irresistible. It can do everything it wants to with the fire of avenging judgement, but for its ultimate constructive object, the creation of a just, peaceful and blessed human community, it is dependent on the free, unforced response of human souls. It might be possible to evade this conclusion by appealing to a doctrine of predestination, in which even the human response would be governed by the sovereignty of God. Ch. 6 employs such an idea in a negative sense: the power of God *prevents* the proper human response, though only through the agency of the messenger; but there is little else in the book which suggests it. Even in 30.21: 'If you stray from the path, you will hear a voice from behind you sounding in your ears saying "This is the way; follow it"', compulsion is not implied.[20]

[19]Cf. Roberts, op. cit. (n. 9), p. 134.

[20]Roberts is prepared to speak (ib., p. 136) of the experience of judgement and deliverance *forcing* the survivors to 'hallow the Holy One of Jacob'; this may indeed be the point of some passages in 1–39, but not of the book as a whole, I think.

These reflections suggest a slightly different way of reading the book from that with which we began, when we saw in it visions of a paradise to be fulfilled by the creative power of God in this world. Now we must see the visions as expressing the result of free human submission to the sovereignty of God, as possibilities which in themselves transcend human history but are also capable of at least partial realisation in history, if people take them seriously and live them out. But on the whole, people will not, or rather cannot, do that. This is a truth that the book acknowledges in a good many places. Repentance can be envisaged as a possibility, and yet dismissed as a practical likelihood, as in 30.16. For the newly-commissioned messenger who is addressed in 6.9f. this truth takes a notably terrible form: the refusal to repent is intended by God, and to be achieved by the messenger's agency.

But there is another mode in which the realisation of the possibilities of human existence is presented to us in the book of Isaiah, which may suggest a way out of this impasse. I am referring to the poems about Yahweh's servant in 42.1-4; 49.1-6; 50.4-9 and 52.13–53.12, and also 61.1-3, I did not list these passages above[21] because they are not, on the face of it, visions of community. But this may be a superficial view. They are visions of an individual, but he is called 'to restore the tribes of Jacob' (49.6) and himself bears the name Israel (49.3); and further, he is called to set *mishpaṭ* on earth (42.1, 3, 4) and bring Yahweh's salvation to earth's farthest bounds (49.6). He is in fact a messianic figure,[22] the human agent of God's saving righteousness and ordering justice. Yet in his calling some apparently unmessianic things happen to him: he is persecuted, humiliated, arrested and brought to and beyond the point of death. This might be taken as illustrating what is realistically likely to happen when the Isaianic ideals come into contact with the world as it really is.[23] But this series of poems is not a tragedy. The servant of Yahweh is victorious. Yahweh's cause

[21]On p. 30.

[22]Eaton, op. cit. (n. 2), pp. 47ff., 61ff., 67ff., 75ff., 90f.

[23]Not to mention the possibility canvassed by Eaton (ib.) that these events are those of a ritual drama in which the pre-exilic king in Jerusalem was the protagonist.

prospers in his hands (53.10), not in spite of but through the suffering that he endures.

And this begins, I would suggest, with the people who speak 53.1-9, who recognise in shame that it is their guilt that the Servant has borne. Here the hope of true community is presented not as something dependent on the prior establishment of righteousness, but as arising out of the acknowledged unrighteousness and disobedience of our present human existence. This makes it possible to conceive of this vision's being embodied in known events. David Clines has suggested that the poem of Isa. 53 may be treated as imaginative literature, which creates a more or less realistic world and invites us to enter it and reflect on its correspondence to the world we know.[24] Beyond any other part of the book, its Christian readers have found in this poem a picture of the reality of their own world. If we recognise Jesus of Nazareth in the suffering Messiah, we are enabled thereby to recognise ourselves in the speakers of 53.1-9. The passage represents repentance as a vivid reality which takes place before our eyes: more than that, it enables it *to take place* when the readers thus identify themselves with characters in the drama. And this opens the door for justice to be established on earth in the midst of injustice, 'like a young plant whose roots are in parched ground'.

But this may be true also of other passages of the book. The function of the visions of Isaiah is not merely to tantalise us with what might be, but to convict us of what should not be, and to enable us to struggle for what ought to be. As the vision engenders repentance and conversion, it becomes embodied in human existence.

To sum up, while on the surface the book of Isaiah leaves all the initiative and power with God in the establishment of his kingdom, it acknowledges the necessity of human response, and at a deeper level actually enables that response to be offered. Thus, although it does not envisage a dichotomy between the world to come and a just society in this world, and

[24] J. A. Clines: *I, He, We and They* (Sheffield:JSOT Press, 1976), pp. 53ff.

in that respect shows a sharp contrast with the Reformed view with which we began, it does see this world as the proper stage for the activity of the grace of God responded to in faith in the creation of a just, peaceful and blessed human community, and to that extent may legitimately be seen as part of the underpinning of the Reformed view. As literature Isaiah as a whole, not merely ch. 53, offers a vision of an alternative world, which appeals to the imagination and so enables action, but is more in line with what may be considered rational expectations than has often been thought. Theologically it may rather be seen as an instrument by which God's purposes for this world, whether recognised as realistic or not, are realised in human time and space and through willing human minds and hands.

# 4

# The Kingdom of God and the Psalms

## by Paul Joyce

The Psalter is a book of worship — indeed, as its Hebrew title acknowledges, a book of 'Praises' (*tehillim*). The theme of the reign or sovereignty of God is here both prominent and pervasive.

Most recent study of the Psalms has been characterised by the conviction that the background out of which the Psalter comes is that of Temple worship. Before the present century, it was generally assumed that each of the psalms had been composed by particular individuals reflecting specific periods. This was the case whether it was (according to the traditional view) David in about 1000 B.C.E. or (as many nineteenth century liberals held) poets in the Maccabean period of the second century B.C.E. In the early years of the twentieth century, however, Hermann Gunkel placed new emphasis on the notion that the Psalms have their background in a worshipping community active over a long period; here he was building upon older insights, but his work did much to encourage the view that the Psalms were produced in worship, in community, and in the spoken (or sung) word. They are themselves, or at least they reflect, typical forms for use in worship and we can discern a range of categories into which they fall.[1]

[1] H. Gunkel, *Ausgewählte Psalmen* (Gottingen, 1904); 'Psalmen', in *Die Religion in Geschichte und Gegenwart* 4 (1913; 2nd edn, 1927; Eng. Tr.: *The Psalms* (Philadelphia, 1967); *Die Psalmen* (Göttingen, 1926; reprinted, 1986). It should be noted that Gunkel himself argued that many psalms represented the private devotions of

Because our theme involves nothing less than the thoroughgoing establishment of the purposes of God, reference will be made to a wide range of psalms. However, two categories of psalm in particular are especially relevant to the theme of the sovereignty of God in the Psalter. We refer here to the Enthronement Psalms and the Royal Psalms. These categories need to be distinguished carefully, for their names are potentially confusing. By Enthronement Psalms we mean psalms which proclaim God's reign as King, whereas the Royal Psalms are concerned with the kingship of the Davidic monarchs. Let us comment briefly on each of these in turn.

The Enthronement Psalms celebrate Yahweh's kingly reign over all. 'The LORD reigns; he is robed in majesty; the LORD is robed, he is girded with strength. Yea, the world is established; it shall never be moved; thy throne is established from of old; thou art from everlasting' (Ps. 93.1-2).[2] The most characteristic phrase of this kind of psalm is that translated here 'The LORD reigns', in Hebrew *Yahweh Malakh* (Ps. 93.1; cf. 96.10; 97.1; 99.1). Scholars have differed in the precise interpretation they have given to this phrase. Gunkel himself argued that it was to be understood primarily in eschatological terms, that is as an affirmation that ultimately Yahweh's reign over all people and all things would be vindicated; this was originally a prophetic declaration about the future (cf. Isa. 52.7), which was only later adapted to liturgical use. Gunkel's Scandinavian pupil Mowinckel, on the other hand, gave a somewhat different emphasis. For him the declaration of God's kingship is first and foremost a cultic event, a moment in the liturgy, albeit eloquent both of the original creation and of God's ultimate victory in

individual Israelites, and indeed that some were late literary imitations of earlier liturgical prototypes. Nevertheless, his work and, more especially, the method which he popularised are justifiably seen as ushering in a period of scholarship in which more thoroughgoing corporate and liturgical readings were to become very widespread.

[2]Quotations from the Psalter are from the Revised Standard Version, unless indicated otherwise. It should be noted that the verse numbers are sometimes one higher in the Hebrew text than in the English Bible; the verse numbers cited in this essay are as in the English Bible.

the future.[3] Sometimes these interpretations of the Enthronement Psalms are presented in a way which polarises them, but this is a mistake. A crude dichotomy between the establishment of God's reign as an accomplished fact of liturgy and as a longed-for hope of eschatology is to be avoided, for there can undoubtedly be a significant eschatological dimension to liturgical enactment. The Enthronement Psalms are to be seen as affirming Yahweh's eternal sovereignty, which is seen partially in the present and may thus already be celebrated in worship, but whose ultimate fulfilment and vindication awaits the future, a hope to which worship itself bears witness. This 'now . . . and yet to come' pattern, which seems to characterise the Enthronement Psalms, has struck a chord in human experience down the centuries, and may be one reason for the abiding power of these psalms.

Reference was made earlier to the possible prophetic background to the affirmation of God's reign in the Psalter. In particular, close affinities have long been observed between the Enthronement Psalms and material in Isaiah 40–55, so-called Deutero-Isaiah. This rests in part on the occurrence in Isaiah of phrases similar to *Yahweh Malakh*, e.g. Isa. 52.7; cf. 44.6. Another phrase is found in both contexts, namely 'Sing to the LORD a new song' (Ps. 96.1; 98.1; Isa. 42.10), and these two groups of texts also share other expressions of the establishment of Yahweh's victorious sway. Gunkel and Mowinckel diverged here too, Gunkel regarding the references in Deutero-Isaiah as the earlier and the Enthronement Psalms as dependent upon them, Mowinckel, conversely, regarding these psalms as primary and Deutero-Isaiah as secondary. Others have preferred, perhaps more plausibly, to speak of a broad tradition of shared language rooted in worship.

The other main category of psalm dealing with royal themes is the so-called Royal Psalm, speaking of the kingship of the Davidic monarchs, as in Psalm 72: 'Give the king thy justice, O God, and thy righteousness to the royal son!' (Ps. 72.1). Such psalms share much, of course, with the Enthronement Psalms.

---

[3] S. Mowinckel, *Psalmenstudien* 6 vols. (Kristiania (Oslo), 1921-24; reprinted Amsterdam, 1961); *The Psalms in Israel's Worship* 2 vols. (Oxford, 1962).

The language of dominion and rule is used in the one case directly of the God of Israel and, in the other, of the human ruler of Israel. The human king is presented as chosen and blessed by God, and frequently as mediating the kingly rule of God, rather as a viceroy (cf. Ps. 110.1). Indeed, it has been said that the office of the Davidic king 'had no other meaning but to be the agent of God's reign'.[4] We shall return to discussion of this parallelism or 'mirroring' between divine and human rule. The number of Royal Psalms to be found has been a matter of dispute. Gunkel listed less than a dozen. Eaton, on the other hand, attributes some sixty-four psalms to this category, this reflecting a conviction that the role of the king in ancient Israel was, above all, a cultic one and that, correspondingly, the worshipping life of the Temple was profoundly imbued with royal themes.[5] Among psalms acknowledged as 'Royal' by all we may cite, for example, Psalms 2, 45 and 110. Even the relatively short list of Gunkel would seem to reflect a wide range of occasions in the royal life, including Coronation (e.g. Ps. 2) and Royal Wedding (Ps. 45).

These, then, are the two main categories of psalm dealing with royal themes. As indicated earlier, however, we are concerned with the full range of ways in which the Psalter speaks of the establishment of the sovereignty of God, and thus other kinds of psalm too, such as the Zion Psalms, will be found to yield evidence relevant to our enquiry.[6] We must ask next what shape the hope of the establishment of God's sovereignty takes, as presented in the Psalter.

[4] J. H. Eaton, writing in *The Expository Times* 101/8 (May 1990), 247-8, reviewing M. Z. Brettler's *God is King* (see note 14 below).

[5] J. H. Eaton, *Kingship and the Psalms* Studies in Biblical Theology, 2nd series, 32 (London, 1976; 2nd edn., Sheffield, 1986). Another scholar who has placed a strong emphasis on the link between the cult and royal themes is A. R. Johnson; see especially his *Sacral Kingship in Ancient Israel* (Cardiff, 1955).

[6] Cf. Pss. 46, 48, 76, 87. On the Zion Psalms, see further H.-J. Kraus, *Theology of the Psalms* (Minnneapolis/London, 1986), ch. 3; W. H. Schmidt, *The Faith of the Old Testament: A History* (Oxford, 1983), pp. 207-220.

## *This World or Another?*

To what extent is any future hope in the Psalter 'this worldly' or 'other worldly'? There is little if any real evidence of a developed belief in an afterlife in the Psalter. *Sheol* is featured in a number of psalms, but this is certainly not presented as a fulfilment of hopes. On the contrary, it seems a shadowy and unattractive underworld, a place of no real life worth speaking of. Psalm 88 is not untypical in its portrayal: 'Dost thou work wonders for the dead? Do the shades rise up to praise thee?' (Ps. 88.10). Some have thought Ps. 73.24 to yield evidence of resurrection hope ('Thou dost guide me with thy counsel, and afterward thou wilt receive me to glory'; cf. also 49.15), but this is improbable. No, it is vindication in this life for which the psalmists seem to look. Many a lament strains for assurance of such vindication and indeed, in many, it is given (e.g. Ps. 12.5, 'Because the poor are despoiled, because the needy groan . . . I will place him in the safety for which he longs'). It is important that such hope of vindication is intimately related to the vindication of God's own sovereignty (again, Ps. 12.5, ' "I will now arise," says the Lord'), but the precise form that this is to take is unclear. Of course, regardless of where particular psalms may fit on the map of developing Israelite ideas about an afterlife (and we must be cautious about drawing such maps), later believers, Jewish and Christian, have frequently expressed their laments and their hopes through these psalms in terms which do entertain hope in an afterlife (sometimes more, sometimes less 'other worldly'). These are to be seen as entirely legitimate appropriations of scriptural texts within later contexts. Hope is one of the recurrent themes of the Psalter. 'Out of the depths I cry to thee, O Lord! . . . I wait for the Lord, my soul waits, and in his word I hope' (Ps. 130.1, 5). The capacity to hope, in the darkest of circumstances, is one of the great and abiding features of the human spirit, as affirmed by writers as diverse as Buber, Moltmann and Bloch.[7] It is

---

[7]Cf. M. Buber, *Kingship of God* (New Jersey/London, 1967); J. Moltmann, *Theology of Hope* (London, 1967); E. Bloch, *The Principle of Hope* 3 vols. (Oxford, 1986).

perhaps in part the Psalter's telling evocation of this theme which accounts for the book's persistent appeal. But the precise shape of that hope remains unspecified. Indeed, it is part of the very power of the Psalms that they are so 'indeterminate' and therefore endlessly open to use and reuse. They lend themselves to ever new partial fulfilments, ever new fresh hopes. But for all their open-endedness and all their variation, time and time again it is for the establishment of the reign of God that the Psalms long.[8]

### God's Act or His People's Act?

Upon what, in the Psalter, depends the accomplishment of the will of God, the establishment of his reign in the lives of his people? Where falls the balance between divine power and human response, between God's 'grace' and Israel's responsibility? The Psalter is a very diverse collection of poems, and so it is not surprising that a broad range of emphases is attested.

There are certainly elements within the Psalter which impose heavy demands upon the faithful. There are, for example, psalms which appear to stand in the tradition of Sinai and the wilderness wanderings. 'Hear, O my people, while I admonish you! O Israel, if you would but listen to me! There shall be no strange god among you; you shall not bow down to a foreign god . . . But my people did not listen to my voice; Israel would have none of me. So I gave them over to their stubborn hearts, to follow their own counsels' (Ps. 81.8f., 11f.), or, again, 'O that today you would hearken to his voice! Harden not your hearts, as at Meribah, as on the day at Massah in the wilderness . . . therefore I swore in my anger that they should not enter my rest' (Ps. 95.7b-8, 11). Another group of psalms in which the 'responsibility' pole, as we might call it, tends to be emphasised is that of the so-called Wisdom Psalms, e.g. Psalm 1 (the 'two ways', of righteousness and wickedness), or, again, Psalm 37,

---

[8]Cf. R. Alter on the historical indeterminacy of the language of poetry: R. Alter, *The Art of Biblical Poetry* (New York, 1985), p. 141.

especially verse 25, 'I have been young, and now am old; yet I have not seen the righteous forsaken or his children begging bread'. We are reminded too of those lines in some of the laments which proclaim the unblemished virtue of the psalmist (e.g. Ps. 7.3-4, 'O LORD my God, if I have done this, if there is any wrong in my hands, if I have requited my friend with evil or plundered my enemy without cause...'; cf. Ps. 15). We think also of the so-called Torah Psalms, such as the monumental Psalm 119 (cf. Ps. 19.7ff.). Here 176 verses are devoted to extolling the commands of God, and although specific stipulations are not reviewed and a spiritualising tendency is probably to be discerned, it is surely the case that the establishment of God's reign is here seen as achieved in large part through the loyal performance of Torah by the people of God. Thus the Psalms yield much evidence that the establishment of God's purposes must involve action on the part of his people.

However, Psalm 119 also reminds us that dichotomies between responsibility and 'grace' are generally inappropriate to the Hebrew Bible. For the ancient Israelite (as for the modern Jew) God's commands constitute a gracious gift rather than an onerous imposition, and this is nowhere better exemplified than in verse 20, 'My soul is consumed with longing for thy ordinances at all times' (119.20). Indeed, even among the Wisdom Psalms, things are not as straightforward as might at first appear, for Psalm 73 questions the 'just deserts' pattern in a manner not unlike the book of Job, whilst Psalm 127 provides a marvellous corrective to any incipient 'Pelagianism': 'Unless the LORD builds the house, those who build it labour in vain. Unless the LORD watches over the city, the watchman stays awake in vain' (127.1). The very genre of lament is essentially an appeal to the gracious mercies of God (e.g. Pss. 22; 130); closely connected with this is thanksgiving, of which there is a great deal in the Psalter, and here too the pole of 'grace' is prominent (e.g. Ps. 30.1, 'I will extol thee, O LORD, for thou hast drawn me up'). But perhaps nowhere more than in Psalm 51 are we reminded that 'grace' is at the heart of the faith of Israel: 'Create in me a clean heart, O God, and put a new and right spirit within me' (51.10; cf. also Ps. 79). Here we have a clear statement of a belief in God enabling his people to do his will, as part of the establishment of his divine reign.[9]

Thus both poles, responsibility and 'grace', are strongly represented in the range of the Psalter as a whole. Indeed, the Royal Psalms themselves provide some of the best examples of the internal tension which can exist within a single psalm. Let us take two examples. In Psalm 89 we read 'If his children forsake my law and do not walk according to my ordinances, . . . then I will punish their transgression with the rod and their iniquity with scourges' (Ps. 89.30-32; cf. vv. 38ff.), but the verses which immediately follow affirm, in the strongest terms, that 'I will not remove from him my steadfast love . . . His line shall endure for ever, his throne as long as the sun before me' (vv. 33-37; cf. vv. 21, 28). Psalm 132 appears to speak of permanent blessing (v. 14, 'This my resting place for ever'), and yet the conditional element is present in verse 12, 'If your sons keep my covenant and my testimonies which I shall teach them'.

### Open to All, or Only for Some?

Closely related to the polarity between 'grace' and responsibility is that between inclusion and exclusion. If salvation depends upon repentance and right behaviour, these conditions will often tend to mean that it is selective — some are excluded (or exclude themselves). On the other hand, where salvation depends upon God's initiative and power, the tendency will often be for all (potentially at least) to be included. However, it is never as simple as this contrast might suggest and there are many different ways in which these themes interrelate. As with the biblical witness as a whole, the Psalter tends to exhibit a tension between what we might call 'inclusiveness' and 'exclusiveness'. We shall not illustrate this in detail here, but simply observe that one form which it takes is the tension

---

[9]Cf. Jer. 31. 31-34; Ezek. 36.22ff.; Deut. 30.6.

Whilst continuing to use the language of 'grace', it is important to give serious attention to the critique of R. P. Carroll, who interprets such language as an 'internalisation' of religion which threatens to undermine ethical endeavour; see esp. R. P. Carroll, *From Chaos to Covenant* (London, 1981), pp. 215-25.

between universalism and nationalism. Here, as elsewhere, the patterns are less predictable than one might expect. Even a strongly 'grace-oriented' presentation can assume an Israel-only context: this would seem to be true, for example, of Psalm 51 and, all the more so, of Psalm 79: 'Return sevenfold into the bosom of our neighbours the taunts with which they have taunted thee, O LORD!' (Ps. 79.12). Where, if anywhere, in the Psalter is a genuine universalism envisaged? There are certainly rhetorical appeals to the whole created order, including the nations of the world, to praise Yahweh, as in Psalm 148: 'Kings of the earth and all peoples, princes and all rulers of the earth . . .' (148.11). But this theme is not much developed, and one cannot help thinking that the expectation of the subordination of the nations is never very far away, as in Psalm 2: 'Now therefore, O kings, be wise; be warned, O rulers of the earth. Serve the LORD with fear, with trembling kiss his feet, lest he be angry, and you perish in the way' (2.10-11). If a more positive universalism is largely absent, this is perhaps because the context of the Psalter is essentially that of the faithful worshipping community of Israel.

## The One and the Many

The Psalter is full of tensions between what we might call the 'one' and the 'many', the individual and the group. Among the categories of psalm isolated by the form critics have been laments, both individual (e.g. Ps. 22) and communal (e.g. Ps. 80), and thanksgivings, again both individual (e.g. Ps. 9) and communal (e.g. Ps. 136). Prior to the twentieth century, the individual dimension was given considerable emphasis. This was understandable when the Psalms were generally regarded as the personal compositions of David. The more individual emphasis continued (though under a very different guise) into the nineteenth century, a period much influenced by the theory that most of the Psalms were compositions from the Maccabean age; many of the liberal scholars of the last century argued (erroneously, in the view of the present writer) that the alleged individualism of the Psalter could be added to the arguments for its late date, a judgement resting upon unwarranted assumptions about evolutionary development in Israel's thinking.[10] With the rise of form criticism in the early twentieth century and the wider recognition of the liturgical matrix of the Psalter, the pendulum began to swing towards a more communal emphasis. Frequently, the 'I' of the so-called individual laments has been interpreted as a representative figure (whether king, cultic prophet, or priest), thereby preserving a corporate reading even in these cases. The Psalter was, moreover, one of the books to which Wheeler Robinson particularly applied his theory of 'Corporate Personality', claiming that the ancient worshipper lacked a clearly defined sense of individual identity.[11] In more recent times there have been fresh attempts to strike an appropriate balance between the individual and communal aspects, as in S. E. Gillingham's work on personal piety in the Psalms.[12] The very range of emphases and interpretations with regard to the 'one' and the 'many' in the Psalms is evidence that they lend themselves to being read differently in various settings. As Christians and Jews have reflected upon the establishment of the kingly rule of God through the medium of the Psalms, sometimes more communal and at other times more individual emphases have, in vastly varying circumstances, been given greater prominence, further evidence perhaps that the very 'indeterminacy' of this scriptural text makes it all the richer as a 'soil' in which reflection and devotion can flourish.

[10]P. M. Joyce, *Divine Initiative and Human Response in Ezekiel* JSOT. Supplement Series 51 (Sheffield, 1989), ch. 5.

[11]H. Wheeler Robinson, 'The Hebrew conception of corporate personality', in *Werden und Wesen des Alten Testaments* BZAW. 66 (Berlin, 1936), pp. 49-62; reprinted in *Corporate Personality in Ancient Israel* (Philadelphia, 1980; London, 1981), pp. 25-44; cf. J. W. Rogerson, 'The Hebrew conception of corporate personality: A re-examination', in *Journal of Theological Studies* 21/1 (1970), pp. 1-16; reprinted in B. Lang (ed.), *Anthropological Approaches to the Old Testament* (Philadelphia/London, 1985), pp. 43-59.

[12]S. E. Gillingham, *Psalmody and Poetry in the Old Testament* Oxford Bible Series (Oxford, forthcoming).

*Is the Idea of Kingship Outmoded?*

What of the very notion of rule itself? Is this a relevant and usable theological model today?

As we noted earlier, there is a close paralleling or 'mirroring' between language concerning the Davidic monarch and that concerning God as king. Indeed, it is not clear which came first. Those biblical narratives which present the adoption of political monarchy as an undesirable step employ the motif of Israel already having a (divine) king (e.g. 1 Sam. 8.7: 'And the LORD said to Samuel, "Hearken to the voice of the people in all that they say to you; for they have not rejected you, but they have rejected me from being king over them"'). Nevertheless, one cannot help suspecting that such theological models as divine kingship are generally based on the down-to-earth realities of human social and political organisation. Is it the case, perhaps, that language about Yahweh as king only came to the fore after the demise of Davidic monarchy at the start of the sixth century B.C.E.?[13] This is possible, but both human and divine kingly models were available in plenty long before the rise of Israel, and so the temporal primacy of the one or the other within the Israelite context should probably be regarded as an open question.[14] Be that as it may, there can be no doubt that the reciprocal relationships between political and theological modelling are complex and profound, as is evidenced in David Nicholls' important recent study *Deity and Domination*.[15]

When we think of the crude political despotism which was the Davidic monarchy we may indeed feel that this does not

---

[13]Such a view would cohere with Gunkel's interpretation of the relationship between the Enthronement Psalms and Deutero-Isaiah, noted above, according to which these psalms are seen as dependent upon the work of the anonymous exilic prophet.

[14]A valuable recent treatment of these questions is found in: Marc Zvi Brettler, *God is King: Understanding an Israelite Metaphor* JSOT. Supplement Series 76 (Sheffield, 1989). On the Davidic monarchy, see Keith W. Whitelam, 'Israelite kingship. The royal ideology and its opponents', in R. E. Clements (ed.), *The World of Ancient Israel* (Cambridge, 1989), pp. 119-139.

[15]D. G. Nicholls, *Deity and Domination* (London, 1989).

provide a good field of association for a central theological concept of our tradition. It might, of course, be claimed that 'God as King' language can itself offer a vital *corrective* to the abuse of earthly power, both in the better example of the exercise of just rule which it provides and also through the motif of the earthly king as subordinate 'viceroy', sitting at God's right hand (cf. Ps. 110.1). Yet we may be sure that the Davidic kings would have been as ready to exploit such divine sanction for their often bloody rule as have many more recent despots. Also we need, in any case, to press the critique of the royal model further, onto the divine plane itself. Is an image of God which is so hierarchical and power-based adequate or desirable? Moltmann, Vanstone and others have helped us question such assumptions about God over recent years.[16]

Such a paradigm may also be criticised from a feminist perspective, not only because of its hierarchical, power-based assumptions, but also in the light of the overwhelmingly masculine imagery employed. It is, needless to say, the rule of the 'King' of heaven rather than the 'Queen' of heaven which is affirmed in the Enthronement Psalms. Moreover, and intimately related, the Davidic monarch is, of course, described as the 'son' of God (Ps. 2.7). Not even Psalm 45 does much to redress the strongly masculine emphasis; this psalm may praise the princess, bedecked in her wedding finery, but the underlying assumptions are clear: 'The king will desire your beauty. Since he is your lord, bow to him' (Ps. 45.11). All of this, of course, is hardly surprising, given the patriarchal assumptions of ancient Israelite society and its political structures. It may be conceded that there are some resources for a feminist critique within the Psalter itself, for example the likening of the repose of the soul to the comfort of a child at its mother's breast (Ps. 131.2). Nevertheless, the overwhelmingly masculine nature of the language about God as king and about his earthly viceroy must be acknowledged, as must the fact that it has a profoundly alienating effect upon significant and growing numbers of people.

[16]Cf. J. Moltmann, *The Crucified God* (London, 1974); W. H. Vanstone, *Love's Endeavour, Love's Expense: The Response of Being to the Love of God* (London, 1977).

Is not monarchy, in any case, a rather dead metaphor in our setting, in which we are familiar with, at most, only a vestigial, constitutional monarchy? The cultural context which generated language about God as king can seem very remote. Some may wonder whether more democratic images would be more suitable for our day.

It may be that such considerations, taken together, cast so much doubt on the use of the royal model that continuity of tradition is at this point ruptured: should we abandon talk of 'the Kingdom of God' altogether? Such a response would be premature. To stand in a tradition is to be called to work and rework images, many of which may remain potent long after they have begun to feel 'archaic'. Continuity of sorts can be maintained, as long as the most rigorous and radical of critiques is permitted. Such may include, for example, the image of the King of Israel hanging tortured upon a gallows, and reflection upon the intimate involvement of the King of Heaven with this paradox.[17]

### The Psalms in Synagogue and Church

The Psalter is the shared heritage of both synagogue and church. Indeed, whilst it is true that these two traditions share the whole of the Hebrew Bible, there is arguably no part of the 'Old Testament' which has played a more prominent part within Christian tradition and liturgy than the Psalter, frequently bound in with the four gospels and in many groups read on a daily or weekly cycle. This shared heritage is both cause for joy and occasion of division.

With the end of the Davidic monarchy in the sixth century B.C.E. the wealth of powerful language formerly associated with the dynasty was left without a referent. In the event, it came to feed a tradition which hoped for 'the King who is to come', the Anointed One, the Messiah.[18] Moreover, although

---

[17]It is interesting to note that it was during the period of the great European totalitarian dictatorships of the twentieth century that the Roman Catholic Church instituted and popularised the feastday of 'Christ the King'.

[18]Cf. S. Mowinckel, *He that Cometh* (Oxford, 1956).

language about God as king probably already by then had a long pedigree, it is likely that the end of Davidic monarchy provided a fresh impetus to such language. Thus the imagery of Davidic monarchy was projected onto what we might call the eschatological and the transcendental 'screens'. One day God's Messiah, the ideal Davidic king, God's viceroy, would come; meanwhile, God himself was already reigning in heaven, and at the appointed time his sovereignty would be fully manifested on earth.

Not surprisingly, the first followers of Jesus drew upon these ideas (as well as other traditions within the Scriptures) as they attempted to make sense of the impact their master had made upon them. Christological interpretation of the Psalms goes back at least as far as the New Testament. The language of the Royal Psalms has generally in Christian tradition been taken to refer to Christ. It is he who is 'Son' of God (Ps. 2.7; cf. Matt. 3.17; Acts 13.33), seated 'at God's right hand' (Ps. 110.1; cf. Mark 14.62; Col. 3.1), 'Priest for ever after the order of Melchizedek' (Ps. 110.4; cf. Heb. 5.6; 6.20). The Enthronement Psalms too have sometimes been read as references to Christ as King, both within the New Testament (e.g. Heb. 1.6, quoting Ps. 97.7) and in Patristic exegesis (from Justin Martyr onwards).

However, there is reason to be less than happy with certain aspects of the legacy of christological reading of the Psalms. For such texts came to be understood simply as predictions of Jesus, and very plain predictions at that. There was an implicit assumption behind this — that the Jews must have been wilfully blind and hard of heart to reject a Messiah so clearly announced in their own Scriptures. Christians through the ages have held that, in not acknowledging Jesus, the Jewish people made a grave and culpable error, and that Christianity has consequently superseded the religion of the Jews, who failed to fulfil their vocation as the people of God. In so doing, Christians have not taken seriously the continued existence of Judaism as a living and faithful reality, or given an adequate account of the purposes of God with his people Israel. We should not underestimate the role played by such 'supersessionist' forms of Christian doctrine (together with a complex range of other factors) in the shaping of the antisemitism which has claimed millions of Jewish lives in the course of the twentieth century.[19]

It is vital to recognise that the Psalms have been and continue to be read within two distinct contexts of interpretation, one Jewish and the other Christian (leaving aside Islam for present purposes). The particularity of each context of interpretation must be acknowledged, as must the great diversity represented within each of the two traditions.[20] There is nothing to be gained by attempting to find a reading of the Psalms which could do real justice to both. It is, moreover, essential to work with a model of the relationship between Judaism and Christianity which takes Judaism seriously as a living reality, and so eschews triumphalism and the 'supersessionism' which regards Judaism as a religion only of the past. Such an approach might speak of two divergent religious traditions, sharing many common roots, but shaped by very different histories. Judaism and Christianity should not be thought of as 'mother' and 'daughter', but rather perhaps as two sisters, whose stories have been distinctive and particular. Each sister has defined her identity in the light of many factors, including of course reaction against her 'sibling'. This is reminiscent of the picture presented earlier this century by the Anglican clergyman James Parkes, whose important contributions in this area are still too little known. According to Parkes, Patristic Christianity and Talmudic Judaism were to be seen as two parallel streams of developing tradition, each with its own valid way.[21]

We may usefully reflect here on how such an understanding might be expressed in terms of the more recent important work of George Lindbeck on *The Nature of Doctrine*.[22] Having reviewed other approaches, Lindbeck puts forward what he

[19]Cf. A. R. Eckhardt, *Elder and Younger Brothers* (New York, 1967); R. R. Ruether, *Faith and Fratricide: the Theological Roots of Antisemitism* (New York, 1974).

[20]It is, of course, not possible to do justice to either of these traditions here. The Midrash on the Psalms is one classic of Jewish interpretation of the Psalter, available in English translation in W. G. Braude, *The Midrash on Psalms*, 2 vols, Yale Judaica Series XIII (New Haven, 1959; 3rd edn., 1976). A history of Christian use of the Psalms is given in J. A. Lamb, *The Psalms in Christian Worship* (London, 1962).

[21]E.g. James Parkes, *The Conflict of the Church and the Synagogue* (London, 1934; reprinted, New York, 1981).

[22]George A. Lindbeck, *The Nature of Doctrine: Religion and Theology in a Postliberal Age* (London, 1985).

calls a 'cultural-linguistic' model of religious traditions, within which he understands doctrine as the 'grammar' of a religion and characterises being religious as analogous to learning and speaking a language. Relating this to our own theme, we may suggest that, though sharing much, Judaism and Christianity each represent a separate (and internally highly complex) 'cultural-linguistic' community, developing through time. The Psalms are naturally and appropriately read very differently in each of these two contexts of interpretation, the criteria which govern such reading being primarily those of coherence with community norms. This is not to abandon the notion of ultimate truth or to slide into sheer relativism, but it is to recognise that judgements between 'worlds of meaning' (which can each only be fully appreciated from within) can only be resolved transcendentally and eschatologically, in other words they must rest finally with God.[23]

It is in the interpretation of the Royal Psalms that the sharpest divergence is found between the two contexts of interpretation, Jewish and Christian. Within the Christian tradition, Christ has, of course, been seen as the fulfilment of the best hopes of Israel which had focused on the Davidic king and the Messiah. It might at first sight seem that divergence between the two traditions has been much less marked in the case of the Enthronement Psalms, celebrating God's kingship, for whilst these have sometimes been read as referring to Christ (e.g. Heb. 1.6), Christians have frequently used these psalms to affirm God's sovereignty without direct christological reference. However, within the framework of Christian theology, this is always at least indirectly in relation to Christ, in whom the establishment of God's kingly rule on earth is seen as at least partially realised. For those who stand within the Christian tradition there are many ways of handling these

---

[23]In arguing here that the distinctive stances of Judaism and Christianity must be respected, it is certainly not implied that we should not strive for a close and cordial relationship. It is fully recognised that Christians and Jews may work together (for example, in the cause of justice and peace), read the Bible together and even pray together.

issues; this essay closes with a development of one particular approach.

### Humanity Fulfilled in Christ

Christians affirm that in Christ not only are the royal, messianic hopes of Israel realised, but also humanity is brought to fulfilment. These themes are intimately related. What is affirmed of Christ as 'King' and Messiah may also, in a sense, be affirmed — 'in Christ' — of all humankind. This solidarity between Christ and renewed humanity can be shown to be a significant motif in the New Testament.[24] It may also be said to cohere with certain important features of Old Testament theology. The representative function of the monarch in ancient Israel, where the king embodied and stood for the people as a whole, is well attested.[25] Moreover, it is likely that the 'image of God' in Gen. 1.26ff. includes among its connotations the idea of humankind's kingly rule over creation as God's viceroy.[26]

The Psalter provides a rich context for reflection upon the establishment of the Kingdom of God as the renewal of humanity and the whole of creation. In Christ, every human being is called to be a son or daughter of God (cf. Ps. 2.7; Rom. 8.14), to sit at God's right hand, sharing responsibility for the whole created order (cf. Ps. 110.1; Ps. 8.5ff.; Col. 3.1ff.), forming part of a holy priesthood (cf. Ps. 110.4; 1 Peter 2.5). As the Davidic king was to be the channel of God's favour, the agent of God's *Shalom* (cf. Ps. 72.7), so we, as God's viceroys, co-creators, are called to remake the world, establishing peace with justice. Thus will the creation be consummated, brought to fulfilment in accordance with the good purposes of God (cf. Ps. 104). Thus, in the end, what was intended in the beginning

[24]Cf. C. K. Barrett, *From First Adam to Last: A Study in Pauline Theology* (London, 1962).

[25]Cf. A. R. Johnson, *Sacral Kingship in Ancient Israel* (Cardiff, 1955), p. 127.

[26]A line of interpretation which has been favoured particularly by Scandinavian scholars, such as I. Engnell and T. N. D. Mettinger. See G. A. Jonsson, *The Image of God: Genesis 1.26-28 in a Century of Old Testament Research* Coniectanea Biblica, Old Testament Series 26 (Lund, 1988), pp. 126-131.

will be brought about. The 'image of God' will be fully realised in vice-regal humanity. 'For the creation waits with eager longing for the revealing of the sons of God . . . the creation itself will be set free from its bondage to decay and obtain the glorious liberty of the children of God' (Rom. 8.19, 21). This establishment of the Kingdom of God demands our active participation, as individuals and in community, but ultimately depends upon the power, 'grace' and will of God. Such an interpretation would maintain a theocentric focus in which God is worshipped as God, and humankind and indeed the whole of the created order reaches fulfilment in dependence upon God. It would also be eschatological in that, though we already enjoy the first fruits of our liberation, its ultimate realisation remains in the future.

However, for the Christian, the realisation of messianic hopes in Christ is not simply a fulfilment of the humanity into which all are called. The Church has properly affirmed the Lordship of Christ, as the Son *par excellence*, the true King. This picks up an important dimension of the Psalms, which speak of kingship as the divinely ordained means of sustaining order and justice. This is a characteristic feature of God's direct reign (cf. Ps. 82.8) and also of the reign of the ideal king ordained by God (e.g. Ps. 72). Here we find affirmed the proper place within theology of a concern for government and polity. The poor and the oppressed need order; anarchy is the enemy of the weak and the helpless. It is in their name that Christians hail Jesus Christ as Lord. 'May he judge thy people with righteousness, and thy poor with justice . . . For he delivers the needy when he calls, the poor and him who has no helper . . . From oppression and violence he redeems their life; and precious is their blood in his sight' (Ps. 72.2, 12, 14).

# 5

# Constitutional Aspects of the Kingdom of God

## by William Horbury

*Introduction*

'The kingdom is departed' from the central height which it formerly held in Christian social and political discussion. The distancing of such discussion from the biblical passages on the kingdom of God results in part from trends in biblical exposition. The kingdom of God in the gospels in particular has been widely interpreted for much of this century as non-national and non-political. This understanding has been shared by exegetes of very different schools. In the early years of the century it was common to the liberal interpretation of the gospels represented by Adolf Harnack, and the reaction against it represented by Johannes Weiss and Albert Schweitzer. A timeless moral understanding of the kingdom was thus confronted by an ultimate, apocalyptic interpretation, but neither school recognised a national or political dimension in the kingdom teaching. For many years afterwards these two positions were successively influential in the English-speaking world.[1]

---

[1]A sketch of Christian teaching on the kingdom of God from the New Testament to the present day, with an annotated bibliography, is given by B. T. Vivano, *The Kingdom of God in History* (Wilmington, Delaware, 1988). Valuable studies of Jewish and New Testament source material are gathered in M. Hengel and A.-M. Schwemer, edd., *Königsherrschaft Gottes und himmlischer Kult* (Tübingen, 1991).

In recent years other exegetical views have come to the fore, partly in restatements of the understanding of Jesus and his followers as revolutionaries, partly in gospel study laying emphasis on the continuities between this group and the Jewish and the emergent Christian communities. More notice is now given to the contacts between the kingdom teaching and the biblical themes of the Israelite nation and the people of God. This essay is devoted to aspects of the treatment of the kingdom which are close to the ideas surrounding the polity and politics of Israel, but for which 'constitutional' seems a better adjective than 'political'.

Thus, in biblical thought the kingdom of God can be represented to some extent by rightly-ordered human government, it is often connected with the kingdom of Israel, and it can accommodate the realities of gentile rule; even Nebuchadnezzar can represent the divine kingdom for a time. Yet, as Nebuchadnezzar's story in Daniel shows, an emphasis on righteousness is never lost, and the adjective 'constitutional' evokes the connections made with the Israelite body politic and the kingdoms of this world on the one hand, and the righteous government of God on the other. These aspects of the kingdom of God emerge especially in post-exilic passages of the Old Testament, reappear in the gospels and other early Christian writings, and can perhaps (so it is suggested here) illuminate the approach to contemporary political issues.

There is, at any rate, some contact between these aspects of the kingdom in the Old and New Testaments, and the later traditions of Christian political thought. The biblical links between the kingdom and the people of God can be developed in at least two ways. Sometimes the biblical assertions of the kingdom of God are adversative, implying for the Israelite or Christian community a distinction from and a victory over the gentiles, the world, or the evil for which the enemies seem to stand. 'The Lord is king for ever and ever: the heathen are perished out of his land' (Ps. 10.16). This stance can re-appear in post-biblical Christianity, for example in Augustine and in later teaching which sharply distinguishes church and state, as in much modern Reformed and Roman Catholic thought. Sometimes, however, there is a more unitive biblical understanding of the kingdom, continued especially in Eusebius and in the political traditions of the modern Orthodox, Lutheran and Anglican Churches. Here Israel is both church and nation, and even alien rulers and political institutions can subserve the kingdom of God. It is possible to stumble in either attitude, but there is biblical ground which either attitude can properly claim.

Thomas Hobbes saw these constitutional aspects when, reading the Bible with the eye of a political philosopher, he stated trenchantly 'I find THE KINGDOM OF GOD to signify, in most places of Scripture, a *kingdom properly so named.*'[2] Yet, to recognise that the biblical passages have political as well as ethical and spiritual dimensions is also to see that they may, for that very reason, seem unfitted to offer guidance. They are often closely bound up with political ideology, and can seem no more than early examples of propaganda for a nation or a regime. The Bible reader might wearily conclude that the adversative texts at their crudest simply support Israel or the Christians as a quasi-national body, while the unitive passages at their most carnal serve to legitimise government of almost any kind.

The passages on the kingdom, when further considered, usually in fact resist reduction to such crude and carnal propaganda. There is no doubt, however, that they bear an earthly as well as a heavenly image. Criticisms of this kind have gained emphasis against the background of liberation theology. Thus, in discussion of the social motivation of biblical thought, some texts have been identified with the monarchy, others with the disadvantaged, and the latter group of texts has then been thought more suited to speak a word in season to the modern West.[3] Rather similarly, but from within a situation of acute political difficulty, the authors of the South African *Kairos Document* rejected 'church theology' and 'state theology'

---

[2] T. Hobbes, *Leviathan* (1651), Part 3, Chapter 35; edited by Michael Oakeshott (Oxford, 1960), p. 266.

[3] This approach is discussed and exemplified by W. Brueggemann, *Revelation and Violence: a Study in Contextualisation* (Milwaukee, 1986).

— phrases which can evoke, respectively, the adversative and the unitive tendencies in the kingdom teaching.[4]

What can be said in response to such preliminary objections to the use of the material considered below? First, to discern social or political motivation in a text is only part of a general evaluation. Thus the psalm quoted above is the cry of those who felt themselves oppressed (see Ps. 10.17-18), and so far it might commend itself to those looking for passages which do not legitimise power, but its zeal for the extermination of non-Jews from the land cannot be taken over without question. Secondly, the kingdom of God seems to be invoked in the Bible not only to support the people of God or the government, but also to arouse the conscience and to strengthen faith and hope. Various motivations can intertwine. Thirdly, this point can be true of the texts which are perhaps most likely to encounter objection, those which legitimise Jewish or alien government. In this respect the biblical material can be compared with an influential ancient literary work of legitimation, Virgil's *Aeneid.* This poem is a strongly political celebration of the Augustan settlement, but many of its narratives constitute profound criticism of war and power politics, and there is lively discussion of the poet's stance.[5] Virgil's literary service to the state was not inconsistent with religious and moral depth. Somewhat comparably, a passage like Exod. 19.3-9 shows that employment of the kingdom terminology to strengthen national identity ('you shall be to me a kingdom of priests, and a holy nation') is not inconsistent with emphasis on the moral demands of a kingdom belonging to God.

In what follows, attention is directed to constitutional aspects of the kingdom, as treated first in the Old Testament, then in the teaching of Jesus, finally in Paul, Revelation, and second century Christian teaching. The attempt to connect all these in a single essay is made in order to pick out a continuity and consistency which can be less obvious when each area is studied

---

[4]*The Kairos Document, 1985* is reprinted in C. Villa-Vicencio, *Between Christ and Caesar: Classic and Contemporary Texts on Church and State* (Cape Town & Grand Rapids, 1986), pp. 251-69.

[5]J. Griffin, *Virgil* (Oxford, 1986), pp. 102-6.

individually. In all these contexts, the kingdom is related not only to individual obedience and faith, but also to the ordering of the kingdoms of this world and the people of God.

The more unitive biblical understandings of these aspects of the kingdom receive special notice in conclusion, in the belief that they deserve attention in Christian social and political thought. They suggest a positive recognition and exploration of contemporary overlaps and intermingling between faith and public opinion, ecclesiastical and civil community, church and state.

### The Old Testament and the Second Temple Period

To turn now to the biblical texts themselves is to be confronted by the irregular distribution of words which may be rendered by 'kingdom' in connection with words for 'God'. The post-exilic portions of the Old Testament, and the Synoptic Gospels, immediately stand out as particularly important witnesses to expression in terms of a 'kingdom' of God. When the search is widened to include affirmations that God is king, extensive further Old Testament material comes into view, notably Second Isaiah, from the exilic period, and the Enthronement Psalms, which probably reflect affirmations of the kingship of God made in pre-exilic worship.[6] Related poems were put into the mouth of Moses and Balaam, and incorporated into the Pentateuch, which will have reached substantially its present form by the end of the fifth century B.C.E.

As far as the Old Testament is concerned, attention is concentrated here on post-exilic passages, including Pentateuchal texts. This material is not often given special notice in study of the kingdom of God,[7] but the constitutional

---

[6] J. Day, *Psalms* (Sheffield, 1990), pp. 71-82.

[7] Exceptions are O. Camponovo, *Königtum, Königsherrschaft und Reich Gottes in den frühjüdischen Schriften* (Freiburg, Schweiz & Göttingen, 1984) and (published after this paper was first written) M. J. Selman, 'The Kingdom of God in the Old Testament', *Tyndale Bulletin* xl (1989), pp. 161-83; apocalyptic passages, rather than the range of post-exilic kingdom texts, are prominent in J. Gray, *The Biblical Doctrine of the Reign of God* (Edinburgh, 1979) and G. R. Beasley-Murray, *Jesus and the Kingdom of God* (Grand Rapids & Exeter, 1986).

aspects here discussed emerge in it clearly, and it is of obvious importance in consideration of the antecedents of gospel usage. The passages surveyed include early and later attestations of the employment of a noun meaning 'kingdom' in connection with God, and examples of the scattered Pentateuchal kingship texts, which exerted great influence because of their place in the books of the law. The period concerned, that of the Persian and Hellenistic monarchies, was one of intense ethical and political discussion of kingship in the Greek-speaking world;[8] Jewish literature, especially but not only in the wisdom tradition, has some approximations to this interest.

Constitutional aspects emerge first of all in the link made in Chronicles (probably of the fourth century B.C.E.) between the kingdom of the Lord and the kingdom of Israel. 'Thine is the kingdom, O Lord, and thou art exalted as head above all' (1 Chron. 29.11); but also Solomon is chosen 'to sit upon the throne of the kingdom of the Lord over Israel', and Jeroboam is warned not 'to withstand the kingdom of the Lord in the hand of the sons of David' (1 Chron. 28.5; 2 Chron. 13.8). An inherited view that the Davidic king in Jerusalem is viceroy of the God of Israel (see, e.g., Psalms 2; 89; 110; Ezek. 37.24-5) is here expressed, in contrast with earlier attestations of it, through the employment of nouns meaning 'kingdom'.

The conception of the kingdom of God in Chronicles has two features which apply to many other kingdom texts. First, in the passages quoted above, sovereignty is primarily in question, but the thought of a territorial dominion and a body of subjects is not far away. It is important to note the primacy of the meaning 'sovereignty' or 'reign' in many biblical contexts in which English 'kingdom' appears, but the semantic range of the words will often be comparable with that noted in Chronicles, and their sense should not be too rigidly restricted to the abstract 'sovereignty'.[9] The Chronicler does not expressly identify the kingdom of the Lord with Israel or the house of

[8]See F. W. Walbank, 'Monarchies and monarchic ideas', in F. W. Walbank, A. E. Astin, M. W. Frederiksen & R. M. Ogilvie, edd., *The Cambridge Ancient History*, Second Edition, vii. 1, *The Hellenistic World* (Cambridge, 1984), pp. 62-100.

[9]The point is stressed by G. W. Buchanan, *Jesus: The King and His Kingdom* (Macon, Georgia, 1984), pp. 15-25.

David, but a concatenated phrase like 'the throne of the kingdom of the Lord over Israel' shows that Israel, like the Church in a strand of Christian thinking, could be considered as approximating to the realm of God.

Secondly, however, even the concatenated phrases of Chronicles save the independence of God's own sovereignty. This independence was stressed in the inherited traditions concerning the Davidic covenant. Even with a king of David's line it might happen that God would 'profane his crown' (Ps. 89.39). This thought was clothed in kingdom terminology, probably before the time of Chronicles. 'He has profaned the kingdom, and its princes' (Lam. 2.2). The divine independence is a regular presupposition of biblical understandings of the kingdom of God. With this fundamental proviso, however, it remains true that the kingdom in Chronicles has an important constitutional aspect; the kingdom of the Lord is represented by the throne of David.

The influence of inherited views of the monarchy apparent in Chronicles forms the background against which the Pentateuchal kingship passages will have been understood in their context, from the fifth century B.C.E. onwards. Here too the kingdom of Israel will have been thought to represent the kingdom of God. 'The shout of a king' in Israel is the counterpart of God's presence (Num. 23.21), Moses was king when he ordained the God-given law in the national assembly (Deut. 33.4-5),[10] and the thought of the occupation of the holy land and the building of the Temple evokes the cry that the Lord shall be king (Exod. 15.17-18). The constitutional aspect of the divine kingdom is comparably to the fore on the one occasion in the Hebrew Pentateuch when a noun is employed for a kingdom pertaining to God. 'You shall be to me a kingdom of priests, and a holy nation' (Exod. 19.6). Election is primarily asserted here, but the occurrence of a word for kingdom would evoke the thought of Israel as the kingdom belonging to God, especially when the passage was viewed together with those just

---

[10]The Septuagint translation (third century B.C.E.) shows that the passages were understood in this way, as noted by Camponovo, pp. 386-7.

noted. Probably in accordance with this thought, a striking tendency to lay separate emphasis on the noun 'kingdom' emerges in the ancient versions of the text, and is reflected in Rev. 1.6, 'he made us a kingdom, priests, to his God and Father'.[11] As noted already, the ethical associations of a kingdom of *God* are important in Exodus 19 (as in Deut. 33.4-5, similarly connected with the giving of the law); but the representation of God's rule by the kingdom of *Israel* is also important. It is of the greatest significance for the understanding of the kingdom of God by Jews in the Greek and Roman periods that this constitutional sense of 'kingdom' was thought to be embedded in the Pentateuch.

Further constitutional aspects are illustrated by the familiar observation that the kingdom of God is both present and to come. Throughout the Second Temple period the kingdom vocabulary is used to express the earlier Israelite conviction that all earthly government is subject to the God of Israel, who will at the last rule openly. Just as God is the king of all the earth and its princes (Ps. 47.7-9), kings reign by the divine wisdom and are to be feared next after God (Prov. 8.15; 24.21), the Assyrian is the rod of God's anger and Cyrus his anointed (Isa. 10.5; 45.1); so, with nouns for 'kingdom', it can be said that God's kingdom rules over all (Ps. 103.19) and is everlasting (Ps. 145.13; Dan. 4.3, 34), that he gives it over to whosoever he will, whether Nebuchadnezzar or the saints (Dan. 2.37, 44; 4.17, 25, 36; 7.14, 18, 26-7), and that the kings of the earth are its servants or officers (Wis. 6.4). Just as the divinely-guided king of Israel was to succour the poor and oppressed (Ps. 72.1-4, 12-14), so 'the kingdom' of the Lord both will and does bring nourishment and succour (Ps. 22.26; 145.13-15). The expected 'day' of the Lord is envisaged as the day of his kingship (Zech. 14.1, 9), and the day when 'the kingdom' would be mainly his (Obadiah 15 and 21); the victory over Israel's enemies expected in this last passage contrasts with the assembly of gentiles at Israel's sacrificial feast adumbrated in Psalm 22, as just cited. The differing attitudes adopted in these two places are both

[11] Much of the evidence for the ancient versions of Exod. 19.6 is presented by Camponovo, pp. 384-6, 411.

consonant with the view that Israel represents the kingdom of God, but other constitutional aspects have appeared in some of the kingdom passages just considered. Emphasis on the kingdom of God in the present can carry with it a far-reaching recognition of non-Jewish kingdoms as in their turn, for as long as it may be ordained, representative of the kingdom of God.

This reiteration of earlier beliefs concerning divine kingship in the kingdom vocabulary characteristic of the post-exilic period is by no means surprising. Recognition of the kingdom of the Lord in the government exercised both by Israel and the nations corresponds to a very widespread ancient conviction that tutelary deities may both protect a nation and permit its defeat, showing favour to its enemies.[12] In post-exilic Israel, however, the belief that the God of Israel is the universal king and law-giver has given the constitutional aspects of the kingdom, close as they are to common ancient views, their characteristically Israelite ethical seal.

These aspects of the kingdom of God usually receive less attention than its general association with the eschatological hopes of the Second Temple period. The importance here claimed for them is consistent, however, with the observations sometimes made — for example, by T. W. Manson — that the kingdom of God in the Old Testament is eternal and present as well as future, and that expectations concerning Israel were at the heart of eschatological hopes in the Second Temple period, however other worldly the expression of those hopes might seem.[13] How far were these post-exilic Old Testament conceptions of the kingdom, and their prominent constitutional aspects, determinative for Jesus and his followers?

References to the kingdom of God occur no more than occasionally in the Jewish literature of the later Second Temple

[12]See E. Bickerman, 'Nebuchadnezzar and Jerusalem', reprinted from the *Proceedings of the American Academy of Jewish Research* xlvi-xlvii (1979-80) in E. Bickerman, *Studies in Jewish and Christian History*, III (Leiden, 1986), pp. 282-98.

[13]T. W. Manson, *The Teaching of Jesus* (Cambridge, 1931), pp. 136-141 and *The Servant-Messiah* (Cambridge, 1956), pp. 9-10; similarly, in more recent years, G. W. H. Lampe, *God as Spirit* (Oxford, 1977), pp. 26-8 (on biblical understandings of the kingdom) and E. P. Sanders, *Jesus and Judaism* (London, 1985), p. 125 (on eschatological hopes).

period. Some have therefore concluded that the conception was neither central nor well-defined at the time of Christian origins.[14] There is evidence, however, to suggest that it continued to be well-known and influential, despite this sparse attestation.

The importance of the Pentateuch in this regard has been noted already. One trace of its widespread influence appears in the incorporation of Pentateuchal kingdom texts into the catena of texts known as 'Kingdoms' (*malkuyyôt*), one of three such catenae inserted into the Eighteen Benedictions at New Year in the time of the Mishnah (see *Rosh ha-Shanah* iv 6), at the end of the second century C.E. This custom was probably of some standing, but in any case it presupposes a well-established interest in identifying texts concerned with the kingdom.

Here Pentateuchal influence verges on a second piece of evidence, the currency of the kingdom vocabulary in Jewish prayer. Thus Tobit's thanksgiving, perhaps of the third century B.C.E., begins 'Blessed be God who lives for ever, and his kingdom' (Tob. 13.1); and a response uttered in the temple ran, according to the Mishnah (*Yoma* iv 2) 'Blessed be the name of the glory of his kingdom for ever and ever'. A formula of praise used in prayer is probably reflected when the words of Ps. 145.13, 'Thy kingdom is a kingdom of all ages, and thy dominion in every generation' recur at Dan. 4.3 and 34. The convergence of pre-rabbinic texts with the Mishnah, here referring to the Temple, strongly argues for the familiarity of mention of the kingdom of God in prayer throughout the Second Temple period — a prayer habit which Ps. 145.10-12 indeed seem to recommend.

Lastly, other traces of the kingdom of God in non-biblical Jewish writings suggest its familiarity. To begin with Greek examples, in the Letter of Aristeas (second century B.C.E.) Hellenistic kingship is an important concern, but the 'sovereignty' (*dynasteiā*) of the God of the Jews is central to its treatment; and in his apology for Judaism, at the end of the first century C.E., Josephus significantly chose the term 'theocracy'

---

[14] So J. Jeremias, *New Testament Theology*, i (ET London, 1971), pp. 32, 97-8 and Camponovo, pp. 437-46.

(*theokratiā*) to describe the Pentateuchal constitution.[15] In each case, the biblical 'kingdom of God' can be discerned behind the Greek political vocabulary. At a greater remove, the currency of the concept is implied in Josephus' reports that the rebel leader Judas the Galilean and his followers, in C.E. 6 and later, 'held God to be their only governor and master'.[16] In Hebrew and Aramaic, however, biblical words for 'kingdom' are used of God's kingdom in the Targums, and especially in the rabbinic literature; Solomon Schechter devoted three chapters of his *Aspects of Rabbinic Theology* to the kingdom, laying great emphasis on the place of the concept in Jewish prayer. The varied times and atmospheres in which the influence of the biblical 'kingdom of God' can be traced confirm the continuing importance independently suggested by its place in the Pentateuch and in Jewish prayer.

This evidence also suggests, however, that the constitutional aspects presented by the kingdom in the Hebrew Scriptures continued to be important. Thus Israel is thought to represent the kingdom both in Josephus' description of 'theocracy' and, with very different practical politics in view, in the principle on which Judas the Galilean urged revolt. The ministration of non-Jewish rule to the kingdom, on the other hand, as in Wisdom, is suggested by the Letter of Aristeas.

The position reached after this discussion of the kingdom of God in the Old Testament and the Second Temple period can now be summarised as follows. In the Hebrew biblical writings of the post-exilic period the earlier Israelite affirmations of eternal, present and future divine kingship over Jews and non-Jews were expressed with a vocabulary of words which can be rendered by 'kingdom'. Constitutional aspects emerge in the striking association of the kingdom of God not only with Israel, as in Chronicles and the Pentateuch, but also with the nations of the world, as in Daniel. These understandings of the kingdom

---

[15]Letter of Aristeas 13, 37 & 219, among other paragraphs; Josephus, *Against Apion*, ii 165.

[16]Josephus, *Antiquities*, xviii 23, discussed with parallels by C. T. R. Hayward in E. Schürer, G. Vermes, F. Millar & M. Black, *The History of the Jewish People in the Age of Jesus Christ*, ii (Edinburgh, 1979), pp. 599, 603-4.

correspond to convictions widely held in the ancient world, but they inherit the ethical emphasis of much Israelite tradition connected with the monarchy, and the constitutional aspects of the kingdom are also associated with the righting of wrong. They can be called constitutional not only because the kingdom may be represented by Israelite or non-Jewish kingdoms, but also because it stands for the righteous government of God. Both the general concept of the kingdom of God, and these particular constitutional aspects, continued to be well-known and influential throughout the Second Temple period.

## The Teaching of Jesus

The concentration of kingdom sayings in the Synoptic Gospels is therefore by no means without antecedent, and Jesus could be expected to have been familiar with the understandings of the kingdom just described. It remains a question, however, how far the constitutional aspects specially considered here were characteristic of his mind and teaching.

References to the kingdom will have been multiplied in transmission, but the topic is likely to have been important in Jesus' teaching. Emphasis on the kingdom is consonant with the Israelite tone of Jesus' activity, notably the calling of the Twelve, although the treatment of the topic in the sayings tradition is not such as his activity would lead one to expect.

The concern with Israel suggested by the activity has of course been underlined by writers who associate Jesus with the revolt ideology of Judas the Galilean, notably Robert Eisler (1929-30) and S. G. F. Brandon (1967). A different attempt to do justice to this evidence appears in the interpretation of Jesus as a prophet of national restoration. This line of thought, important in B. W. Bacon (1930), has more recently been developed by G. B. Caird (1965), B. F. Meyer (1979) and E. P. Sanders (1985).[17] Both these approaches, however, encounter

---

[17]Eisler and Brandon are discussed, among other writers who associate Jesus with revolt ideology, by E. Bammel in E. Bammel & C. F. D. Moule, edd., *Jesus and the Politics of His Day* (Cambridge, 1984), pp. 11-68 (32-43); on Caird and Meyer see Sanders, pp. 116-7 with n. 81, and pp. 47-9, respectively; in B. W. Bacon, *Studies in Matthew* (London, 1930), see especially pp. 421-35.

difficulty in the kingdom sayings, which for the most part strikingly lack any reference to Israel. The principal exception is the appointment of a kingdom to the disciples and the promise that they shall judge the tribes (Luke 22.29-30, cf. Matt. 19.28); but, partly because it is exceptional, its authenticity is doubtful.[18]

The kingdom sayings in general are markedly theocentric, as is the Old Testament material just discussed, but they more often lay emphasis on individual obedience than on the national and constitutional aspects which were prominent in the Hebrew biblical texts. It is of special interest, therefore, that G. W. Buchanan (1970 and 1984), in an interpretation of Jesus as campaigning for revolt, argues that the kingdom of God in his teachings would have been understood, against the background of the Hebrew Scriptures and Jewish thought, as referring to the kingdom of Israel.[19] Buchanan gives healthy Hobbes-like reminders that, when the kingdom is mentioned, the thought of the nation is unlikely to be far away; but his interpretation is one-sided enough to recall that it is precisely the kingdom sayings which have often been thought, as by J. K. Riches (1980), to distance Jesus from national hopes.[20] Politics can seem scarcely to fall within the purview of these sayings. This consideration works equally against the presentation of Jesus as a prophet of national restoration. So W. D. Davies commented on Caird's statement of this view: 'Caird has sacrificed the personal and transcendent dimensions of the Kingdom to an exaggerated politico-national concern.'[21]

---

[18]Bacon, pp. 421-6, 432-3 and Sanders, pp. 98-106 argue that the saying is basically genuine; this is regarded as on the whole unlikely by W. D. Davies, *The Gospel and the Land* (Berkeley, Los Angeles & London, 1975), pp. 363-5 and W. Horbury, 'The Twelve and the Phylarchs', *New Testament Studies* xxxii (1986), pp. 503-27 (524-5).

[19]Buchanan, *Jesus* (n. 9, above) developing his earlier *The Consequences of the Covenant* (discussed by Bammel (n. 17, above), pp. 52-3).

[20]John Riches, *Jesus and the Transformation of Judaism* (London, 1980), pp. 87-111, especially 107-8 (stressing not only the content of the kingdom sayings, but also their context in a ministry expressing love and forgiveness to sick, poor and outcasts).

[21]Davies, *Land*, p. 348.

Such a criticism does not mean neglect of the communal reference of the teaching of Jesus, which W. D. Davies himself emphasises, but it indicates the difficulty of integrating the kingdom teaching with any national interpretation of Jesus' activity. E. P. Sanders shows that the two need not be inconsistent, but chiefly stresses that the national perspective of the activity seems to be so reliably attested that it must be regarded as basic to any interpretation.[22]

Debate will continue, but it seems clear that, in the teaching and activity of Jesus, a political element — the national orientation of significant actions — must be recognised as co-existing with an ethical element centred on individual obedience to God—evident especially in the kingdom teaching. There is a comparable co-existence in rabbinic thought between hope for the restoration of the kingdom of David and the individual acceptance of the yoke of the kingdom in the recitation of the Shema. These differing understandings of the kingdom are both distinguished and linked in rabbinic sources,[23] and one should probably allow for a comparable link in the case of Jesus (the point rightly made, but over-pressed, by Buchanan). In the gospel tradition as it has reached us, however, the juxtaposition of the two types of understanding works not only to 'nationalise' individually-oriented sayings, but also and more obviously to 'ethicise' a national outlook.

Thus, in Mark 10.13-45, the sayings on child-like reception of the kingdom, and on how hard it is for a rich man to enter the kingdom, form the context of the political request of the sons of Zebedee for places at the right and left. Here, although the kingdom is unmentioned, its association with Israel is concretely exemplified. The answer to the request takes up the assertion of divine independence noted above in the Chronicles passages on the kingdom of the *Lord* over Israel, and it is

[22]Sanders, pp. 118, 156, 235-7.

[23]Thus the Shema (Deut. 6.4) is quoted at the climax of a strongly patriotic rendering of the 'Kingdoms' by Yose ben Yose, probably fifth century C.E. (W. Horbury & B. McNeil, edd., *Suffering and Martyrdom in the New Testament* (Cambridge, 1981), p. 163).

followed by an ironical reference to gentile monarchs, made to sharpen teaching on rule as service.

Here ethical aspects of the kingdom are to the fore. Notably for the present purpose, however, it is also possible to recognise the first of the constitutional aspects considered above, the association of the kingdom of God with the kingdom of Israel. This presupposition of the disciples' request is not repudiated by their master, but he underlines its theocratic aspect, and is then represented as continuing with a patriotic contrast between non-Israelite rule and that to be exercised among the Twelve. On the other hand, an approach to the second constitutional aspect, the recognition of foreign rulers as servants of the kingdom, appears in the famous answer on the tribute-money, 'Render to Caesar . . . and to God' (Mark 12.17). Here too the atmosphere of Jesus' saying is patriotic. A potential opposition between Caesar and God is allowed for in the answer as well as in the question. Nevertheless, the answer firmly contradicts the principles of Judas the Galilean, and makes it impossible to suppose that his interpretation of the kingdom of God was fully shared by Jesus. The teaching of Jesus seems rather to be true to the pattern discerned in the post-exilic kingdom passages, interpreted with a certain patriotic bias; Caesar is not expressly hailed as a servant of the kingdom, but obedience to him is consistent with obedience to the kingdom, just as the kingdom of God is most closely associated with, but in the end not subsumed by, the kingdom of Israel.

It may then be concluded that the constitutional aspects of the kingdom of God emerge in the teaching of Jesus, particularly when it is viewed together with his actions. This implies no failure to recognise the theocentricity of his kingdom teaching, or its emphasis on individual obedience. Nevertheless, in this teaching as in its antecedents in Israel, the kingdom of God is not far from the thoughts of the kingdom of Israel, and of the kingdom granted for a time to the gentiles.

In an influential history of Christian social teachings Ernst Troeltsch assigned social problems to an entirely different group of interests from those related to the ethic of Jesus, in which 'the Kingdom of God is the rule of God and not the rule of the Jewish people'; in Jesus' kingdom teaching there is no thought of the state at all.[24] Judgements of this kind could be made not only in the liberal Ritschlian school of thought which Troeltsch and Harnack represented, but also, as noted already, on the basis of the ultimate, apocalyptic interpretation of the kingdom advanced by Johannes Weiss and Albert Schweitzer. Such judgements are questioned, however, when the aspects of the kingdom considered here are recognised. The primacy of the rule of *God* in the kingdom sayings was justly affirmed in the exegesis which Troeltsch grandly and positively expounded, but no notice was taken of the constitutional aspects of the rule of God which emerge when the gospels are considered against the background of the Hebrew Scriptures and their interpretation in the Second Temple period. When these aspects are also recognised, concern for the body politic and right government no longer seems alien to the kingdom teaching of Jesus.

*Early Christianity*

These constitutional aspects reappear in early Christianity. The association of the kingdom of God with the kingdom of Israel is hinted at in the gospel Passion narratives, in which the Son of God is crucified as King of the Jews. Paul presents the pattern inherited from the Hebrew Scriptures more fully. He probably shares the expectation of a messianic kingdom (1 Cor. 15.20-28),[25] which will constitute a redemption of Israel after the flesh (Rom. 11.25-6); but he still saves the independence of God's own kingdom, for Christ 'shall deliver up the kingdom to God' (1 Cor. 15.28). Christians owe primary

---

[24]E. Troeltsch, *The Social Teaching of the Christian Churches* (1911, ET London, 1931), i, pp. 58-9.

[25]W. D. Davies, *Paul and Rabbinic Judaism* (2nd ed., London, 1962), pp. 288-98 represents those who argue, against Johannes Weiss, Albert Schweitzer and others, that here the coming of Christ (verse 23) is thought of as the culmination of a hidden reign which began at his resurrection; but on the view that, instead, the coming is understood as the beginning of a new, manifest kingdom the passage agrees with the widespread Jewish and early Christian interpretation of the Danielic kingdom of the saints as a messianic kingdom.

allegiance to God's sovereignty in their own common life, as is assumed in the hortatory Pauline references to the kingdom studied in Frances Young's contribution; but that sovereignty is exercised in a delegated and particular way by non-Jewish and non-Christian government. In Paul's famous assertion of the divine ordination of 'the powers that be' (Rom. 13.1-7) the kingdom is not mentioned, and his thought overlaps with contemporary non-Jewish ideas of monarchy, but precisely in the overlap he also reproduces an aspect of the kingdom familiar from Second Isaiah on Cyrus, Daniel on Nebuchadnezzer, and subsequent Jewish tradition; here in Romans, as in Wis. 6.4, gentile rulers are 'officers of the kingdom'.[26] This combination of hope for a messianic kingdom of Israel (to be governed by Christ) with recognition of the divine authorisation of gentile rulers, saving the independence of the kingdom of God over all, corresponds to the pattern of constitutional aspects of the kingdom already discerned in the Hebrew Scriptures.

In Revelation the patriotic note audible in the sayings of Jesus is intensified, but the understanding of the kingdom is not so different from that found in Jesus and Paul as may at first appear. Rome is the enemy, as in the comparable Jewish apocalypses of Ezra (2 Esdras or 4 Ezra 3–14) and Baruch (2 Baruch or the Syriac Apocalypse of Baruch); but the kingdom of God 'rules over all' (Ps. 103.19), and the three apocalypses simply reflect the hope that, since Roman oppression of Jews or Christians must offend the divine righteousness, there will now be an end to the time of delegated sovereignty allotted to Rome, identified with the fourth gentile kingdom in Daniel.

---

[26]Monarchs regarded in post-biblical Jewish writings as governing by divine appointment include Xerxes or Artaxerxes (Rest of Esther 16.16), Ptolemy Philadelphus (Letter of Aristeas 19, 37, 219), and the Flavian emperors (Josephus, *Jewish War* v. 2); Wisdom, Paul and Philo are set in the context of abundant classical references to the divine appointment of kings, with a douche of cold water, by R. G. M. Nisbet and Margaret Hubbard, *A Commentary on Horace: Odes, Book 1* (Oxford, 1970), pp. 164-5 (on i. 12, 50); by contrast with the interpretation offered above, special features of Romans 13 in this Jewish and gentile setting are emphasised, and the particular situation of Christians in Rome is taken to have been strongly influential, in the study of the passage by E. Bammel in Bammel & Moule, pp. 365–83.

Thus 'the kingdom of the world is become the kingdom of our Lord, and of his Christ' (Rev. 11.15) represents the same faith in the ultimate manifestation of God's kingdom as is met in Jesus, Paul and the Old Testament — a point doubtless recognised when the text was inscribed by Dean Stanley over the high altar of Westminster Abbey. The association of the kingdom of God with the kingdom of Israel is present in the conception of the 'kingdom' of the Christians (Rev. 1.6, alluding to Exod. 19.6, as noted above), and in the expectation of the messianic kingdom of the saints (Rev.20.1-6); while the association of the kingdom with non-Jewish rule is represented in the hope that the time of the fourth gentile kingdom is up. The constitutional aspects of the kingdom once again form the same pattern.

The consistency with which this pattern has appeared makes it unsurprising that second century Christians embraced the hope for a messianic kingdom suggested by the gospels and Paul, expressed in Revelation, and shared by their Jewish contemporaries on the basis of the same biblical inheritance.[27] At the same time Christian authors, again like contemporary Jews when in more favourable circumstances, reverted to the positive recognition of pagan rule found in Paul and the Wisdom of Solomon. Justin Martyr and Tertullian both look forward to a kingdom of Christ in Jerusalem, but Justin regards the Romans as instruments of divine providence (*First Apology* 32, 63), and Tertullian claims Caesar as more truly the Christians' lord than the pagans' — 'because he was appointed by our God' (*Apology* xxxiii 1).[28] In many ways, therefore, they anticipate the political theories of the post-Constantinian Church as outlined above,[29] but they do so by continuing the

---

[27]R. L. Wilken, 'Early Christian Chiliasm, Jewish Messianism, and the idea of the Holy Land', *Harvard Theological Review* lxxix (1986), pp. 298-307; on the kingship of Christ in the early church, P. Beskow, *Rex Gloriae* (Stockholm, 1962).

[28]For Justin's view of Rome see H. Chadwick, 'Justin Martyr's defence of Christianity', *Bulletin of the John Rylands Library* xlvii (1965), pp. 275-97 (286-7); on Tertullian, M. Sordi, *The Christians and the Roman Empire* (ET London & Sydney, 1983), pp. 172-3.

[29]H. Chadwick and M. Sordi, as cited in the preceding note, both make this point.

inherited pattern of constitutional aspects of the kingdom. These embrace a hope for the kingdom of the saints, which is the kingdom of (true) Israel, and a contrasting potential for the recognition of alien rule as divinely ordained; the two aspects are often but not invariably reconciled by affirmation of the present kingdom of God (including delegation to gentile rulers) as well as the future kingdom (to be manifest in the kingdom of the saints).

*The Approach to Contemporary Political Issues*

The pattern of ideas here described as some constitutional aspects of the kingdom can properly be called 'biblical'. It appears with consistency and strength in the Old Testament and the New, in ancient Judaism and early Christianity. Nevertheless, its full range is not regularly recognised, and its bearing on the approach to social and political questions deserves further notice. Here three implications of the more unitive biblical understandings of the kingdom of God are picked out.

First, the association of the kingdom with Israel carries with it what would be to a modern the conjunction of church and nation in one body called to represent the kingdom of God. This contrasts with the situation of 'churches in the modern state', to quote the title of Neville Figgis' study. It corresponds, however, to one aspect of contemporary British society which sociological inquiry has highlighted, the coexistence of a lack of churchgoing with widespread manifestations of belief in God.[30] To link the kingdom of God with this sociological observation is to meet afresh what Raymond Plant, discussing some characteristic contemporary Christian approaches to British politics, calls the 'Christian nation' view.[31] Such a view is but too clearly prone to unreality, yet it need not be merely tied to the phenomenon of churches 'by law established' in England and Scotland; it can

---

[30]Grace Davie, in G. Ahern & G. Davie, *Inner City God: The Nature of Belief in the Inner City* (London, 1987), pp. 41-56, surveys sociological study of this phenomenon, concluding with D. Martin that it sets a query against descriptions of modern British society as 'secular'.

[31]R. Plant, 'The Anglican Church and the secular state', in G. Moyser, ed., *Church and Politics Today* (Edinburgh, 1985), pp. 313-36 (317-23).

also claim to reckon more seriously than other views with the complex overlap and intermingling between Christian faith and practice and popular tenets and customs, and between ecclesiastical and civil community.

Secondly, the associations of the kingdom with the entire nation of Israel and with the nations of the world set a query against neat distinctions between the sacred and the secular. Government by those who expect to inherit the kingdom can become secular, as in the story of the sons of Zebedee ('You know not what you ask'); conversely, there can be something sacred about the honestly undertaken work of government, even gentile government ('By me kings reign'). Christians, accordingly, can expect to learn from 'secular' political views or social policies. D. M. MacKinnon piercingly criticises excess reverence for the powers that be as ordained of God, but still stresses that Christian thinkers must be prepared to learn as well as teach in the school of statesmanship.[32] He is thinking of international problems, but the observation can be extended to national politics and social action.

Lastly, a recognition of the constitutional aspects of the kingdom in their full range discourages Christian dissociation from political questions. This is strikingly shown in the second century apologists, in whom the millenarian views already noted were not a sign of despair with this present evil age. Second century Christians inherited from the biblical tradition sketched above a quasi-national consciousness of themselves as a body of heirs of the kingdom; but they also followed the same biblical pattern of ideas in acknowledging the delegated sovereignty of Caesar, and in acting as a 'conscience' of the Roman state.[33] The modern Christian can approach social and political questions as one who stands in a biblically grounded tradition suggesting such an approach. This essay has endeavoured to bring out the links made with remarkable consistency in the biblical writings between the kingdom of God, the kingdom of Israel, and the kingdoms of this world.

[32]D. M. MacKinnon, *Themes in Theology: the Three-fold Cord* (Edinburgh, 1987), p. 105.
[33]Chadwick, p. 286.

# 6

# From Reimarus to Sanders: the Kingdom of God, Jesus, and the Judaisms of His Day

## by Robert Morgan

Jesus did not explain what he meant by 'the kingdom of God'. 'We conclude from this that the term must have been quite clear to the Jews of that day and that Jesus referred to it thus; hence there is no other way for us to find out what Jesus' intention was concerning the Kingdom of heaven than to concern ourselves with the usual meaning of this phrase among the Jews of the time.' So argued Hermann Samuel Reimarus (1694-1768)[1] — in what Albert Schweitzer celebrated as 'perhaps the most splendid achievement in the whole course of the historical investigation of the life of Jesus ... the magnificent overture in which are announced all the *motifs* of the future historical treatment of the life of Jesus ...'.[2]

Reimarus' enunciation and pursuit of that principle governing the historical investigation of Jesus' life and teaching

---

[1]'Fragments' of his *Apologie, oder Schützschrift fur die vernünftigen Verehrer Gottes*, written over thirty years and completed in 1767, were published by Lessing, concealing the author's identity, in 1774-8. The complete work was first published in 1972 (2 vols., Frankfurt), but the important passages can be found in English in C. H. Talbert's 1970 edition, *Reimarus: Fragments*, in L. E. Keck's Fortress and SCM *Lives of Jesus* series, from which this quotation is taken (pp. 123f.).

[2]*The Quest of the Historical Jesus: A Critical Study of its Progress from Reimarus to Wrede* (London, 1910), pp. 23, 26. On Schweitzer's books on the NT see especially E. Grässer *Albert Schweitzer als Theologe* (Tübingen, 1979).

earns him pride of place in any account of historical Jesus research. Respect for that principle also suggests E. P. Sanders' *Jesus and Judaism* (1985) with its fine grasp of Palestinian Judaism as a high note on which to mark a modern phase of the discussion. But the similarities between these two perceptive and well-equipped NT historians in our own title could also suggest a presumption in favour of one set of conclusions concerning the meaning of 'the kingdom of God'. The shape of the problem needs therefore to be explored before filling in some details.

'From Reimarus to Sanders' is of course an echo of Albert Schweitzer's *Quest*. The original German was called *Von Reimarus zu Wrede* (1906). It might more accurately have been called *Von Reimarus zu Schweitzer*, as it covered most German and French research from Reimarus not only to Wrede but to Schweitzer's own 'sketch' of the life of Jesus.[3] This had appeared on the same day in 1901 as Wrede's epoch-making *Messianic Secret*, but had been generally ignored. The main purpose of Schweitzer's magnificent but highly tendentious account of his predecessors was to support his own conclusion that the gospels were to be understood in terms of Jesus' eschatological understanding of his whole ministry, teaching and passion.

This eschatological key to the 'historical Jesus' had been overlooked, suppressed, denied, underplayed or spiritualised by liberal Protestant life-of-Jesus research, but recovered by Johannes Weiss' account of *Jesus' Proclamation of the Kingdom of God* first published in 1892[4] — and then expanded from 67 to 214 pages in the definitive second edition of 1900. It was then applied by Schweitzer not only to the preaching of Jesus but to the whole history of his ministry and passion.

---

[3]*Das Abendmahl im Zusammenhang mit dem Leben Jesu und der Geschichte des Urchristentums*. Only Part 2, the 'sketch' of the Life of Jesus (*Das Messianitäts und Leidensgeheimnis*) was translated as *The Mystery of the Kingdom of God* in 1914; the rest as *The Lord's Supper* in 1982.

[4]This first edition was finally translated and edited with an introduction by R. H. Hiers and D. L. Holland (SCM and Fortress series, n.1, 1971). The more important and influential second edition has not been translated. The best recent discussion is B. Lannert, *Die Wiederentdeckung der neutestamentlichen Eschatologie durch Johannes Weiss* (Tübingen, 1989).

It was the sober research of Weiss, not the fireworks of Schweitzer, which carried the eschatological understanding of Jesus' teaching to its dominant position in twentieth century NT scholarship. But it is the ghost of Schweitzer that despite the valiant efforts of C. H. Dodd (see below) and T. F. Glasson[5] still needs to be laid. More colourful than either Reimarus or Sanders, Schweitzer eulogised the one and adumbrated the other, and in England especially was responsible for the way the so-called 'eschatological' interpretation of Jesus was received.[6] Many still talk of a 'near consensus' about what 'the kingdom of God' meant for Jesus, following the impact of Weiss and Schweitzer.[7] E. P. Sanders has much in common with both and is today the most powerful proponent of their type of solution. The presumption lurking in a title based on Schweitzer and referring firstly to his great hero and then to his most impressive modern representative is the suggestion that with all its variations their type of interpretation has carried all before it. That is not so.

At one level of generality it is so. Virtually everyone insists that on Jesus' lips the phrase is 'eschatological', and that (as Weiss and Schweitzer insisted) this is very different from the Kantian-Ritschlian idealist reference to a human moral

---

[5] Among Glasson's many writings on this theme, 'Schweitzer's influence — blessing or bane' (*JTS* 28, 1977) is reprinted in B. D. Chilton (ed.) *The Kingdom of God* (London, 1984) pp. 107-20. Dodd comments on his reaction to Schweitzer in his 1961 Preface to *The Parables of the Kingdom.*

[6] See W. Sanday *The Life of Christ in Modern Research* (Oxford, 1907), G. Tyrrell *Christianity at the Cross-Roads* (London, 1909), F. C. Burkitt 'The eschatological idea in the Gospels' in *Biblical Essays* ed. H. B. Swete (London 1909), and Preface to the *Quest* (1910), B. H. Streeter in *Oxford Studies in the Synoptic Problem* (Oxford, 1911) and 'The historic Christ' in *Foundations* (London, 1912); C. W. Emmett *The Eschatological Question in the Gospels* (Edinburgh, 1911) is negative about it. Latimer Jackson *The Eschatology of Jesus* (London, 1913) gives a balanced judgment.

[7] T. F. Glasson op. cit. in Chilton (1984) p. 107 quotes B. Lindars' T. W. Manson memorial lecture (1974): 'Modern scholarship has largely accepted the results of Albert Schweitzer's classical study of this issue . . .'. Cf. also H. Schürmann *Gottes Reich — Jesu Geschick* (Freiburg, 1983), p. 21 'Since Johannes Weiss there is almost a consensus'. J. T. Sanders *Ethics in the NT* (London, 1975), p. 3 drops the 'almost' but then discusses 'dissenters' who do not share it (Dodd, Kasemann, Funk). There are several others, e.g. G. B. Caird and now M. Borg (nn. 5, 38), but the rhetoric prevails where argument is weak.

community, as reflected in the older liberalism from Renan's *Vie de Jésus* (1863) to Harnack's *Wesen des Christentums* (1900, ET *What is Christianity?* 1901). But that word 'eschatological' has accumulated a wide range of meanings and needs more precise definition. In some criticism it means that Jesus expected the end of the world soon and was evidently mistaken, as M. Tindal has claimed. In other theological writing (e.g. K. Barth, *The Epistle to the Romans* (1921² ET Oxford 1933) p. 314) it means the action of the transcendent God, in contrast to purely human inner worldly activity. Where there is no reference at all to the end of the world, the word is inappropriate, but unlike catastrophe theory it belongs to discourse about God and therefore cannot be isolated from talk of human existence, personal and social. In the reaction against Ritschlianism the ethical and ecclesiological dimensions of 'the kingdom of God' were sometimes lost to view but some subsequent discussions have recovered the relationship of the phrase to individual behaviour, the Messianic community, and religious worship and belief.

Contemporary interpretations of this admittedly eschatological gospel phrase vary considerably, but these variations are less striking than what divides most critical NT scholars today from their nineteenth century predecessors: a new uncertainty about how many of the words attributed to Jesus in the Synoptic Gospels were actually uttered by him, and a recognition that we can only guess at the precise nuances of the underlying Aramaic, and at the original contexts in which the parables were told and sayings uttered. In this respect Schweitzer belongs firmly with the biographers of Jesus that he criticised. His reconstruction was less a modernisation than theirs, but he shared their confidence that the historian could give a full and accurate picture out of the available sources, especially Matthew.[8]

---

[8]'The historical problem of the life of Jesus cannot be recognised, much less solved, from the fragmentary record of Mark. The differing narratives of the two oldest Gospels are equally valuable, but Matthew's fulness gives it greater importance.' (*Quest* p. xi, from the Introduction to the third edition (1950).) Contrast Sanders (op. cit.) pp. 4, 13–17, 149.

The relatively favourable reception of the *Quest* in England, in contrast to the hostility shown to Wrede's *Messianic Secret* (1901, not translated until 1971) and to Bultmann's *History of the Synoptic Tradition* (1921, 1933,[2] not translated until 1963; revised 1968), illustrates how unwilling English theology was to follow the German lead up the 'history of traditions' path. The great liberals were widely followed — Wellhausen on the OT, Holtzmann in NT, Harnack in church history. The history of traditions research pioneered by Wrede, and in Wellhausen's never translated gospel commentaries (1903-5) and advanced by K. L. Schmidt in *The Framework of the Gospel History* (1919, never translated)[9] and by the form critics, was not widely accepted until later. But these scholars mark out the path of twentieth century gospel criticism even more clearly than does the ambiguous label 'eschatology'.

In flagging as the fourth great alternative facing modern criticism, *either* his own 'consistent eschatology' *or* Wrede's 'consistent scepticism', Schweitzer at least saw the significance of Wrede's book, even if he totally failed to see how far Wrede was right. But this alternative proved a false one. Most scholars (including Wrede) accepted the importance of eschatology for Jesus without accepting Schweitzer's fanciful reconstruction of his ministry,[10] and Wrede's path proved to be the main line for historical criticism of the gospels. The title *Von Reimarus zu Wrede* thus revealed more of the shape of things to come than the more accurate *Von Reimarus zu Schweitzer* would have done. There is no escaping the implications of Wrede's scepticism for our questions about the historical Jesus.

But there is no escaping Schweitzer either. His powerful reading of the early history of the *Quest* has mesmerised his

---

[9]*Der Rahmen der Geschichte Jesu* (Berlin, 1919, reprinted Darmstadt, 1969). Excerpts are translated in W. G. Kümmel *The NT. The History of the Investigation of its Problems* (Eng. tr. Nashville, 1972, London, 1973) pp. 328-30.

[10]Cf. Bultmann *History* p. 137, n. 2 on Schweitzer's 'fantasies'. The best survey (up to 1947) is G. Lundström *The Kingdom of God in the Teaching of Jesus. A History of Interpretation from the Last Decades of the Nineteenth Century to the Present Day* (Diss, Uppsala, 1947, ET London, 1963). See also N. Perrin *The Kingdom of God in the Teaching of Jesus* (London, 1963), and Wendell Willis (ed.) *The Kingdom of God in Twentieth-Century Interpretation* (Peabody, Massachusetts 1987).

successors. One has to discuss some of the same older scholars without being seduced by Schweitzer's siren which either sucks them into support for his own eccentric conclusions or else stigmatises them as the enemy of eschatology.

The way in which any late twentieth century discussion of the historical Jesus must revise while revisiting Schweitzer's *Quest* is by counterbalancing the Weiss and Schweitzer question about Jesus' eschatology with Wrede's question about the historicity of the sources. Both questions combined in a pincer movement to destroy nineteenth century liberal interpretations of Jesus, but the scepticism of Wrede was equally fatal to Schweitzer's reconstruction. It transferred from Jesus to the account of the early Church much of the evidence for Jesus' messianic convictions and so undercut accounts which made this the key to Jesus' understanding of 'the kingdom of God'. The question of Jesus' understanding of his mission remains central to any quest for the historical Jesus, but answers to it have become so uncertain that it no longer provides the base from which interpretations of 'the kingdom of God' can be derived. On the contrary, this is now a main plank in our tentative assessments of Jesus' self-identity.

It is now his historical scepticism, much more than his raising the question of eschatology, that makes Reimarus that 'magnificent overture in which are announced all the *motifs* of the future historical treatment of the life of Jesus' (n. 2). Writing in the mid-eighteenth century (over a period of thirty years, completing his manuscript in 1767) he anticipated Wrede's central insight that all the gospels represent Christian interpretations of Jesus which differ in some crucial respects from the historical reality. Nineteenth century liberals from Strauss to Schweitzer attributed the stories of the supernatural and most of the Johannine discourse material to subsequent Christian experience, but Reimarus like Wrede perceived subsequent interpretation in the synoptic sayings on which the liberals built their reconstructions first of Jesus' life, and then when it was realised that 'a life of Christ cannot be written' (Ritschl), of his teaching.

Reimarus' *explanation* of what he judged, with a remarkable prescience, to be non-authentic material in the gospels is not plausible now that the gospels are dated late in the first century. He thought their unhistorical elements originated in a deliberate fraud perpetrated by the apostles immediately after the crucifixion to save their skins and their cosy religious jobs. This was based on his pre-critical acceptance of the apostolic authorship of Matthew's Gospel, plus a bit of anti-clericalism. D. F. Strauss (see below) and his successors saw that the fictional elements in the Gospels developed more slowly and unconsciously. But Reimarus' fundamental insight, that the historical truth about Jesus has to be sifted out of accounts that aim to give a different picture, adumbrates twentieth century treatments of the historical Jesus, as Schweitzer in his critical innocence does not.

Justified doubts about the authenticity of much of the evidence make the historical reconstruction of Jesus' ministry and teaching far more tentative than Schweitzer was prepared to accept. Only a reckless NT scholar would now claim to know with any certainty what exactly Jesus meant by the phrase 'the kingdom of God', even though nearly all agree that he used it, and that it was central. We all have our guesses, and some are more educated than others, and a few like Schweitzer get carried away by their enthusiasm and inspirations. But much of the data is suspect, and all the arguments for assigning one saying to the early Church and another to Jesus himself are based on total reconstructions of both, and these in turn depend on an historian's judgement about the origin of each individual piece of tradition. All reconstructions therefore involve an element of circularity. We try to sharpen our criteria of authenticity, but they remain rules of thumb (cf. n. 81). We aim to tell a plausible story about Jesus and his preaching of the kingdom of God, and another one about the beliefs of the early churches, recognising that the pieces of evidence in the gospels may belong to one or to the other or to both. Coherence becomes the main criterion, but we also look first for what seems most probably to belong to one picture or the other, and are helped in this by what we know about early Christianity from the rest of the NT, and what we know from other sources about Palestinian Judaism prior to the destruction of Jerusalem in C.E. 70.

Reimarus was therefore right to look at both Judaism and subsequent Christianity in order to reconstruct the history of Jesus and his followers. But over two centuries of further research has inevitably revealed deficiencies in his picture of Judaism. Schweitzer thought he could improve on Reimarus here, thanks to the discovery, especially in the 1850s, of 'apocalyptic' as an important strand in the Judaism of Jesus' time. But was this the key to Jesus' message and activity? In particular was it the key to the phrase 'the kingdom of God'? The most important investigator of Jesus' Aramaic language thought not: G. Dalman in *The Words of Jesus* (1898, ET 1902, pp. 91-147) shows how common the idea is in Judaism — and how rare in apocalyptic writings. Weiss had to agree (second edition, p. 19). Opinion remains divided. The question of Jesus' background was rightly raised by Reimarus, but given the variety of Judaisms[11] in the time of Jesus it is less easily answered than either Reimarus or Schweitzer thought.

The question of Jesus' *usage* of the phrase 'the kingdom of God' is no less important than its background, as again Reimarus perceived. His conclusion that Jesus used the term 'kingdom of God' in the same way as his contemporaries is based on his observation that Jesus does not explain it: 'The parables that he uses about it teach us nothing or certainly not very much if we do not already have some idea that we can connect with the phrase' (p. 123). Reimarus was right to infer that both the disciples and the crowd must have understood the phrase, but over-confident about his historian's ability to reconstruct their understanding, and premature in excluding any novelty or creativity on Jesus' part. It is difficult to deny all originality to Jesus, in view of the impact he made. Certain meanings can be excluded as historically impossible, and incompatible with what he is known to have said and done, as Weiss was powerfully to demonstrate. But those who like Bousset[12] responded to Weiss by emphasising the novelty in Jesus' teaching are unlikely to have been entirely wrong. It may also be the case that when

---

[11]Cf. J. Neusner, W. S. Green, E. Frerichs (eds.) *Judaisms and their Messiahs at the Turn of the Christian Era* (Cambridge, 1987).

[12]*Jesu Predigt in ihrem Gegensatz zum Judentum* (Göttingen, 1902).

interpreting how an ancient thought about God an element of conscious modernisation or self-involvement, properly controlled by what is known of first century thought, will take us closer to the heart of the matter than a deliberate exclusion of all modern religious sensibility. The nature and functions of eschatological language are more elusive than some who have used the slogan in justifiable reaction against Ritschlian interpretations have understood. Their arguments about whether it is 'here' or 'near' have not been notably successful in specifying what the 'it' is or will be.

Retracing now a few of Schweitzer's steps in an attempt to escape the spell cast by his brilliant rhetoric, we can at least join hands with him in saluting Reimarus. This great Hamburger rightly reconstructed both the historical Jesus and early Christianity in terms of his understanding of contemporary Jewish messianism. He identified two strands in Jewish eschatology (not his words) and attributed one to Jesus and the other to the disciples after his death, as they rewrote the script to cover up the fiasco of failure. Jesus saw himself as a political, Son of David Messiah, bringing worldly deliverance to Israel, provocatively entering Jerusalem on an ass with a foal to fulfil the coming king prophecy of Zechariah 9.9, and committing an act of violence (John 2.15) in the Temple. He was justly executed as a messianic pretender, and died with his hopes frustrated, a cry of dereliction on his lips (pp. 135-50).

The other minority view current in first-century Judaism was (Reimarus thought) that 'the Messiah would come twice, and each time after quite a different manner. The first time he would appear in misery and would suffer and die. The second time he would come in the clouds of heaven and receive unlimited power' (p. 213).

Justin's Jewish interlocutor Trypho, to whom Reimarus appeals, has proved an unreliable witness, and 'the Talmud and other Jewish writings' (ibid.) give scant support to the idea of a suffering Messiah and second coming. But Reimarus' general approach foreshadows the correlation of history of religions and history of traditions methods characteristic of twentieth century research. His accounts of Jewish messianism were only as good as the state of research at the time allowed, but he was right about there being some variety of eschatological beliefs in first-century Judaism, and it is quite credible that the disciples' views, shaped at least in part by the death of Jesus and what followed it, were not identical with those of their master during his ministry.[13] Reimarus' anticipation of Wrede's history-of-traditions separation of the different layers in the gospels, and his correlation of these with the two eschatologies he thought were to be found in the Jewish milieu of Jesus and the first disciples, are even more impressive. His judgements about what material came from Jesus and what from the early Church (e.g. the passion predictions) have found a large measure of agreement in the present century, and it is to his credit that he described what he judged authentic without suppressing either the ethics of Jesus which he approved or the messianism which he did not. The resulting amalgam is not historically satisfactory, but it flags a real problem which some others have evaded.

On the one hand a deist like Reimarus could value those parts of Jesus' teaching which 'referred man (*sic*) to the true great goal of religion, namely, eternal salvation' (p. 64). But on the other, 'it is regrettable that Jesus so soiled and obscured his other services for the active religion of humanity by his aim to become Messiah of the Jews' (1972 complete ed., vol. 2, p. 170).

The lack of historical perspective here is plain, but that makes it all the more striking that in contrast to Kant and later Ritschl, Reimarus does not extend his modernising treatment to the phrase 'the kingdom of God'. His political interpretation is historically argued and has had a long life.[14] It is surely mistaken, but hard to refute on account of the evidence being

---

[13]This point is well made by E. P. Sanders: 'The question of just what Jesus expected is hard to answer, for obvious reasons. Here, if anywhere, the crucifixion and the resurrection would have influenced the expectations of Christians after Jesus' death, and consequently may have affected the evidence' (p. 228). But Sanders in practice gives too much weight to the continuities, Reimarus to the discontinuities.

[14]Cf. E. Bammel 'The revolutionary theory from Reimarus to Brandon' in *Jesus and the Politics of His Day* (eds. E. Bammel and C. F. D. Moule (Cambridge, 1984) pp. 11-68).

uncertain. The discussion has also been hindered by false alternatives. One can deny that Jesus was violent, but social and political implications can scarcely be excluded from Jesus' ministry altogether.[15]

The second great hero of Schweitzer's *Quest* is David Friedrich Strauss (1808-74) whose *Life of Jesus* (1835)[16] presents Jesus as 'a Jewish claimant of the Messiahship, whose world of thought is purely exchatological' (*Quest* p. 95). Like Reimarus, Strauss adumbrates twentieth century history of traditions research as well as its interest in eschatology. But he is less sceptical about the historicity of Jesus' sayings, and therefore stands closer to Schweitzer than to Wrede. He agrees with Reimarus and many contemporary NT scholars in denying the authenticity of some passion and resurrection predictions (p. 567) but unlike a growing number of specialists today, accepts the eschatological Son of man sayings. He therefore concludes from that material that Jesus saw himself destined to return as Messiah — Son of man. But the way he struggles to make sense of the disparate materials that he accepts as authentic is superior to Schweitzer's fatal fluency, and more revealing of problems in the gospels which cannot be conjured away by waving a wand called eschatology. His exploration of the authenticity of the discourses on the Second Advent at §115-16 points a modern reader towards more sceptical conclusions.

Coming some 300 pages after his brilliant discussion in Chapter 4 on 'Jesus the Messiah', Strauss' unwarranted conservative conclusion that Jesus expected to come on clouds does not infect everything else, as it does with Schweitzer. His discussion of 'the kingdom of God' is not distorted by an apocalyptic lens drawn from the eschatological Son of man material. Even though Strauss naturally supposed that 'the Son of man' must be the Messiah, and that at some point in his

---

[15]See J. H. Yoder *The Politics of Jesus* (Grand Rapids, 1972), R. Cassidy *Jesus, Politics and Society* (Maryknoll, 1978), M. Borg *Conflict, Holiness and Politics in the Teachings of Jesus* (New York and Toronto, 1974), C. Rowland *passim*.

[16]George Eliot's celebrated translation (1846) of *Das Leben Jesu* (1835) is conveniently available in P. C. Hodgson's 1972 edition in the same series as Reimarus and Weiss (nn. 1, 4).

ministry Jesus meant himself when he used the phrase, since in the majority of cases (e.g. Matt. 18.11(!); 9.6; Mark 8.31ff.; cf. 16.22) a self-reference is plain (p. 283), this does not prevent him from seeing other elements in Jesus' teaching.

Writing before Lachmann (1835), Wilke (1838) and C. H. Weisse (1838) had made out the case for the priority of Mark, finally established by H. J. Holtzmann in 1863, Strauss still believed in the priority of Matthew. Those who make Matthew their main source and like Strauss accept the authenticity of most of the Son of man sayings are almost bound to be misled by the quotations of Dan. 7.13 and the passage concerning the Son of man coming in his kingdom (Matt. 16.28) to correlate and in effect subordinate 'the kingdom' to the eschatological Son of man, as happens in Dan. 7 which (Strauss thought) Jews of Jesus' time interpreted messianically. It is therefore all the more impressive that Strauss is sensitive to aspects of the evidence which point in other directions.

Holding it (pre-Wrede) to be 'an indisputable fact' that 'Jesus held and expressed the conviction that he was the Messiah' (p. 284) Strauss naturally discussed 'the kingdom of heaven' or 'messianic kingdom' in terms of Jesus' 'messianic plan', considered in terms of its 'half religious, half political' Jewish background. Like Reimarus, he thought it impossible to avoid an element of temporal rule in Jesus' messianic self-consciousness, because 'the fact is that the prevalent conception of the messianic reign had a strong political bias; hence when Jesus spoke of the Messiah's kingdom without a definition, the Jews could only think of an earthly dominion, and as Jesus could not have presupposed any other interpretation of his words, he must have wished to be so understood' (p. 293). More importantly, he sent out to announce the Messiah's kingdom (Matt. 10) apostles who could dispute about their status on the right and left hand of the messianic king (Mark 10.35ff.) and who even after the resurrection expected a restoration of the kingdom to Israel (Acts 1.6 — Reimarus also had laid great weight on Luke 24.21a). Jesus thus sent them out knowing that they would disseminate a political conception of his messiahship. Even if he was speaking spiritually at Matt. 19.28 the disciples must have understood him literally, and

Jesus must have recognised this. He therefore intended to nourish their temporal hopes. And then there was the entry into Jerusalem, deliberately fulfilling the prophecy of Zechariah.

But Strauss also saw there was much to be said on other sides than eschatology and political messianism, and that the historian has to take account of *all* the evidence considered reliable, not pick out bits to fit a thesis. 'In the parables by which Jesus shadowed forth the kingdom of heaven, in the Sermon on the Mount in which he illustrates the duties of its citizens, and lastly in his whole demeanour and course of action, we have sufficient evidence that his idea of the messianic kingdom was peculiar to himself' (ibid.). There is no trace of Jesus forming a political party; he withdrew when the people wanted to make him king (John 6.15). Strauss adumbrates Harnack's interpretation of Luke 17.20f. — 'the messianic kingdom comes not with observation but is to be sought for in the recesses of the soul' (p. 295) — and he even accepts the authenticity of John 18.36 — 'My kingdom is not of this world'.

In seeking to strike a balance between the evidence adduced by Reimarus, and the orthodox spiritualisation of Jesus' teaching, Strauss finally comes quite close to Schweitzer without using the word eschatology, and even to E. P. Sanders' association of Jesus with 'restoration Judaism'. Like Sanders he accepts and gives weight to Matt. 19.28, and like the eschatologists (and against Reimarus) attributes that sitting on thrones judging the twelve tribes of Israel not to a political revolution but to 'a revolution to be effected by the immediate interposition of God' (p. 296). Rebirth (*palingenesia*), he points out,

> was not a political revolution any more than a spiritual regeneration, — it was a resurrection of the dead, which God was to effect through the agency of the Messiah, and which was to usher in the messianic times. Jesus certainly expected to restore the throne of David, and with his disciples to govern a liberated people; in no degree, however, did he rest his hopes on the sword of human adherents (Lk. 22.38, Mt. 26.52), but on the legions of angels which his heavenly Father could send him (Mt. 26.53). . . . Thus we conclude that the messianic hope of

Jesus was not political, nor even merely earthly, for he referred its fulfilment to supernatural means, and to a supermundane theatre (the regenerated earth): as little was it a purely spiritual hope, in the modern sense of the term, for it included important and unprecedented changes in the external condition of things: but it was the national, theocratic hope, spiritualised and ennobled by his own peculiar moral and religious views. (p. 296)

This is the synthesis of one who accepts the general reliability of the synoptic sayings and struggles to hold together conflicting tendencies within it. A later generation would not share that confidence and would therefore be far more selective in its choice of data — and would therefore inevitably run the risk of picking and choosing evidence to support a particular and more coherent thesis. Strauss not only demolishes his supernaturalist and rationalist predecessors, he also anticipates (as did Reimarus) the liberals' spiritualising and the theocratic political interpretation of the kingdom. But he also anticipates the later 'apocalyptic' other worldly interpretation of Jesus by Weiss and Schweitzer which Reimarus (like some today) assigned to the early Church.

Gospel criticism after Strauss' 1835 *Life of Jesus* established the two-source hypothesis — the priority of something like our Mark, and the use by Matthew and Luke of another early source, now lost, in addition to Mark. That became important for the liberal lives of Jesus which followed Renan's (1863), as these mostly depended on the Marcan outline. But that framework buckled in the early twentieth century, and source criticism of the synoptics has in the longer perspective proved only indirectly important for historical Jesus research, i.e. through its contributions to understanding the history of the gospel tradition.

All sources and strata of tradition have to be sifted for reliable information, regardless of their data. But belief that Matthew used Mark allows some of his divergencies to be judged redactional rather than original. The double tradition, by contrast, contains much that on grounds of coherence seems original, whether or not one believes in Q as a literary source. However, if we believe that Luke used Matthew, while altering him sometimes in the light of alternative versions of a saying known to him, and sometimes for editorial reasons, then some of the material most confidently accepted as Q and original (e.g. Matt. 10.7) has to be re-examined. Matthew might be following earlier Jewish Christian tradition (he usually is), but the existence of a Lucan parallel no longer guarantees this, for Q sceptics. He might have modelled the disciples' proclamation, like the Baptist's, on that of Jesus (4.17). This latest turn of the sceptical screw illustrates how scholars' understanding of the historical Jesus depends very largely now on what material is considered original, and how conversely these judgements about authenticity are influenced by one's hypothesis about Jesus' mission and message. Source criticism is no longer the royal road to the historical Jesus, but one line of questioning which assists us in evaluating the sources.

The next, and most important, advance in historical Jesus research was made along the lines that Reimarus had laid down when he asked about 'the usual meaning of the phrase (kingdom of God) among the Jews of the time' (op. cit.). The apocalyptic character of the OT book of Daniel, its difference from OT prophecy and its similarities with the book of Revelation, had been recognised in the eighteenth century, but the new factor was the discovery of intertestamental Jewish writings beginning with 1 Enoch (Ethiopian Enoch) which an English traveller in Africa discovered, and Sayce published in 1800.[17] 2 Esdras (4 Ezra), pushed out of the canon by Luther[18] and so sidelined for Protestants, gained new attention, and in 1832 F. Lücke attempted a 'complete introduction to the Revelation of John and the whole of apocalyptic literature' on the basis of the two canonical writings, plus 2 Esdras (4 Ezra) in the Apocrypha, the Sibylline Books, and the Ethiopic Enoch. By the mid-nineteenth century 'apocalyptic' was established as a label for several

---

[17] See J. M. Schmidt *Die jüdische Apokalyptik. Die Geschichte ihrer Forschung von den Anfängen bis zu den Textfunden von Qumran*, (Neukirchen-Vluyn 1969, 1976²). More popular, K. Koch *Ratlos vor Apokalyptik* (Gütersloh, 1970, ET *The Rediscovery of Apocalyptic*, London, 1972).

[18] In his Preface to the Book of Revelation he rightly compared 4 Esdras (Vulgate) to that book of 'visions and figures' — see Kümmel's *History* p. 26.

intertestamental writings and Daniel 7–13 soon became generally recognised as deriving from the second century. The outstanding Strasbourg historian E. Reuss wrote on the 'Johannine Apocalypse' in 1843 and analysed the concept 'apocalyptic' with its doctrine of the two ages.[19] Enoch had made little impression in Germany where few theologians could read Ethiopic or even English[20] but in 1853 A. Dillmann translated it. Finally A. Hilgenfeld's classic *De Jüdische Apokalyptik in ihrer geschichtlichen Entwicklung* (1857 rp Darmstadt 1966) appeared and the new field of study was established.

Further materials became available later in the century: *The Assumption of Moses* (from the Old Latin) in 1861, 2 Baruch (from the Syriac) in 1866, *The Ascension of Isaiah* from Ethiopic manuscripts in 1877, 3 Baruch in 1886 (Slavonic) and 1896 (Greek), 2 Enoch in 1896 and the *Apocalypse of Abraham* in 1897, and it was natural to suppose that these might contain the key to 'the usual meaning of the phrase (the kingdom of God) among the Jews of the time'. In fact the phrase barely occurs in this new material. But it contributed to an understanding of Jewish thought from the second century B.C.E. and contains some points of contact with other sayings attributed to Jesus in the gospels. In retrospect the decisive question is whether these *other* sayings are original to Jesus, in which case they will determine our picture of Jesus, or whether (as Reimarus thought) they originated in the early Church, in which case they must not be allowed to determine our picture of Jesus or what he meant by 'the kingdom of God'.

There were several developments in Jewish eschatology subsequent to the prophets and Psalms that had clearly expressed the idea of God's kingship or rule. These developments include a variety of expectations that God would intervene in this present evil age and establish his rule, some thought by the agency of a messianic Son of David figure

---

[19]This article from the *Allgemeine Encyclopädie der Wissenschaften und Künste* is reprinted in the Wissenschaftliche Buchgesellschaft 'Wege der Forschung' Vol. 365 *Apokalyptik* (ed. K. Koch and J. M. Schmidt, Darmstadt 1982).

[20]Archbishop R. Laurence had published his English translation at Oxford in 1821.

(Psalms of Solomon 17 — not an apocalypse). But only *The Assumption of Moses* 10 speaks of God's rule appearing. That is too slender a basis for interpreting Jesus' sayings about the kingdom of God in terms of the apocalypses. The justification for understanding Jesus (who never wrote an apocalypse) in this way comes from a darker corner.

In the later apocalypse 4 Ezra, written around 100 C.E., and in the perhaps equally late *Similitudes of Enoch*, a 'Son of man' is depicted in imagery drawn from Daniel 7. This seems to provide the key to the gospel sayings of Jesus about the eschatological Son of man. So long as the authenticity of these was taken for granted these parallels in two Jewish apocalypses provided some grounds for interpreting Jesus' teaching in similar terms. But when the authenticity of these sayings is challenged (as it was by Colani as early as 1864[21] and has been by a minority of scholars ever since) it becomes questionable whether the apocalypses provide the key to Jesus' teaching. His use of the phrase 'the kingdom of God' and talk of its coming then has to be weighed in the light of other possible Jewish backgrounds and meanings. 'Eschatological' interpretations of 'the kingdom of God' have survived the now widespread belief that 'the apocalyptic Son of man' sayings reflect early post-resurrection expectations rather than Jesus' own, but that is to anticipate . . .

The two most important books in establishing the near consensus within NT scholarship that Jesus' teaching was in some sense 'eschatological' were those of Baldensperger and Weiss. Albert Schweitzer was important for the subsequent English discussion, but at that time advances in gospel criticism came from Germany, and there Schweitzer was not highly regarded. By the time his *Quest* appeared in 1906 Weiss' second edition (1900) had already won a large measure of acceptance.[22]

In *Das Selbstbewusstsein Jesu im Lichte der messianischen Hoffnungen seiner Zeit* (1888) W. Baldensperger drew on E. Schürer's great *History of the Jewish People in the Time of Jesus Christ*

---

[21] *Jésus-Christ et les Croyances Messianiques de son Temps* (Strasbourg, 1864).
[22] So Lannert op. cit.

(initially 1874, but expanded in subsequent editions) to analyse first the messianic hopes of Judaism and especially the concept of apocalyptic. He then discussed the self-consciousness of Jesus, i.e. his messianic self-consciousness, against that background. In accord with the rising tide of history of religions research, he placed Jesus more firmly than most other NT scholars had done in his first century Jewish context, understanding this with the help of the new discoveries of Jewish documents from the period. Apocalyptic, he thought, involved a 'renunciation of secular political ideals and the intensification of messianic expectations into the realm of the supernatural'.[23] This explained Jesus' apparent lack of a political programme and his talk of the Son of man.

From a later perspective one of the many merits of Baldensperger's book is that it begins the discussion of Jesus' self-consciousness with an account of his preaching of the kingdom of God, with the result that what now seem the most questionable data do not seriously distort the picture. That is even more true of Weiss' decisive monograph four years later. Here, the limited focus on *Jesus' Proclamation of the Kingdom of God* (1892 ET 1971) sharpened the impact of the case incontrovertibly made for interpreting the phrase eschatologically. 'The kingdom of God has drawn near' (*engiken*) is well-attested in Mark 1.15 and Q (Matt. 10.7; Luke 10.9, 11), in which Weiss like most critical scholars then and later believed. The meaning 'seems quite clear: the Kingdom (or the rule) of God has drawn so near that it stands at the door. Therefore, while the *basileia* is not yet *here*, it is extremely near' (Eng. tr. pp. 65f.). Thus Weiss begins his strong exegetical argument, moving on to Matt. 12.28, parallel Luke 11.20, where *ephthasen eph' hymas* is similar, the verbs providing variant translations of the Aramaic *mt'* at Dan. 4.8.

One might object that Mark 13.29, which does not mention the kingdom, has been illegitimately introduced ('at the door') to reinforce the notion of an imminent (temporal) expectation. These verbs are more commonly spatial, but they can have a

[23] Quoted from the excerpt in W. G. Kümmel op. cit. p. 216.

temporal sense, and it is reasonable to refer to the Jewish doctrine of the two ages and other gospel passages (e.g. Mark 14.25) in support of a temporal meaning here. Kümmel later saw that parable of the fig-tree as the clearest evidence 'that Jesus' proclamation of the nearness of the coming reign of God can only have been meant in the temporal sense that God's unqualified rule is soon to be actualised'.[24]

In his second (1900) edition Weiss regretted that the debate about this 'concept' (*Begriff*) of God's rule had concentrated one-sidedly on the unfruitful debate over how far Jesus had thought of it as still future, and how far already present (p. 69). He rejected too sharp a contrast between present and future, insisting that it is essentially future, as the Lord's Prayer makes clear. It is not yet here, even though in 'moments of sublime prophetic enthusiasm, when an awareness of victory comes over him' (Eng. tr. p. 78) Jesus speaks of it as already present. The point is not how imminent the crisis is but Jesus' certainty of it. 'The time of waiting is past; the turn of the ages is here' (second ed. p. 69). When we see thunder clouds we might say 'there's a storm coming', or (proleptically) 'it's a storm' (p. 70). As this analogy and the word *proleptisch* make clear, the present sayings are interpreted in the light of the essentially future coming of God's rule. The notion of imminence is surely implicit, but Weiss (unlike Schweitzer) places no emphasis on it. He is concerned to stress its futurity and transcendence — God will establish his rule — and can admit that there is no direct evidence that Jesus had at times 'hoped that he might yet live to see that great event' (Eng. tr. p. 85).

The force of Weiss' historical case lay not in clarifying the elusive nature of the kingdom of God, but in showing that the Ritschlian concept which had dominated liberal theology, and which he himself shared at the theological level, could not exegetically be identified with Jesus' own meaning. If on occasion Jesus 'speaks of a Kingdom of God which is present, it is not because there is present a community of disciples

---

[24]See 'Eschatological expectation in the proclamation of Jesus' (1964), reprinted in Chilton (1984) p. 38.

among whom God's will is done, as if God's rule were realised from the side of men' (Eng. tr. p. 78). Jesus was not the 'founder' of the kingdom of God in the Ritschlian sense. His belief in a God beyond this world, who is making his power felt and about to transform it, should not be confused with modern religious humanism or inner-worldly development.

Weiss' sharp contrast between his own theological Ritschlianism and his historical understanding of early Jewish conceptions could be challenged by reflection about the nature of religion and talk of God. Positivists who talk of Jesus' 'imminent expectation' in terms analogous to our expectation of the general election which will come soon, we know not when, are further from 'the kingdom of God' than Ritschlians who realise that talk of God involves talk of this world and the mystery of human existence. But Weiss' historical corrective was needed. His awareness of the difference between modern liberalism and the New Testament was correct, and his perception of this as a task for modern theology was more constructive than that of conservatives (Sanday) and neo-conservatives (Barth) who saw in it only a weapon against liberal Protestantism.

The second edition of Weiss' book is still arguably the best treatment of the subject available. Part of its merit lies in its sobriety and care not to outrun the evidence which he accepted as reliable. Admittedly he accepted more material as original to Jesus than many would today, and was led by this to make a suggestion that now seems speculative about how Jesus' mind changed in the course of his ministry: that he was compelled by the general lack of response to reckon with a longer period (twenty or thirty years) before the end came (Eng. tr. p. 86; second edition pp. 101f.). The same acceptance of doubtful material led Weiss to interpret Jesus' self-consciousness in terms of his expecting to become the apocalyptic Son of man.[25] But he recognised that so far as we can see Jesus did not specify

---

[25]Eng. tr. p. 82 'Thus, since Jesus is now a rabbi, a prophet, he has nothing in common with the Son of man, except the claim that he will *become* the Son of man. Thus even he cannot intervene in the development of the Kingdom of God. He has to wait, just as the people have to wait.'

what the coming salvation would be like. 'We possess not one certain saying in which Jesus expressed himself' concerning the future transformation (second edition, p. 110). He used the eschatological language of his day but placed no great weight on it. He used it unreflectively, allowing his hearers to fill out his language with all their hopes of messianic salvation (p. 115). As with Strauss, these good observations about the kingdom material scarcely cohere with the apocalyptic Son of man sayings which like most nineteenth century scholars they still accepted.

The reticence which Weiss ascribes to Jesus leaves room for the religious dimensions of Jesus' words which are lost when the language of eschatology is pressed more literalistically. It is not at all easy for any modern interpreter to be sure how Jesus or even Paul understood this imagery. The modern fundamentalist and adventist analogies that spring to mind are probably grossly misleading. But Weiss' religiously sensitive discussion in the second edition, pp. 85-121, is persuasive and points in some ways towards the Rudolfs, Otto and Bultmann. Schweitzer, on the other hand, described the debate from the perspective of his own construction, and his description needs to be challenged. Instead of his unhelpful alternative, 'eschatological or non-eschatological', his account of 'the struggle against eschatology' (*Quest* ch. 16), and his attempt to force a simple choice between 'the sceptical and eschatological schools' (*Quest* p. 334) i.e. Wrede and himself, it should be recognised that Wrede accepted the eschatological character of Jesus' preaching of the kingdom.[26] Granted that Jesus spoke of God in some of the eschatological language of first century Judaism it remains a question how this is to be understood and whether it can even be described without a strong element of interpretation.

Weiss was determined to keep historical description and theological interpretation firmly separate. Like Gunkel on *The Influence of the Holy Spirit* (1888, Eng. tr. 1979) he represented

---

[26]*Vorträge und Studien* (Tübingen, 1907) contains a lecture given in 1894 summarised by Lundström op. cit.

the history of religion school's determination to clarify the historical distance between then and now, however important it is for theology or hermeneutics to bridge the gulf that historical research has ascertained. The merits of this position are as clear as its difficulties. It allowed Weiss to remain a Ritschlian in theology without compromising his integrity as a historian, but it left him with a theology that had lost its scriptural warrants.

Nobody can dispute the historians' right to interpret the biblical sources in ways that serve their own constructions. Much good has accrued to theology from other disciplines doing their own business with integrity. But even historical knowledge is fragile here. By refusing to fill in the gaps in the evidence and attribute to Jesus convictions which he may not have held (on the weak grounds that a few other visionaries held them) Weiss left the interpretation of Jesus' eschatology open, and while holding exegesis and modern theology apart, himself introduced some theological reflection into his exegetical discussion. As a Christian theologian specialising in the interpretation of Scripture he was not disposed to let his historical knowledge and exegetical skills serve a positivistic anti-theological bias.

Jesus' expectation of God's future eschatological intervention (our metaphor, not his) at the end of the age, to save and judge the world, is reflected in the prayer he taught his disciples. 'Thy kingdom come', like the synagogue prayer from about this time with which it invites comparison[27] is not a forlorn hope but a confident expectation based on the inner certainty of faith. The images in which such faith and hope in God are expressed are usually those found in one's religious tradition and are easily varied. Paul, for example, can make contradictory statements about the end, which suggests that he did not intend them literalistically. Statements of time are unavoidable in eschatological discourse but it is a category mistake to treat them like a railway timetable. Jesus warned against this (Luke

---

[27]On the Kaddish prayer (see below p.110) cf. B. F. Meyer *The Aims of Jesus* (London, 1979) p. 289.

17.20) and that should guard his interpreters against jumping to premature conclusions about his discourse concerning God. When it all was assumed to be about himself, his messianic status and role, it was natural to timetable it more precisely to correspond with his own human life-span. Once this connection is loosened by doubts concerning the authenticity of the eschatological Son of man sayings, the elusive character of Jesus' parabolic talk of God's rule can be better appreciated.

Even Weiss was quite cautious on the question of imminence. The main argument for an imminent expectation is the Matt. 10 account[28] of his sending out the Twelve on a mission through Israel with instructions to move on fast if rejected (Eng. tr. p. 85). Weiss also appeals to several sayings whose authenticity is now widely doubted, including Matt. 19.28, which Dalman rejected on the grounds that *palingenesia* lacks an Aramaic equivalent. When he comes to filling in some detail about the end Weiss like his predecessor turns to sayings about the parousia of the Son of man (Luke 17.22ff. and Mark 13.24f., 29 (pp. 92f.)). Rev. 6.12-17 is also drawn in, and 2 Pet. 3.10 and especially 4 Ezra 4.26ff. These passages do not speak of the kingdom, and when analysing the actual kingdom material Weiss says very little about its content. But anyone who accepts the authenticity of the Danielic Son of man sayings has a route into 'apocalyptic' and can then draw upon all kinds of remote parallel material with which to fill in the picture of Jesus. Mark 14.25, for example, the eschatological saying at the Last Supper, is taken to imply cosmic transformation. None of the kingdom sayings demands anything so specific. Their interpretation is inevitably determined by other material and much depends on which other material is deemed most reliable.

Those who now assign the Danielic Son of man sayings to the post-resurrection enthusiasm of the disciples may regret that

---

[28]Mark 6.7-13 will not bear this weight at all. There is no mention there of the disciples preaching 'the kingdom of God has drawn near'. Those sceptical about Q might suppose that this phrase at Matt. 10.7 is redactional, as at Matt. 3.2, both based on Matt. 4.17 which follows Mark 1.15. Matthew typically repeats formulae in this way. Luke 9.2 and 10.9, 11 would then also be redactional, based on his having read and used Matthew, though working mainly with Mark.

for all his admirable caution when analysing the kingdom sayings, Weiss finally interprets Jesus in the light of these early Church hopes. These are part of the historian's data, as are what we know of first century Jewish beliefs. A plausible account must be given of the relationship between any reconstruction of Jesus' beliefs and those of his contemporaries and disciples, partial as our knowledge of these is too. But a simple identification of Jesus' views with those of either Enoch or St Paul is no more plausible than too wide a gulf (cf. n. 13). If we concentrate first on those few sayings generally deemed authentic, as Weiss does for most of his monograph, there is less reason to press a literalistic sense on sayings like Mark 9.43ff. Weiss' view that these verses imply that Jesus' hearers 'will live to see the coming of the Kingdom' (Eng. tr. p. 98) is credible only if one is already convinced that Jesus thought in such literal terms. All we know about his poetry, parable telling and exaggerated language tells against any such supposition. A new interpretative key seems called for.

One was provided by Weiss' greatest pupil a generation later, but not before the eschatological construction had been pushed to literalistic extremes by Schweitzer. Like Weiss, Schweitzer thought that Jesus saw himself as the future messianic Son of man, which his contemporaries read into Daniel, and is reflected in the *Similitudes of Enoch*, but whereas Weiss stuck closely to the sayings of Jesus which he considered authentic and argued his case exegetically, Schweitzer thought he could reconstruct both the history of Jesus' ministry and its inner motivations. His theory about Jesus going to Jerusalem to force God's hand and bring about the parousia is sheer fantasy, depending upon an uncritical use of Matthew's compilation in chapter 10. Everything hinges on the Son of man saying in v. 23 — and Schweitzer was not the last eschatologist to make a highly doubtful Son of man saying bear the weight of his whole construction.

The vulnerability of Schweitzer's theory needs no further demonstration. The more interesting question is how much of Weiss' more cautious construction remains in place once the supporting buttresses have been challenged.

That the 'apocalyptic' interpretation of the kingdom remained more or less in place even after Wrede had introduced a more sceptical attitude to the synoptic sayings material owes much to the prestige of Weiss' one-time doctoral pupil Bultmann. The apocalyptic kingdom survives in Bultmann's historical construction (which he regards as theologically unimportant) partly because the apocalyptic Son of man supporting buttress remains in place, even if eroded by the rejection of several sayings (Mark 13.26; 14.62; Matt. 10.23 etc.). While accepting Wrede's view that the messianic secrecy theme in Mark cannot be traced back to Jesus, Bultmann accepted the authenticity of some of the eschatological Son of man sayings. He thought Jesus had been referring to someone other than himself, and so broke with theories of messianic self-consciousness, but by retaining some of the apocalyptic Son of man language as authentic and intended literally he still supposed that Jesus was dominated by apocalyptic categories.[29] Like Weiss and Schweitzer (and Reimarus and Strauss) he still thought Jesus was mistaken about the end and could not exclude the possibility that he may have died in despair.[30]

Bultmann sat light to such pre-Christian (!) matters as the life and teaching of Jesus and reduced his proclamation to a 'call to decision' (*Theol. NT* p. 9). But in referring the kingdom of God to 'the transcendent event, which signifies for man the ultimate Either-Or, which constrains him to decision' (*Jesus and the Word* p. 37), he sketched a historical interpretation of Jesus' eschatology which was not very different from that of Weiss. It was open to challenge on the basis of his own and Wrede's history of traditions approach to the sources, and in 1957 Philipp Vielhauer took that further step and disputed even the eschatological Son of man sayings accepted by Bultmann.[31]

Vielhauer argued that the eschatological 'kingdom of God' and eschatological 'Son of man' were associated neither in the

---

[29]Cf. *Theology of the NT* I (1948, ET London, 1952) pp. 26-30: *Jesus and the Word* (1926, ET 1934) p. 36.

[30]*Exegetica* (Tübingen, 1967) p. 453.

[31]'Gottesreich und Menschensohn in der Verkündigung Jesu' (Dehn Festschrift, 1957), rp in Vielhauer's *Aufsätze zum Neuen Testament* (Munich, 1965)).

relevant Jewish nor in any authentic saying of Jesus,[32] and so are unlikely both to have derived from Jesus himself. This case against the authenticity of each and every eschatological Son of man saying is a strong one, but its plausibility was undermined by Vielhauer's acceptance of the unwarranted German consensus (following Sjöberg and others) against the authenticity of the *earthly* Son of man sayings. This led Vielhauer to conclude that *all* the Son of man sayings are secondary, which seems so wildly improbable that, despite its acceptance by Käsemann and Conzelmann, younger Germans such as Hahn and Tödt[33] continued to maintain the Bultmann position and accept some apocalyptic Son of man sayings as authentic. But there is an alternative possibility. If Jesus spoke of himself as Son of man in a non-titular sense, as he does at Matt 8.20 (Luke 9.58) and 11.19 (Luke 7.34), it is easy to suggest how the eschatological sayings accrued to him when the early Church searched the Scriptures trying to understand what had happened, and fastened onto Dan. 7.13. He had called himself a son of man (*bar enash*) and so was with hindsight identified as the vindicated 'Son of man' prophesied in Daniel. This preference for some of the earthly sayings, rather than some of the eschatological sayings, as the origin of the tradition is now increasingly favoured outside Germany.[34] It is supported by

[32]Mark 8.38 and 9.1 are separate sayings placed together by the evangelist. Luke 17.21 and 22 are separate sayings combined by the evangelist who has also editorially introduced 'the kingdom of God' into the synoptic apocalypse at 21.31. References to the kingdom at Matt. 24.14 and 25.1 are also editorial.

[33]Their doctoral dissertations were translated into English (*The Titles of Jesus in Christology*, 1963, ET London, 1969; *The Son of Man in the Synoptic Tradition*, 1963, ET London, 1965). Vielhauer's fine critiques of both, reprinted in his *Aufsätze*, like his original essay, were never translated. The obvious alternative solution, that some of the earthly sayings are authentic, was defended in the Bultmann school by E. Schweizer (*ZNW* 50, 1959; *JBL* 79, 1960) but without the necessary linguistic support it was lightly dismissed e.g. by Vielhauer, *Aufsätze* p. 120.

[34]Due mainly to G. Vermes 'The use of *barnash/bar nasha* in Jewish Aramaic' (Oxford lecture, 1965, published in M. Black *An Aramaic Approach to the Gospels and Acts*, Oxford, 1967[3]), *Jesus the Jew* (London, 1973). See also B. Lindars *Jesus Son of Man* (London, 1983) admitting his conversion from his earlier adherence to 'the apocalyptic Son of man' (*NTS* 22, 1975-6).

growing doubts about the whole 'apocalyptic Son of man' theory even in the Judaism of Jesus' day.[35] The Danielic cryptogram evidently was later referred to an individual figure, but perhaps after Jesus' death.[36]

This detour around the apocalyptic interpretation of 'the kingdom of God', which looks inescapable so long as the eschatological Son of man sayings are taken to provide the key to Jesus' self-consciousness, has brought us right back through Vielhauer's scepticism to T. Colani, who in 1864 first denied the authenticity of the synoptic apocalypse and all the gospels' parousia material (n. 21). He claimed Mark 13.5-27 was a Jewish–Christian apocalypse placed on Jesus' lips in the early Church. This later became the majority view of Mark 13, but Colani and Vielhauer went further in judging all the eschatological Son of man sayings secondary. If we agree, then our understanding of Jesus' phrase 'the kingdom of God' will also be less coloured by the apocalypses.

The use of the word 'apocalyptic' to refer to an imminent expectation and the otherworldly character of the event is now widely recognised to be inappropriate. But that is a recent development.[37] In all these discussions over the past century the central question has not been how far Jesus used similar imagery to that of some apocalypses, but whether he expected the end of the world soon, and if so, how he conceived it. There is little doubt that he shared in the eschatological vocabulary of his time and spoke of resurrection and judgement, rewards and punishment, perhaps also of this age and the age to come, and that he looked forward in hope to God establishing God's rule on an earth somehow transformed or renewed. But from Weiss to Sanders, these eschatological assumptions have been

[35]E.g. R. Leivestad 'Exit the Apocalyptic Son of Man' (*NTS* 18 1971-2). An earlier (1968) essay had called it 'a theological phantom'. See now in popular form *Jesus in His Own Perspective* (Minneapolis, 1987, Norwegian 1982). See especially M. Casey *Son of Man* (London, 1979). Also N. Perrin *Rediscovering the Teaching of Jesus* (London, 1967) pp. 164-206.

[36]4 Ezra and probably the *Similitudes of Enoch* were written shortly after 70 C.E.

[37]Cf. J. J. Collins *Apocalypse: The Morphology of a Genre* (*Semeia* 14, Missoula, 1979), C. Rowland *The Open Heaven* (London, 1982) pp. 48, 71 etc., Sanders op. cit. pp. 375f.

moulded into specific constructions of Jesus' alleged expectation of an imminent end to the present world order. These constructions have been built out of sayings whose authenticity is doubtful and which do not cohere with material less open to question. If the historical sceptics' challenge is taken seriously, and the eschatological Son of man sayings eliminated, this literalistic treatment of Jesus' eschatology is far less plausible. There is no solid evidence left that Jesus was driven by an *imminent* expectation.[38] What he expected is sufficiently unclear to make one doubt whether he was specific, and his use of the conventional imagery of the period is poorly suited to provide the key to his mission and message because it does not unlock the more obviously authentic material of Jesus' parables and moral teachings.

This is not to reduce the religious urgency of Jesus' self-understanding and message, but to argue for less crude and easily dismissable interpretations. The clue to the key phrase 'the kingdom of God' is probably to be found in how those who use it think of God.[39] That includes, but is not exhausted by, eschatology. It also includes convictions about how human life can and should be lived in the present under the protection and claim of God. The destiny of individuals and the future of the world are related to ethics in a religious vision. Eschatology is not futurology, but a necessarily temporal language for speaking of God who is beyond time and space and who impinges only indirectly on human experience. God's rule in

[38]See above, p. 102 on Matt. 10. For a denial of the authenticity of the 'imminent expectation' texts see E. Linnemann *Parables of Jesus* (London, 1966) pp. 132-6. J. T. Sanders op. cit. p. 5 thinks the strongest proof that Jesus expected an imminent end is his endorsement of John the Baptist, Matt. 11.7a-11a, 16-19 par. (E. P. Sanders, p. 371, seems to agree). If that is the strongest argument the case is not strong. M. Borg 'An orthodoxy reconsidered: the "end-of-the-world Jesus",' in L. D. Hurst and N. T. Wright (eds.) *The Glory of Christ in the NT* (Oxford, 1987) p. 212 argues that without the coming Son of man sayings the basis for claiming an imminent expectation for Jesus is slim. Käsemann would presumably agree.

[39]On the Targums' use of the phrase as a synonym for God see Dalman *The Words of Jesus* (1898 ET Edinburgh, 1902, p. 101). Followed by J. Jeremias *NT Theology* (1971 ET London 1971, p. 102) and B. F. Meyer *Aims* p. 136. See also n. 45.

Jesus' teaching is evidently an eschatological hope, a future passionately yearned for. It is acknowledged to be exercising its power in his earthly activity. But this sense of the nearness or immediacy of God which naturally finds expression in temporal terms (e.g. Rom. 13.11) as a future hope of salvation, and in ethical terms as a demand in the present for obedience to God's will, is to be cashed out (like all talk of God) in terms of the present existence of those who use the language. Understood as theology (Godtalk, which has an eschatological as well as an ethical aspect) it may still be dismissed as fantasy by those who reject this code, but it cannot be dismissed, as it was by Reimarus, simply on grounds of the non-arrival of the parousia.

It is possible that Jesus expected an imminent end to the present world-order, in which case he was mistaken. But that case depends on a particular reading of some evidence which may not have originated with Jesus, a reading which is open to serious question on account of its failure to do justice to those sayings of Jesus which seem to envisage an on-going life in this world. What kind of transformation he anticipated is quite unclear, and when he expected it to happen, or whether he was specific about this, is even more uncertain, despite one or two sayings which, if reliably reported and rightly understood, suggest that he thought it would happen with the present generation.[40]

Twentieth century Christians can cheerfully live (as their predecessors have done) in ignorance of such beliefs of Jesus as remain obscure or unexpressed in the tradition of his sayings. Their faith is not dependent on certain answers being given where historical certainty is not available. Faith requires only enough historical information to identify the one in whose life and death (and subsequent vindication) a variety of factors, including a little historical information, leads them to find the decisive revelation of God. But the believer's reverent agnosticism will not satisfy the modern historian who will want to make an educated guess about the motivations of Jesus, even

---

[40]Mark 13.30; Mark 9.1, on which Kümmel placed most weight, is more doubtful.

though this means going beyond the available evidence. Such constructions remain hypothetical and may fall well short of historical knowledge, but intellectual curiosity craves to be satisfied, and the quest goes on. Its value to the theologian lies in the testimony it bears to the historical reality of Jesus, and the warnings it carries against taking anyone's guesses too seriously, and the arguments it provides against improbable theories which return from time to time in anti-religious propaganda and sensationalist journalism.[41]

All these constructions go beyond the evidence of the gospels and some are wildly at odds with it, ignoring or rejecting most of what the gospels highlight and filling in the picture from other Jewish writings deemed more relevant. Against this, the moral dimensions (individual and social) of Jesus' message will have to be included in a study of the phrase if the synoptic evangelists are followed and 'the kingdom of God' (heaven) is taken to embrace his whole message and activity. But before referring to some of the twentieth century attempts to do better justice to these moral dimensions of the phrase neglected by some consistent eschatologists, it is necessary to note some diversity within the 'eschatological (near) consensus'.[42] Setting aside modernising misuses of the word and reserving it for references to a temporal future within a first century Jewish framework of thought that contrasts this age with the age to come and the rule of God with that of Satan, interpreters still disagree when they try to explain a teaching about what lies beyond human experience. How literally did those ancient Jews understand their imaginations? When they speak of a new social order by analogy with the old, how hard can their details be pressed? And how strong in Jesus' teaching is the note of imminence, and how literally is that to be understood?

---

[41]E.g. after 200 years the canard that Jesus did not die on the cross can still be aired in a reputable medical journal and excite the popular press. On this theory of Karl Bahrdt, renewed in the BMA journal, 1991, see *Quest* pp. 39-47.

[42]See n. 7.

It is Paul's moral instructions (e.g. 1 Cor. 7) more than his apocalyptic imagery which lead most scholars to assume that he at any rate intended his language of imminence literally. This test of measuring the eschatological predictions against the moral prescriptions is sensible because actions show what beliefs are held. But the test gives a different result in the case of Jesus. Attempts to understand his 'ethics' as an *Interimsethik* have not won much support.[43] The case for saying that Jesus' talk of God was cast largely in eschatological terms is very strong. The case for interpreting this literalistically and with reference to an imminent expectation is not. We have found reasons to question the reliability of Schweitzer's inference from the Matt. 10 account of what Hiers[44] calls 'the urgent mission of the twelve'. The poet, parabler and aphorist speaks of God's rule more allusively than most of his interpreters.

One good reason for interpreting Jesus' message in temporal terms is the conclusion of the Kaddish prayer believed to have originated as early as Jesus: 'And may he (God) establish his kingdom in your lifetime, and in your days and in the lifetime of the whole house of Israel, speedily and in a time that is near.' The natural assumption is that Jesus' language about the 'coming' of the kingdom, e.g. in the Lord's Prayer, echoes the same idea of some dramatic intervention by God. But how soon did he expect it? The parallel indicates a religious hope rather than an imminent expectation, but its temporal reference is commonly taken to interpret Jesus' other language about the nearness of the kingdom. The theory of imminent expectation stems partly from the Son of man material already discounted, and partly from combining very different kingdom passages in this rather questionable way. In itself the *engiken* of 'the Kingdom of God has drawn near' would more naturally be interpreted spatially. But neither temporal nor spatial categories are adequate to the reality being expressed. The Targumic parallels lead some to understand 'the rule of God' as focussing on *God*

---

[43] J. T. Sanders op. cit. is an exception. R. H. Hiers is another.
[44] R. H. Hiers *The Kingdom of God in the Synoptic Tradition* (Florida, 1970) p. 66.

rather than on the new social order established by God.[45] They cannot be separated, but their connection is reason enough to treat the phrase with all the qualifications due to talk of God. We simply cannot say directly what 'it' is.

The new social order implied by the phrase was discredited by the Ritshlian this-worldly interpretation and neglected in the apocalyptic view. But it has rightly returned in the most powerful recent advocate of a consistently eschatological interpretation of Jesus' ministry and teaching: E. P. Sanders *Jesus and Judaism* (London 1985). This splendid book is afforded more detailed discussion here not least because it responds (pp. 125-9) to the type of literary interpretation represented by Bernard Scott (see below) which the present writer finds ultimately more persuasive, and in doing so shows how differently two contrasting casts of mind engage with this fascinating material.

Sanders stands firmly in the tradition of Weiss and Schweitzer, but draws back from the otherworldly ideas associated with the modern word 'apocalyptic' to an interesting hypothesis about 'restoration Judaism' that, while resisting the loaded word 'political' on account of its associations with theories of revolutionary activity, nevertheless has more of the this-worldly character which Reimarus attributed to Jesus' use of the phrase 'kingdom of God'. Sanders echoes what Reimarus noted in Luke 24.21, that 'we have every reason to think that Jesus had led (the disciples) to expect a dramatic event which would establish the kingdom' (p. 320). In other words, he probably expected it himself, and expected it soon, and was therefore mistaken (cf. pp. 327, 152, 154 etc.).

But Sanders is more cautious than Schweitzer and other consistent eschatologists. Most of them find a reference to imminence in Jesus' kingdom saying at the Last Supper (Mark 14.25). It seems they can imagine abstinence from wine only as a short-term contingency. Sanders (p. 332) by contrast sees this

[45]E.g. B. Chilton *God in Strength* (Linz, 1979) agreeing with Dalman, op. cit., and citing P. Stuhlmacher's observation that in the Isaiah Targum the kingdom is something to be preached. See also Chilton *A Galilean Rabbi and his Bible* (London, 1984).

as no more than a possible implication of the saying. He also has rather little to say about the 'Son of man' material (p. 324). The 'general theme of a heavenly figure who comes with angels is very early and quite possibly goes back to Jesus' (p. 144), and he recognises that our scholarly picture of the 'eschatological Son of man' is drawn from the Synoptic Gospels, not from the Jewish milieu, as is still widely supposed (pp. 124, 376). However, there was in Judaism an eschatological expectation that God would vindicate and restore Israel, and Sanders not only believes that Jesus shared this national conviction but makes it the key to his whole activity and message of a 'future cosmic event and a future judgment' (p. 146).

'Restoration Judaism' was recognised as an element in Jesus' eschatology by Strauss (p. 296) and Weiss (Eng. Tr. p. 93), and explored by his then colleague Ben Meyer (n. 27) before being made central in Sanders' own work. But for clear statement of the problems, trenchant argument, knowledge of the context,[46] boldness in risking a hypothesis coupled with careful assessments of the weight of the evidence at every point, Sanders' book is unsurpassed. It is a delight to read, not least for its respect for the Judaism of Jesus' day — a refreshing change from the attitudes of some scholars a century ago.

Sanders mentions the 'standard difficulty' about drawing far-reaching conclusions from the surviving Greek records of any saying of Jesus: 'In order to make sense of a saying we must detach it from its context (i.e. in the gospels), delete part of it, and reconstruct a hypothetical original. The results of this sort of work can never rate higher than "possible"' (p. 149). He therefore works from the evidence which he considers most secure — the 'almost indisputable facts' (p. 11 cf. p. 326). And yet, even a reader who agrees with him about most of these 'facts' may question him on some salient points and wonder whether this exciting and partly new path brings us nearer to understanding what Jesus meant by the kingdom of God.

---

[46]'Everything which enlarges our knowledge of' (Palestinian Judaism) which is Jesus' environment, 'indirectly extends our knowledge of the historical Jesus himself,' writes Sanders, p. 17, quoting Dahl.

It is very much to Sanders' credit that he reckons with Jesus having spoken of the kingdom in different ways and can even find the rabbinic meaning of 'taking upon oneself the yoke of the kingdom' by obedience to God within the covenant in Jesus' saying about entering the kingdom — an interpretation that concedes much to Dalman (and to Matthew) and weakens the argument of Weiss (Eng. tr. p. 98). No other consistent eschatologist does this, and it might have given Sanders a possible route for integrating Jesus' ethical teaching into his reconstruction. But he does not pursue that, perhaps on account of his scepticism about the sayings. He is accordingly careful about placing much weight on most of even the eschatological sayings of Jesus. It is therefore the more surprising that he thinks he can identify a group of 'kingdom' sayings in which, using dramatic imagery, 'the kingdom will come as an otherworldly, unexpected event in which the righteous will be separated from the wicked' (p. 142-6). The evidence he offers for this (Matt. 13.24, 47) is surely a secondary Matthean editorial formulation. Elsewhere in this section Sanders reverts to the common practice criticised above of using probably inauthentic, 'apocalyptic', sayings which do not even mention 'the kingdom of God' to interpret this phrase.

But all that is tangential to Sanders' own position. The one non-kingdom saying on which he depends very heavily, and whose authenticity he must defend, is Matt. 19.28 (cf. Luke 22.30), in which Jesus speaks of the Son of man (clearly himself) sitting on his glorious throne (Semitism) at the 'rebirth' and promises his disciples that they will sit on twelve thrones judging the twelve tribes of Israel. This saying is without parallel in the gospels and has been widely doubted since Dalman was unable to find an Aramaic equivalent for *palingenesia*. A remote parallel in the early Church is provided by 1 Cor. 6.3, but that does nothing to alter the view that the idea was born out of the eschatological excitement of the early (pre-Pauline) Church and should be bracketed out, along with the other eschatological 'Son of man' material. The nearest supporting material is the request of James and John at Mark 10.37 that they should sit at his right and left hand in his glory. Sanders notes that this request was turned aside by Jesus and that 'in a test of authenticity not many would give high marks' to this or to Matt. 19.28 (p. 147). And of course neither is a kingdom of God saying. But if we agree with all three evangelists in seeing in this phrase the key to Jesus' activity and teaching it is right to allow anything judged authentic to inform one's interpretation. Sanders can therefore appeal to these passages, together with Mark 14.25 and even Matt. 16.18f. as indicating that 'the kingdom will involve a decisive future event which will result in a recognisable social order involving Jesus' disciples and presumably Jesus himself' (p. 146).

Even a moderate scepticism must recognise that the whole construction is built on thin ice. Its most solid foundation plank is Jesus' choice of twelve disciples, presumably (though nothing of this nature is recorded, except Matt. 19.28) symbolising or otherwise relating to the twelve tribes of Israel. Most scholars accept this,[47] but Wellhausen (and Schleiermacher!) had good reasons for seeing post-resurrection theology here too, and his arguments were accepted by Vielhauer.[48] Of course Jesus called some disciples, including Judas, but the post-resurrection list at 1 Cor. 15.5 is more readily explicable if 'the Twelve' did not exactly correspond to the group surrounding Jesus in his ministry. Gospel references to the Twelve, and to Judas as one of them, occur in the editorial narratives which reflect the subsequent identification of these largely overlapping groups, not in any reliable sayings of Jesus.

The other foundation plank of Sanders' theory is his interpretation of the temple incident as Jesus upturning a table

---

[47]B. F. Meyer calls the choice of twelve 'beyond reasonable doubt' (op. cit. p. 154), but ignores Wellhausen's objection. Sanders appeals to R. Meye *Jesus and the Twelve* (Grand Rapids, 1968). In 'Jesus and the Kingdom: The restoration of Israel and the new People of God' (W. Farmer Festschrift, 1988) p. 232 he calls Jesus speaking of 'there being twelve' (i.e. presumably Matt. 19.28) a 'more-or-less incontrovertible fact'.

[48]See n. 31, pp. 68-71. Sanders (p. 99) discusses Vielhauer, but misrepresents him. Far from regarding the betrayal by one of the disciples a legend Vielhauer, like almost everyone else, regards this as 'without doubt' (p. 70) historical. Only the story about Jesus *pointing out* the betrayal at Mark 14.17-21 is a legend based on Psalm 41.10, as Wellhausen argued.

to symbolise its destruction, believing that God would build a new one. This is brilliantly argued and can find some support in the prediction of Mark 13.2, even though this says nothing about a new temple. The evidence for Jesus having expected a new temple built by God (the trial, Mark 14.58; crucifixion, Mark 15.29; and especially John 2.19) is scarcely admissible as it stands, but may contain an echo of Jesus' beliefs. One would not appeal to these passages unless already convinced of a theory which can be based on them. It is a big jump from supposing that Jesus prophesied and symbolised the destruction of the Temple to speculating that he imagined God would build a new one. Not many have been convinced by this second step.

There remains one kingdom saying that may, if authentic, support Sanders' hypothesis, though he places no great weight on it and most scholars have interpreted it differently: Matt. 8.11 ('Many will come . . .'). This can be detached from the secondary v. 12 which makes it refer to gentiles and may have originally referred to the dispersed Jews. But whether it stems from Jesus or an early Jewish Christian prophet is impossible to say.

Other aspects of Sanders' reconstruction arouse misgivings and throw further doubt on his reconstruction. Granted that repentance is a Lucan theme and rarely mentioned in the earlier strata of tradition it is hard to imagine a relationship with God that does not include penitence. Sanders' theory about Jesus accepting sinners without requiring repentance confirms how little his Jesus has to do with religion as most of his followers have understood it, even his first century followers. This allegation of a striking discontinuity between Jesus and his followers' religious sense is perhaps indicative of a certain impatience with traditional religious language. That would explain why this historian emphasises the continuities he finds between Jesus and the early Church in eschatology but interprets them in a way that at times seems peculiarly insensitive to their religious character. It may be that the modernising Ritschlians were groping for something their more secularised successors have lost.

Sanders' cursory treatment of the sayings tradition, especially his rejection of the command to love one's enemies, along with all of Matt. 5.17–6.8 (p. 263) and the saying about food at Mark 7.15, is more sceptical than Bultmann or even Vielhauer. Whether that is right or wrong it makes one wonder how Sanders can associate himself with the historically unsceptical Schweitzer in believing that Jesus was mistaken about the immediate future (p. 327). Even the best historical reconstructions have to stretch some of the evidence and reject what does not fit.

The sober truth is that we cannot be sure how Jesus imagined the future. One possible conclusion to be drawn from what happened is that Jesus spoke of God's future indefinitely, in ways that could be interpreted along different lines, including those which saw in his own vindication the decisive action of God. The standard objection to this view is that it is all too compatible with Christian belief and can therefore be suspected of being apologetically motivated. But accusations of Christian or anti-Christian intent are fruitless. One can only argue openly and historically about this highly ambiguous evidence, setting one proposal against another in the hope of gaining historical insight.

Sanders does that magnificently and the argument over his reconstruction will continue. He himself concedes that 'the sayings material, viewed as a whole, is not what we would expect of a prophet of Jewish restoration. It is not focussed on the nation of Israel . . . The sayings material is markedly individual in tone, and when collective terms are used they do not imply "all Israel"' (p. 222). This failure to integrate much of the sayings tradition, especially the parables, into his reconstruction might be defended by an extreme scepticism which rejects the authenticity of this material. But that is hard to combine with the sober judgement Sanders shows elsewhere in such matters, and the relatively conservative conclusions he reaches about the reliability of other parts of the data. The sceptical card can be played consistently only by those who have no hope of saying anything significant about the historical Jesus. Sanders is historically more ambitious, and rightly so. Such an extreme scepticism is unwarranted. But that leaves him open to the same objections that were laid against Weiss and Schweitzer. Their failure to give due weight to the ethical material was the clearest weakness in their 'consistently eschatological' interpretation of Jesus.[49] Schweitzer's notion of 'interim ethics' — that Jesus called for a heroic effort for the short period before the end — misses the way in which Jesus' teaching seems to envisage a continuing social order. Sanders' hypothesis makes more room for that, while rejecting the 'zealot' theory of Eisler and Brandon (cf. n.14), and repeating the insistence of Weiss that *God* will bring about the new age. The kingdom is not a human social programme. But it had and still has moral, social and even political implications.[50] The highly successful imaginative reconstruction of Jesus' attitude to revolutionary groups in Palestine offered by Gerd Theissen in *The Shadow of the Galilean* (1986, Eng. tr. London 1987) is both historically and theologically suggestive.[51]

But Sanders, unlike Theissen and most NT scholars, is not trying to fertilise theology. His aims are historical and the style of his history is positivistic. His book therefore illustrates most clearly the effect of this kind of historical research on Christian theology at its most sensitive point. A reconstruction rightly based on the small proportion of the gospel evidence judged reliable and interpreted in the light of some suggested material from the Judaism of the period, naturally stands in some tension with the Christian pictures of Jesus provided by the gospels. The evangelists bear witness to a religious reality that includes but is not identical with their historical reference to Jesus of Nazareth. A gospel says more than a biography theologically, and less historically. Modern historians aim to reverse these priorities.

But Christian belief cannot be satisfied simply to note the differences between Jesus as reconstructed by modern historical

---

[49]Important corrections were made by A. N. Wilder *Eschatology and Ethics in the Teaching of Jesus* (New York, 1939, 1950[2]). Also R. Schnackenburg *God's Rule and Kingdom* (1958, ET London, 1963), *The Moral Teaching of the NT* (1962[2], ET London, 1965). The best modern treatment of the ethical dimensions of the Kingdom of God is H. Merklein *Die Gottesherrschaft als Handlungsprinzip* (Würzburg, 1978).

[50]M. Borg (op. cit. pp. 4-20) protests at 'the exclusion of politics'. Richard Horsley's many contributions have been more influential.

[51]As is M. Hengel *The Charismatic Leader and his Followers* (1968 ET Edinburgh, 1981), one of the best books on the subject.

research and this same Jesus as variously confessed by his followers later — or not unless it pretends to be interested in only one or the other. Since it is normally interested in both it must draw historical lines of connection along which believers' eyes can travel as they confess the man from Nazareth their Lord and God. How well a theological theme such as 'the kingdom of God' can travel along the lines linking the history of Jesus to the post-resurrection confession of faith is a question involving the philosophy of history as well as theology and hermeneutics. Some styles of history writing offer a broader gauge than others.

The lines can be sabotaged by a historical hypothesis like the fraud hypothesis of Reimarus which in effect denies any religiously relevant continuity between Jesus and Christian faith. This rationalist hypothesis drew theologians into the historical arena to try and remove the blockage obstructing faith in Jesus. It was broken up and the most dangerous parts removed, but some parts of Reimarus' hypothesis have survived in critical gospel study, and the disturbance caused by historical work in this area of faith's concern has become a fact of modern religious life. Later historical hypotheses proved less destructive of traditional belief than that of Reimarus, but some of them have made it hard to hold on to Jesus as the divine object of faith and worship. Some liberal theologians have therefore changed the theological shape of Christianity by regarding him as the exemplar of faith, not its object.

The reason modern historical research can create havoc in the field of religion when given free rein to pursue its critical vocation is that historians do not normally deal in the coins of theology whose exchange value is contested in a post-Christian culture. Their hypotheses are therefore bound to appear reductive to believers. Only where historians are willing to entertain the reality of what their sources confess are their modern descriptions likely to satisfy believers. The terms in which historians are willing to discuss religious phenomena determine how these sources are interpreted and this history reconstructed. Sanders is reacting against scholars whose Christian faith has apparently distorted their history. But the price he pays for deliberately distancing himself from a more philosophical interpretation of his religious data is that believers are likely to doubt whether he has gone to the heart of what 'God's rule' meant for Jesus. He has come up against the limitations of a positivistic historical knowledge. That is not within his own terms a criticism, since these were the limits within which he chose to write. It simply shows how decisive is one's choice of interpretative framework.

Sanders' book has been discussed at some length, not only because it raises certain issues about the historical Jesus and his proclamation of God's rule most sharply, but because it reflects most clearly some aspects of the current debate about Jesus and the gospels within New Testament scholarship. Writing from outside the German form-critical tradition Sanders (pp. 13-17) criticises that in some respects but also shows how thoroughly its sceptical arguments have now persuaded the majority of critical scholars. Even though judgements about the authenticity of the kingdom material do not vary greatly[52] Sanders' book indicates that much twentieth century gospel criticism is now dated. This allows us to move quickly over the terrain adequately documented by Lundström, Perrin, Willis (n. 10) and Ladd (n. 52).

That discussion within New Testament scholarship was shaped largely by the reception and some correction of the futurist eschatological emphasis of Weiss and Schweitzer. Their accounts of the inter-testamental background and the eschatological character of the phrase were widely accepted[53] as interest in the inter-testamental literature declined. G. F. Moore, P. Billerbeck, Schlatter and Kittel concentrated on the rabbinic literature and most other German scholars pursued their history of religions research in non-Jewish areas until the discoveries at Qumran in 1947 gradually brought intertestamental Judaism

---

[52]Thus the conservative scholarship of G. E. Ladd *Jesus and the Kingdom* (New York 1964; second edition *The Presence of the Future*, 1974, rp. Grand Rapids and London 1980) and G. R. Beasley-Murray *Jesus and the Kingdom of God* (Grand Rapids and Exeter, 1986) represent a broad spectrum of mid-twentieth century writing on the subject.

[53]E.g. E. F. Scott *The Kingdom and the Messiah* (Edinburgh, 1911), F. C. Burkitt *Jesus Christ, an Historical Outline* (London, 1929 and 1932), B. S. Easton *Christ in the Gospels* (New York, 1930).

back to its now more central position. In addition 'historical Jesus' research stood under the theological cloud of dialectical theology in Germany after the First World War. Some liberals continued to work the seam[54] but even such a great book as Rudolf Otto *The Kingdom of God and the Son of Man* (1934, Eng. tr. London 1938) could make little headway in Germany. It was subtitled 'A study in the history of religion' and much of its value lies in its author's having a more clearly thought-out understanding of religion than most of his successors,[55] and a better grasp of history than the contemporary theology of crisis.[56] Otto accepted the Weiss–Schweitzer criticisms of Ritschl but thought that their 'new enthusiasm for logical eschatology obscures the truth just as much as, if not more than, Ritschl' (p. 72).

Otto's book, like Schweitzer's, made a bigger impression in England than in Germany on account of the Barthian reaction against liberalism and its life of Jesus research. Britain was not affected by this black-out and Schweitzer's challenge was still discussed with a mixture of fascination and dismay.[57] His theory was disputed not so much by a deeper study of Judaism, nor by a more sceptical view of the gospel tradition, but by alternative interpretations of the relevant texts.[58]

The most important contribution was C. H. Dodd's *The Parables of the Kingdom* (London 1935). Dodd acknowledged a debt to Otto who had argued that Jesus (in contrast to John the Baptist) thought that the still future eschatological kingdom of God was already exercising its force during his ministry. But

---

[54]E.g. H. D. Wendland *Die Eschatologie des Reiches Gottes bei Jesus* (Gütersloh, 1931).

[55]It reflects *The Idea of the Holy* which Otto had published in 1917 (ET 1923, revised 1929), e.g. at pp. 49, 52, 164.

[56]His colleague Bultmann is occasionally acknowledged but sharply criticised without being named on p. 51 for making eschatology atemporal.

[57]Cf. A. S. Peake: 'We should be sorry to think that the Jesus of history was such as (Schweitzer) has depicted Him ... It was not quite easy to see what kind of gospel he intended to take to the natives . . .' *Recollections and Appreciations* (London, 1938), pp. 165f.

[58]E.g. T. W. Manson *The Teaching of Jesus* (London, 1931). In America B. W. Bacon and also the Social Gospel writers Rauschenbusch and Shailer Matthews maintained older liberal views.

Dodd tried to eliminate the future expectation altogether: Jesus thought the kingdom had already come in his own ministry. This so-called 'realised eschatology' theory has usually been seen as the antithesis to Schweitzer's thesis of *konsequente Eschatologie*, and in the Preface to the 1961 edition Dodd does indeed refer to the impact of the *Quest* upon him. His attempt to deny the future aspect of the kingdom was not persuasive,[59] but his insistence upon its presence found many followers and it again as in earlier generations[60] became customary to talk of its presence *and* future.

What the 'it' is remained remarkably unclear. Dodd insisted on 'the symbolic character of the "apocalyptic" sayings' of Jesus (p. 79) and thought 'these future tenses are only an accommodation of language' because 'there is no before and after in the eternal order' (p. 81). Whether this can be called 'eschatology' may be doubted. His suggestion that 'the Kingdom of God in its full reality . . . is that to which men awake when the order of time and space no longer limits their vision' (p. 82) is reminiscent of Bultmann's modernising interpretation at the end of *History and Eschatology; The Presence of Eternity* (1957): 'In every moment slumbers the possibility of being the eschatological moment. You must awaken it' (p. 155).

Neither of these theological interpretations reflects Jesus' message at all closely at the level of historical description, but both suggest that the road to understanding his use of the phrase 'kingdom of God' may not be by way of exegesis alone. In retrospect the greatness of Dodd's book lies neither in its sometimes forced exegesis, nor in its Platonising theological interpretation, but in the literary sensitivity to Jesus' parables by which it pointed to the 1960s literary attempts to understand his message of the kingdom. At the time, however, the discussion was advanced along more historical lines by Jeremias who proposed in *The Parables of Jesus* (1947 Eng. tr.

[59]Among many criticisms see especially W. G. Kümmel *Promise and Fulfilment* (1945, ET London 1957).

[60]E.g. L. W. Muirhead *The Eschatology of Jesus* (London, 1904).

1954, revised edition 1963) modifying 'realised eschatology' to 'eschatology in the process of being realised' (*sich realisierende Eschatologie*).[61]

Whatever that means. The difficulty in all these mid-century discussions of the temporality of the kingdom, about whether it is 'here' or 'near', is unclarity about what the 'it' is. There was a measure of agreement about what it is not — the moral community specified by Ritschl. But even that denial denied too much. It was important to stress the supernatural intervention of God but not much can be said about this if ideas and ideals of community are excluded. The metaphor of kingship or rule demands them. Jewish eschatology contained some and Sanders was right to insist as strongly as T. W. Manson (in a very different idiom) and other less chastened liberals, that they belong in this discussion. Some of the eschatologists' picture of how the imminent event was imagined by Jews of the time and by Jesus himself were far too dependent on Mark 13. Dodd distanced Jesus from these conceptions, but they continued to provide the backcloth to most interpretations. Jesus no doubt shared in the Jewish eschatological conceptions of his day, but these are inadequately represented by the cosmic fireworks of the synoptic apocalypse, and interpreting Jesus' teaching in the light of that untypical and probably inauthentic passage (vv. 5-27)[62] fails to throw light on the many sayings and parables which have a quite different texture.

The historian's problems are not limited to judging which traditions are most probably authentic. In contrast to most ancient history, having a plurality of sources and being able to gain some understanding of the history of the tradition by

[61] *Parables* (1963 ed.) p. 230 says that Haenchen gave him the phrase in a letter and that Dodd 'to my joy, agreed with it'. Actually Dodd said (*The Interpretation of the Fourth Gospel*, Cambridge, 1953, p. 447) that he 'liked' it but could not translate it. Since he took it as an 'emendation for the avoidance of misunderstanding' of his own realised eschatology one may doubt whether he understood it either. But by *The Founder of Christianity* (London, 1967) he had changed his position on this.

[62] Beasley-Murray's defence of this is in *Jesus and the Future* (London, 1954); *A Commentary on Mark Thirteen* (London, 1957) is a minority view. Cf. Jeremias *NT Theology*, pp. 123-6, for a more common view.

comparing them, makes it reasonable to believe (though impossible to prove to the determined sceptic) that we can get within earshot of some of Jesus' teaching. But there is still the problem of locating these traditions on the larger map of his mission and message. Jeremias' guesswork on the original contexts of individual parables is after all largely guesswork.[63]

In this impasse two strategies are possible. Only one relates to the 'historical Jesus' and so concerns us here, but the other is arguably more important and therefore must be mentioned. That is to focus attention away from the 'historical Jesus' and attend instead to the gospel narratives themselves. This was famously proposed by Martin Kähler in *The So-Called Historical Jesus and the Historic Biblical Christ* (1892, 1896;[2] Eng. tr. 1964), a pamphlet overlooked or ignored by Schweitzer. It suffered from later association with Barth and Bultmann's theological objections to real history and so to historical enquiry about Jesus as such. But what it was actually attacking was the theological over-valuation of the modern liberal historians' speculative reconstructions. Some historical information is clearly needed by theology to identify the Lord of faith, but Christian faith-pictures of Jesus are shaped by the gospel narratives which are repeatedly heard as Scripture, not by historians' tentative reconstructions of what lies behind these. One might want to go further than Kähler and allow historical research a critical role over against aspects of the gospel pictures (e.g. Matthew's account of the Pharisees and John's of 'the Jews') but his main point is clear, and it relativises the whole 'quest' and encourages closer attention to the gospels' presentations.

The new emphasis was pioneered in Britain by R. H. Lightfoot[64] (who was indebted to Lohmeyer) and Austin Farrer,[65] but independently developed within the history of traditions context of German 'redaction criticism' following

---

[63]Cf. J. Drury *The Parables in the Gospels: History and Allegory* (London, 1985).

[64]*History and Interpretation in the Gospels* (London, 1935), *Locality and Doctrine in the Gospels* (London, 1938), *The Gospel Message of St Mark* (Oxford, 1950).

[65]*A Study in St Mark* (London, 1951), *St Matthew and St Mark* (London, 1954). These were not taken seriously by 'normal' NT scholarship of the day.

the Second World War. As every aspect of every gospel yielded new PhD thesis topics scholars considered how each evangelist understood Jesus' phrase 'the kingdom of God'.[66] These investigations have often proved theologically fruitful, suggesting that the way the gospels inform Christian life and thought is by reflection on the witness of the texts more than by the legitimate but subordinate quest of the historical Jesus.

For present purposes it is sufficient to note that the two contrasting styles of historical Jesus research exemplified above by Sanders and below by Scott have been pursued alongside a study of the gospels that is quite differently oriented. If either or both types of historical Jesus research run into the sand, contemporary biblical scholarship will nevertheless have made other contributions to the life of the Church and contemporary culture.

This modern bifurcation in gospel studies, distinguishing sharply between historical Jesus research (pursued in different ways) and a focus on the texts themselves (whether as literature or out of historical interest in the authors and/or communities behind them), also throws fresh light on the history of research already sketched. A good many liberal and conservative judgements about what Jesus meant by 'the kingdom of God' have surely picked up what one or another evangelist understood the phrase to mean. There are some deliberate moves in this direction in Liberation Theology where 'the historical Jesus' sometimes seems to mean 'the Jesus of the Synoptic Gospels'.[67] Earlier, the distinction was less conscious. Thus Harnack's translation of *entos hymōn* at Luke 17.20 as the kingdom of God being 'within you', vital for his understanding of Jesus and now generally rejected, may nevertheless reflect what Luke intended.

---

[66]E.g. A. M. Ambrozic *The Hidden Kingdom* (Washington D.C., 1972), W. H. Kelber *The Kingdom in Mark* (Philadelphia, 1974), M. Pamment 'The Kingdom of Heaven according to the First Gospel' *NTS* 27, 1981, pp. 211-32, J. D. Kingsbury *Matthew: Structure, Christology, Kingdom* (Philadelphia, 1975, London, 1976), *Matthew.* Proclamation Commentaries (Philadelphia and London, 1978), O. Merk 'Das Reich Gottes in den lukanischen Schriften' in *Jesus und Paulus* ed. E. Ellis et al., Göttingen, 1975).

[67]E.g. L. Boff *Jesus Christ Liberator* (1972, ET London 1980).

This consideration is particularly important for Matthew, who used the phrases 'kingdom of God/heaven' fifty times and even more than Mark saw in it a summary of Jesus' proclamation, but who naturally understood it slightly differently from Jesus on account of his different historical position. It is hard to doubt that some interpreters such as T. W. Manson in *Jesus the Messiah* (London 1943) and Dodd in *Gospel and Law* (New York 1951) who have emphasised the moral dimension of Jesus' use of the phrase, have tuned in rather to Matthew. There is a moral aspect to Jesus' usage also (cf. n. 52) but it is arguably more individual and existential than in the evangelist's more ecclesiological understanding. When Matthew introduces ten parables with 'the kingdom of heaven is like . . .' the eschatological aspect has receded. It has not disappeared. Eschatology is important for Matthew too, but differently. He seems almost to mean 'the God happening, i.e. Christianity, is like this . . .'. Even Dodd's theory of 'realised eschatology' may have caught more of the evangelists' perspective than that of Jesus, especially if the phrase at Mark 1.15, 'the time is fulfilled', is redactional.

Recent developments have moved much gospel criticism away from the quest of the historical Jesus. But the quest has continued, and one alternative response to the problems we have noted has been to acknowledge the limits of our historical knowledge but to trace the traditions we have of Jesus' parables (including those in the Gospel of Thomas) back to as early a version as can be detected, and to see whether they can be interpreted without reference to their now lost original contexts. Various steps have been taken in this direction, some sitting more loosely to history than others, some more clearly theologically motivated than others. The main advances have been made in the United States, where literary perspectives have been most systematically applied and the parables treated as 'literary artefacts'.[68] Some of this was

---

[68]Notably D. O. Via *The Parables* (Philadelphia, 1967). See also H. Weder *Die Gleichnisse Jesu als Metaphern* (Göttingen, 1978). Also G. V. Jones *The Art and Truth of the Parables* (London, 1964). Amongst recent works see especially J. R. Donahue *The Gospel in Parable* (Philadelphia, 1988).

stimulated by the 'new hermeneutic' wing of the 'new quest of the historical Jesus'[69] which emerged in the 1950s and 1960s among Bultmann's pupils, but it also had indigenous roots in the work of Amos Wilder.[70]

This chapter, like the earlier one (n. 10), has been told by N. Perrin.[71] For our purposes it will suffice to refer in passing to the books of Eta Linnemann (n. 38) and E. Jüngel,[72] both pupils of Fuchs, and to discuss briefly one excellent book which illuminates what Jesus said while illustrating several aspects of the new trend. B. B. Scott has subsequently published a much larger work on the parables[73] but the book which drew a response from Sanders (pp. 125-9) was *Jesus, Symbol-Maker for the Kingdom* (Philadelphia 1981).

Perrin's 1976 survey had borrowed from P. Wheelwright's *Metaphor and Reality* (1962) and suggested that 'the kingdom of God' is not a concept but a 'tensive symbol'. Scott agreed, but showed that Perrin was still partly trapped in Schweitzer's view of Jesus as an 'apocalyptic' preacher of the end of the world. The later Perrin had no longer understood the kingdom in temporal terms, but still had thought that the symbol derived from the world of apocalyptic and had to be understood in the dualistic terms of that world. Scott himself is critical of the whole approach summed up in our opening quotation from Reimarus, of interpreting 'the kingdom of God' in the light of its supposed meaning for Jesus' Jewish contemporaries. He prefers to concentrate on Jesus' own usage. These two prongs of historical method of course cannot be seen as alternatives. Both are always used, and the results should converge. But

---

[69]Cf. J. M. Robinson and J. B. Cobb (eds.) *The New Hermeneutic* (New York, 1964), discussing the work of Fuchs and Ebeling.

[70]E.g. *Early Christian Rhetoric: the Language of the Gospel* (London, 1964); *Jesus' Parables and the War of Myths* (Philadelphia, 1982) contains an autobiographical preface and also one by James Breech, both of which provide good background. See also J. D. Crossan *A Fragile Craft* (Chico, 1981) and several essays in *Semeia* 12 and 13 (1978).

[71]*Jesus and the Language of the Kingdom* (London, 1976). See also R. Morgan with J. Barton *Biblical Interpretation* (Oxford, 1988) pp. 231-60.

[72]*Paulus und Jesus* (Tübingen, 1962).

[73]*Hear Then the Parable* (Minneapolis, 1989).

Scott's emphasis provides a welcome correction to the now century-long tendency to interpret the phrase in the light of Jewish literature which scarcely contains it.

Reimarus had argued that since Jesus did not define the phrase, its meaning must have been clear to his contemporaries. Scott responds (p. 11) that the disagreements of subsequent scholarship and its failure to reconstruct the meaning show this to be wrong. But that misdirects the discussion. Scott's own theoretical analysis shows that the mistake lay not so much in assuming the intelligibility of the phrase, but rather in misconstruing the nature of its referring. The phrase refers primarily to *God* whose reality, identity, promises and sovereignty were well known by its hearers. It does not itself refer to some datable event when that sovereignty would be established, otherwise the Kaddish prayer would not have had to pray for its establishment. In the Lord's Prayer only the verb refers the petition to the establishment of God's rule — and that leaves entirely open the time and character of this happening. The persecuted Church yearned for a rapid denouement (Rev. 22.20) which would be unpleasant for the persecutors. Jesus (so far as we know) was less specific. A political and historical or quasi-historical cosmic event, and some place or state of being, are implied by his reference to God by means of a political metaphor, but Jesus seems not to have unfolded these implications.

The relevant Jewish background is its belief in God, which includes trust in God's providence, a moral perspective on present human existence, the practice of prayer, and a hope of future vindication and transformation. That could be understood from Scripture (and Targums) with no deep knowledge of intertestamental literature on the part of Jesus' contemporaries. So Scott is right to give priority to a study of how Jesus used the phrase, so far as this can be reconstructed by critical analysis of the synoptic tradition. Understanding anyone's talk of God requires some conceptual apparatus. Scott therefore offers some theoretical discussion. Only in third place is it valuable to seek confirmation of one's analysis in possible Jewish parallels to Jesus' uses of the phrase. Thus one might judge that the Targums provide the closest analogies, and even suspect, with Chilton, that Jesus was influenced by the Targum on Isaiah which in some form was perhaps known to him. But such speculations provide possible confirmations not solid foundations. The chief task is to study the gospels themselves, and when the nature of Jesus' religious language is seen to be important it is natural to turn first to the parables. These once played a subordinate role in discussions of the kingdom because they are ambiguous. But polyvalency may be of the essence and perhaps the single most important thing to say about Jesus and the kingdom is that he spoke of it in parables.

Scott and others[74] build on Dodd's definition of parable as 'a metaphor or simile drawn from nature or common life, arresting the hearer by its vividness or strangeness, and leaving the mind in sufficient doubt about its precise application to tease it into active thought' (p. 13). This even anticipates the reader-response theory[75] which has subsequently become central to literary study and is particularly germane to 'kerygmatic' documents, but it is the role of metaphor, and the distinction between this and discursive speech, which first proved illuminating. Parables are narratives, not metaphors, but their metaphorical character is essential to their definition. All talk of God is indirect and much of it is metaphorical, inviting the hearers to see themselves and their world in a new way. Because the 'kingdom of God' does not belong to discursive language it is impossible to state exactly what it means. We can only reconstruct the 'world' or referential horizon in which the phrase once had meaning for Jesus and his hearers, and relate that to the context in which we hear it.

Scott notes that metaphors are able to direct attention to a referent not otherwise expressable in language, and that this makes them suitable for disclosing religious symbols, which discursive speech cannot fully apprehend. He sees that interpretations are always secondary and can easily violate

[74]E.g. R. W. Funk *Language, Hermeneutic and Word of God* (New York, 1966) p. 133. *Parables and Presence* (Philadelphia, 1982) p. 35. J. R. Donahue op. cit. p. 5.
[75]W. Iser *The Act of Reading* (Baltimore, 1978) is already referred to by Scott op. cit. p. 60.

what they are supposed to be interpreting by closing off the hermeneutical potential of a metaphor or parable. The task of an interpreter is 'to provide an opportunity for meaning's disclosure by creating the necessary conditions for hearing' (p. 15). He says that 'Parable as metaphor is generated from the experiential world of the teller. Parables, expressing the incomprehensible in terms of the comprehensible, are developed out of Jesus' fundamental vision/experience of reality' (ibid.). He is prepared to speak of Jesus' experience of God as symbolised by the kingdom of God, coming to expression in Jesus' parables.

This short account of some landmarks in gospel criticism began with a warning against being misled by the big names and echoes in our title into thinking that 'consistently' or one-sidedly eschatological interpretations of Jesus' phrase are necessarily correct. One aim of this account has been to dispute the widespread opinion that Jesus expected the end of the world and was mistaken, and perhaps died in despair at his failure.

These speculations have been challenged, not (as might be supposed) out of embarrassment about Jesus being wrong. He whom Christians confess as their Lord and God was a man of his time, subject to human limitations, including limited knowledge. According to Mark 13.32 he disclaimed any knowledge of the time of the end, and recently published Qumran material has removed the old argument for its inauthenticity (on account of what was supposed to be an unjewish use of 'the Son'). As for his alleged 'failure', theologians can find plenty of religious significance in that.[76] Christians might take some convincing that Jesus was actually wrong about God, and they have seen improbable theories claiming historical authority for attacking or more subtly eroding their faith. But the main reason for challenging the prevailing view here is that it seems to be historically weakly based.

It has been challenged not by detailed exegetical argument, which the history of research shows is inconclusive on this

[76]E.g. E. Schillebeeckx *Jesus: An Experiment in Christology* (London 1979) pp. 310, 319.

matter, but (in tune with the aim to provide a survey) by showing how it gained its widespread acceptance, and how the supporting struts have now crumbled. The 'apocalyptic' theory about 'the kingdom of God' attained its Weiss-Schweitzer hegemony on the back of newly-discovered intertestamental literature (apocalypses) which do not contain the phrase. Jesus did not write apocalypses but 'That Jesus of Nazareth knew himself to be the Son of Man who was to be revealed is for us the great fact of his self-consciousness . . . the eschatology of Jesus can therefore only be interpreted by the aid of the curiously intermittent Jewish apocalyptic literature of the period between Daniel and the Bar-Cochba rising' (*Quest* p. 365). But Jesus as the coming Son of man is probably an early post-resurrection belief based on reading Daniel in the light of their conviction of Jesus' exaltation.

The drift of this survey has been critical of the conclusions of many scholars from Reimarus to Sanders whom this critic personally admires. It has been more sympathetic to recent literary trends, not in the first place because these are potentially more fruitful religiously but because they take more seriously the nature of this religious language. They too contain the potential to lead the study of the gospels away from theology, especially when they cut loose from history altogether.[77] Conversely, new historical theories about what Jesus intended can prove religiously as suggestive as the old. The recent shift from 'apocalyptic', for example, corresponds to a widespread shift in religious sensibility to the social and political dimensions of Christian commitment. Theories about restoration Judaism or 'Jesus and Israel' may encourage Christian activists and foster Jewish-Christian relations. The Ritschlians were not wrong to be interested in the community ideal in Christianity.

Johannes Weiss, a Ritschlian by conviction as well as by marriage, thought they were only wrong to claim that their convictions corresponded to those of the historical Jesus. Our survey suggests we should be cautious about basing

---

[77]S. Moore *Literary Criticism and the Gospels* (New Haven, 1989) shows the potential of these approaches — for good and for ill.

anything on such historically uncertain foundations —
including attacks on Christianity, which usually show a
stunning ignorance of the historical problems discussed
above. But Weiss' proposal that theologians should live with
the hiatus between their own and Jesus' use of the phrase is
as theologically unsatisfactory as the historical conclusions
on which it was based are uncertain. Weiss' second edition
was both historically and theologically (p. 177) more cautious
than the first which is now (unfairly to Weiss) more widely
read thanks to the American translation of Hiers and Holland.
The second edition rightly distinguishes between subsequent
religious evaluation of a historical figure and the historical
investigation of the life (p. 178), and justifies the Christian
interpretation by reference to the Fourth Gospel. But if
(unlike the Fourth Gospel, on the whole) we use a phrase of
Jesus' in theology and preaching we implicitly claim his
authority and should therefore try to use it in a similar sense,
or at least justify our interpretation by appeal to our
understanding of his teaching.

This can only be an approximation, on account of the
uncertainties already noted. But we can at least be certain
that Jesus used the phrase to speak metaphorically of God's
relationship to the world and involvement with it, at least
partly in future terms. Moreover, the evidence of the gospels
tells strongly against construing that future eschatological
reference in any way that evacuates the present of its
significance — or even reduces its significance to being a
time of decision. Against Bultmann, Fuchs and others are
surely right to speak of a time of salvation, not only in Paul's
preaching (2 Cor. 6.2) but also in Jesus' words and actions.
There is something implausible in all reconstructions,
including those of Weiss (Eng. tr. p. 82) and Bultmann,
which propose a historical Jesus indistinguishable in his
eschatology from the synoptic picture of John the Baptist.
Important as Jesus' association with John is for any historical
reconstruction, the differences between the ascetic preacher
of repentance in face of God's impending judgement, and
the Son of man who came eating and drinking, must be
given due weight. Jesus no doubt echoed Jewish ideas of

judgement (cf. Matt. 11.21-4) — but it is hard to see in these warnings and woes the centre of his message.[78]

It is not plausible, either, to give the apocalyptic imagery used by Paul at 1 Thess. 4.15-7 as much weight as Sanders does for the historical reconstruction of Jesus' teaching, despite the reference to 'a word of the Lord' in v. 15 and the more important echo of 'a thief in the night' at 1 Thess. 5.2. Even those who think that Paul was Jesus' truest interpreter, rather than 'the second founder of Christianity' (Wrede), generally refer not to the occasional echoes of his teaching, but to his unfolding the implications of what God was doing in Jesus. That theological judgement, however well supported by historical and exegetical conclusions, does not imply they had identical eschatological expectations.

Jesus spoke of God's rule in the world, operative in his exorcisms. Its future manifestation was certain; meanwhile it was hidden. It is to be 'entered', whether now (as I think Matthew thought) or in the future (as Windisch thought Matthew thought).[79] It must be received as a gift before it can be entered (Mark 10.15). Jesus' ministry was in fact largely restricted to Israel and yet nothing he said about entering the kingdom restricted it to the chosen people in principle, and it would be hard to claim that the extension epitomised by Matthew (28.19) was inconsistent with Jesus' teaching. If one thinks that the Lord is king, as the Psalter asserts, and the earth is the Lord's and all that is in it, such an extension becomes inevitable. Paul celebrated the gentiles worshipping with Israel (Rom. 15). Whether Jesus envisaged something similar at Matt. 8.11, as its present context at the healing of a gentile's boy suggests, is historically an open question on which nothing theological depends.

The larger question raised by the whole debate from Reimarus on is whether Jesus had a programme at all, and here advocates of the 'restoration Judaism' hypothesis and conservatives who think he founded the Church and instituted the sacraments can unite against those who suppose that his

---

[78]On this cf. M. Borg (1984) pp. 201-21.

[79]*The Meaning of the Sermon on the Mount* (1929, 1937[2], ET Philadelphia, 1951).

God-consciousness found expression in less goal-oriented ways. Both points of view can find support in the gospels and the fundamental disagreement between the Reimarus–Sanders type of construction and the Scott–Funk–Breech type of interpretation may find some explanation in the different religious outlooks and temperaments of different scholars. In other words, which evidence is made the key to one's 'historical Jesus' may sometimes be a matter of personal preference based on one's own personality type,[80] as well as historical and exegetical judgements. How the evidence is interpreted and what is accepted or rejected as 'authentic' is less 'objective' than talk of 'criteria' for authenticity imply.[81] Harnack was not the last to look deep into the well for Jesus only to find the reflection of his own face. Neither was he wrong to do so, despite some mistakes in his reconstruction.

The reason why Harnack was not wrong in principle concerns the kind of self-involvement often present in historical interpretation and always present in religious commitment. The final difficulty in specifying what Jesus meant by 'the kingdom of God' goes beyond even the impossibility of fully translating poetry and metaphor into discursive speech. It is related to this, because poetry and metaphor involve the hearer or reader in more intimate ways than most prose. But a person's talk of God, which Jesus' parabling talk of the kingdom clearly was, has a quite peculiar logic. It can be discussed, but never adequately described. It is irreducibly first person. Something can be said about the metaphors of fatherhood, kingship, and even (for the sake of gender balance) poultry (Matt. 23. 37; Luke 13.34), but the best interpretations of another person's talk of God seem to involve the interpreter's own pre-understanding of this language. Jesus' hearers no doubt understood him well enough to follow him or to turn away, because as Jews they knew who he was talking about, whether or not he confirmed their national hopes (and the

---

[80]Cf. the difference between P types and J types in the Myers-Briggs type indicator: I. Myers *Manual* (Palo Alto, 1962).

[81]Cf. B. F. Meyer *Critical Realism and the NT* (Pennsylvania, 1989) pp. 129-45. He rightly prefers the word 'indices' to 'criteria'.

evidence of his teaching suggests he did not, contrary to Sanders' pp. 116-19 construction). In the same way, interpretation of even the gospels' echoes of Jesus' talk of God are likely to involve the interpreter's prior understanding of this subject-matter.

But here understanding is inseparable from evaluation. Those who are sympathetic to the gospels' claims are likely to interpret them differently from those who are unsympathetic. That is not quite a matter of accepting or rejecting the evangelists' Christian commitments. In practice this division may be reflected in the interpretations chosen, but it is seldom so clear-cut and non-Christians can sometimes be sympathetic interpreters of the gospels and Jesus (e.g. Claude Montefiore). Christians can also be poor interpreters. But a sympathetic interpreter of the gospels, whether a believer or not, will try to understand what is typically involved in speaking of God, and look for traces of that in Jesus' kingdom language, as Otto and Bultmann did. Whether or not one personally speaks of God as ultimate reality and thinks that listening to Jesus can inform one's faith, it is simply good interpretative practice, recognised in the phenomenology of religion, to ask oneself what belief in God is likely to have involved for first century Jews. This consideration raises further doubts about interpretations of 'the kingdom of God' which underestimate its ethical dimensions and strengthens the case of those who, like Wilder and Merklein (n. 49), take this seriously.

Reflection on the nature of religious discourse provides some questions which can be addressed to the gospels. Talk of God involves talk of human existence, behaviour, hopes and aspirations, personal and social identity. All these dimensions might be expected in the phrase 'the kingdom of God' if this epitomises Jesus' message. Such an approach also offers suggestions about how the variegated material of the gospels might be organised and understood, secondary developments in the early Church co-ordinated with the earliest strata in the tradition, and the lines of development between Jesus and the gospels hypothetically reconstructed. This approach not only casts doubt on accounts of the historical figure of Jesus which marginalise either the moral or the eschatological aspects of his message. It also challenges interpreters to relate both to Jesus' presumed experience of God,[82] even though very little can be said about that.

Historians unsympathetic to religion have also made contributions to the study of the gospels. To quote Schweitzer with a grain of salt: 'For hate as well as love can write a Life of Jesus, and the greatest of them are written with hate ... not so much hate of the Person of Jesus as of the supernatural nimbus ... And hate sharpened their historical insight. They advanced the study of the subject...' (pp. 4f.). Hatred blinds and distorts, but it may function to unmask the untruths of its enemies while contributing a few fictions of its own. Historians have rightly discredited some interpretations of 'the kingdom of God' as untenable according to the rational methods used to elucidate texts. They have also provided background information which has illuminated Jesus' use of the phrase. But some have used their historical skills to construct images of the historical Jesus aimed to embarrass those for whom he is the object of religious veneration.

Such anti-religious propaganda is entirely legitimate in a pluralist culture, as is religious propaganda. Since historical research can be used by both sides there is a need for rules of combat. The first is that both sides distinguish between facts and judgements, and avoid such dubious rhetoric as asserting, with whatever authority a chair in Religious Studies at the University of Oregon confers, 'that Jesus held an imminent eschatology will have to be considered a fact'.[83] It is one of the merits of E. P. Sanders' book that he scrupulously distinguishes between facts and judgements. All our overall interpretations of Jesus' elusive language about the future are tentative judgements and it is misleading to claim more for them.

[82]H. Schürmann's profound reflections along these lines and his controversy with the more pronounced eschatological views of A. Vögtle are unsympathetically summarised by H. Bald in Chilton (1984) pp. 139-44. See also F. W. Schmidt *Ethical Prescription and Practical Justification in Selected Apocalyptic Literature and the Teaching of Jesus* (Diss, Oxford, 1986).

[83]J. T. Sanders op. cit. p. 5, cf. p. 29.

Those who think that Jesus was talking of God, and that what he said may well be true and worthy of all to be received, will (like his original hearers) have some prior understanding of that ultimate reality. They will try to make sense of Jesus' teaching in terms of that, allowing their preconceptions to be challenged and perhaps overturned in the process. That involvement of one's pre-understanding is inescapable. The only condition attached is that it must not lead interpreters to ignore or deny uncomfortable evidence. When other historians protest about theological prejudgements playing a role in the hermeneutical process they are either ignorant about the nature of interpretation, or rightly protesting against the evidence being forced — or else they are engaging in anti-religious polemics.

Distorted interpretations have to be uncovered by historical argument and by ideology criticism (which cuts more than one way), not by pretending that historical judgements necessarily contradict those of religious faith. They operate on different levels, and the latter include some of the former. These historical arguments are in principle religiously neutral, though in practice they are often built into religious or anti-religious judgements. They are worth cultivating in their principled neutrality because they provide some guidance in discriminating between better and worse, richer and poorer, even ultimately more and less true understandings of the gospels.

The aim of all interpretation is to read the texts with understanding. Historical research provides valuable and necessary assistance. But there is a plurality of understandings available, as well as many misunderstandings. Discrimination involves more than historical research, but it cannot involve less. It should not be disregarded merely because it rarely gives final answers and has often been abused by religious and anti-religious interpreters. In the interpretation of the gospels final answers are not available to the historian *qua* historian, but provisional judgements are possible and even have theological value in discriminating between true and false statements about Jesus.

Orthodox Christian theologians are also committed to historical research because they identify the Lord of their faith with the man from Nazareth. Like other historians they will want to integrate (i) Jesus' relationship to John the Baptist, (ii) his healing art, and (iii) his violent death within the hypothetical framework they construct (partly from their own pre-understandings) in order to understand him as the religious figure he clearly was. There is uncertainty here. (i) Interpreters are divided between those who stress the continuity between Jesus and the Baptist (Bultmann, the Sanders brothers) and those who stress the differences (Baur, Käsemann, Bornkamm). Both imply that our knowledge of John is more secure than it probably is, despite the brief notice provided by Josephus. (ii) The link Jesus made between his exorcisms and the kingdom (Matt. 12.28; Luke 11.20) is open to more than one interpretation. (iii) The Romans executed Jesus, apparently as 'the king of the Jews'. But that says nothing certain about how he understood his mission. Even the involvement of the high priests is open to more than one explanation, of which John 11.50 perhaps provides the best.

Where so much is historically uncertain the doors stand wide open to both historical and theological construction. The accounts of Jesus most satisfying to Christians are likely to be those which succeed in correlating these two sometimes related interests. Opponents of Christianity have for centuries (since Celsus) realised that historical reconstructions which contradict traditional belief are a potent weapon against the latter. Theologians have shifted their ground to avoid being subverted by (say) scepticism about the raising of Lazarus, and some seem not to mind if Jesus was badly wrong about the future. Others reserve their position on that until more solid evidence that he was mistaken is produced. Some historians despise religion and some theologians despise history, but neither is likely to interpret Jesus of Nazareth sympathetically. The attraction of the newer literary approaches is that they can be combined with both historical research and theological interests in clarifying Jesus' religious language about the kingdom.[84] They can also lead gospel study into new fantasies that have

[84]Cf. Morgan with Barton op. cit. pp. 167-263.

even less to do with Jesus of Nazareth than some of the past 250 years' historical speculations. Freed from historical controls, pictures of Jesus can become arbitrary and no longer command the respect due to historical reality.

Some religiously motivated constructions, especially within Liberation Theology, have been too easily dismissed for failing to conform to the dominant critical assumptions of history of traditions research. Rather than challenge this research on its own ground several scholars have done their history in other ways. It is important to remember that 'history' itself is a contested concept and that there is room for disagreement about its possibilities, method and goals. The quest of the historical Jesus has too often been dominated by a positivistic view of history which was challenged without much success by Bultmann (following Dilthey) and is being challenged on a wider front today.

Historical constructions will continue to be made as long as human curiosity about Jesus survives — i.e. at least as long as Christianity itself survives. So the 'Quest' goes on.[85] Its importance for theology lies in the journey itself, which bears witness to a historical reality that constantly eludes our grasp, and in the good observations it makes on the way, and the false conclusions it discredits, rather than in its ever reaching its ideal goal. We thus return to the interpretation of the gospels themselves, aware of a history behind them to which they refer, but also aware that their meaning for us is partly determined by the questions we ask of them. Christians' understandings of God's rule in the gospels depends on their prior understandings of God, as well (in some cases) as their historical understanding of the Jewish religious tradition. And these are not unrelated, because Christians' understandings of God have already been pre-formed by that matrix, and by what Jesus said and did and suffered within it. Convergences may therefore be expected.

---

[85]Important contributions not discussed here include H. Merklein op. cit. and L. Goppelt *Theology of the NT* Vol. 1 (1975, ET 1981). Both are discussed by H. Bald (op. cit. n. 82). Also G. Bornkamm *Jesus of Nazareth* (1956, ET 1960) Chap. 4, A. E. Harvey *Jesus and the Constraints of History* (London, 1982) Chap. 4.

To assign our understandings of Jesus' use of the phrase in the gospels to 'the historical Jesus' says both too much and too little. It lays claim to a historical assurance which cannot truthfully be claimed, and it distracts from a more important truth which Christians claim to find in the gospels. Historical reconstruction provides an outline picture of the ministry and passion of Jesus from his association with John the Baptist, through his healing and teaching ministry and his gathering of disciples, to his betrayal by one of them, his arrest, his trial and execution by Pilate. It can also approximately reconstruct a few of his aphorisms and parables, some of which contain his phrase 'the kingdom of God/Heaven'. But when it comes to interpreting this phrase in the context of his whole mission and self-consciousness (about which we can make only educated guesses) historical reconstruction is not enough. Literary techniques are necessary too[86] as we try to understand how others have been drawn by Jesus' religious language, whether or not we are so drawn ourselves. As we reflect on this material and see it in the frames provided by historical research on first century Palestine and by our own fragmentary understandings of the mystery of human life, we may find with Robert Browning

That one face, far from vanish, rather grows,
Or decomposes but to recompose,
Become my universe that feels and knows.

(*Dramatis Personae*)

---

[86]E.g. J. Breech *The Silence of Jesus* (Philadelphia, 1983) is suggestive. It is dismissed as 'aggressive ahistoricism' by Sanders (p. 127), but its observations can be set in a historical framework, even if Breech himself does not intend that. Cf. *Jesus and Postmodernism* (Minneapolis, 1989). The work of J. D. Crossan at its best is another example of illumination that historical reconstruction alone does not provide.

# 7

## The Kingdom of God and Ethics: from Ritschl to Liberation Theology

### by Mark Chapman

I. *The Kingdom of God*

Few would deny that the Kingdom of God was the central theme of the preaching of Jesus. It has accordingly provoked more discussion than almost anything else in theology, at least in the last hundred years or so,[1] since to understand the meaning of the Kingdom of God is to understand the message of Jesus. Indeed, throughout Christian history there have been continued attempts to reinterpret this central theme of the gospel in terms of the predominant conception of the Christian religion and its attitude to the world. It thus easily becomes a 'cover-all word with many meanings . . . In short, whatever is of importance for the community is considered under the heading: "mystery of the Kingdom of God".'[2] It is clear that the concept of the Kingdom of God often functions as a mirror of the prevailing understanding of the church and society, and of the

---

[1]Cf. Gösta Lundström, *The Kingdom of God in the Teaching of Jesus: A History of Interpretation from the Last Decades of the Nineteenth Century to the Present Day*, tr. Joan Bulman (Edinburgh and London, 1963); Bruce Chilton (ed.), *The Kingdom of God* (London, 1984); Norman Perrin, *Jesus and the Language of the Kingdom* (London, 1976); Wendell Willis (ed.), *The Kingdom of God in Twentieth Century Interpretation* (Peabody, Massachusetts, 1987).

[2]Johannes Weiss, *Die Idee des Reiches Gottes in der Theologie* (Vorträge der theologischen Konferenz zu Gießen, Gießen, 1901) (hereafter DI), p. 6.

complex relationship between the two and can either subvert or legitimate the dominant ideology in church, theology and state. Perhaps more than any other theological concept, the Kingdom of God carries a profound ethical burden.

The Kingdom of God has sometimes been seen as 'wholly other' where nothing in the world is able to match the goodness of a divine ruler whose sovereignty protests against all finite human constructions. It was the sovereignty of God that became the Protestant principle *par excellence*.[3] Within the present world, however, God functioned as a benevolent autocrat or even as a totalitarian dictator demanding unyielding obedience from the believer until he established his rule on earth. At other times, however, the reign of God was concretely identified with the institutional Church and even with the structure of the state, which meant that God's rule was manifested in divinely inspired human institutions. Yet, all too often, the Church, or the commonwealth of human beings, usurped the divine monarch's prerogative.

The ethical implications of these understandings of the Kingdom of God are clear. On the one hand, when worldly institutions are equated with the Kingdom of God, when the Church is seen as a glorious reflection of the divine will, then the obvious ethical response is not one of isolation but of participation. Yet such participation is fundamentally conservative, since in a world which is divinely inspired and where human institutions are identified with the divine reign, then obedience to earthly rulers and governments is identical to obedience to God's will and the status quo is preserved.

On the other hand, the Kingdom of God, when viewed as 'wholly other', implies an ethic of withdrawal, a longing for an escape from the corrupt and sinful world, which leads naturally to the ethics of the sect (even if such sects, as Weber pointed out, could have profound effects on world history). Yet when the concrete expression of the salvation no longer takes the form of a sectarian community, but is to be found in the mystical domain of the isolated individual confronting the

---

[3]Cf. H. Richard Niebuhr, *The Kingdom of God in America* (New York, 1959).

almighty on his or her own, then there can be little alternative to a resigned passivity in such a one-sided relationship. The rediscovery of apocalyptic by Johannes Weiss and Albert Schweitzer around the beginning of the present century[4] provided a powerful boost for this understanding of the Kingdom of God: when it was God's action alone that could initiate the glorious arrival of the Kingdom, the world was left to pursue its own evil course and again the *status quo* was preserved.

Both conceptions of the Kingdom of God, which appear at first sight to be diametrically opposed, thus have the same practical consequences: an ethical indifference which allows for no change of the *status quo*. To avoid both these extremes is the task for a theology which seeks to stand apart from the world while at the same time retaining its place and relevance within the world. Theology demands not merely a critical distance but also an ethic which prescribes Christian responsibility and codes for behaviour within the world which in turn allows for the possibility of a transformation of history.[5]

Probably the most important attempt in modern theology to grasp the implications of a sovereign God for Christian life in the world was made by Albrecht Ritschl. While pointing to God as the judge of all things he also simultaneously demanded an ethical transformation of the world, and placed these two poles in a creative tension with one another. Thus, as well as offering theological criticism of all finite human structures, he also

---

[4]Cf. Johannes Weiss, *Die Predigt Jesu vom Reiche Gottes* (Göttingen, 1892, 1900²). Except where stated, references are to the English translation edited by Richard H. Hiers and D. L. Holland of the First Edition, *Jesus' Proclamation of the Kingdom of God* (Philadelphia, 1971) (hereafter JP). Cf. Albert Schweitzer, *The Quest of the Historical Jesus; A Critical Study of its Progress from Reimarus to Wrede* (London, 1954³), pp. 237-240, 348ff.; idem. *The Mystery of the Kingdom of God: The Secret of Jesus' Messiahship* (London, 1925), pp. 59-126, pp. 253-273; idem. *My Life and Thought*, pp. 45-75. Cf. Lundström, *The Kingdom of God*, pp. 27-95. For a modern reassessment of Weiss, see esp. Richard Hiers, intro. in JP, and *The Historical Jesus and the Kingdom of God* (Gainesborough, 1973).

[5]On this theological model see esp. Trutz Rendtorff, *Theorie des Christentums. Historisch-Theologische Studien zu seiner neuzeitlichen Verfassung* (Gütersloh, 1972), esp. Chapter 10.

pointed to the positive function of human activity. The object of theology was thus not God alone, but God in relationship to human beings. In turn the world was not understood as dialectically opposed to God, but in dynamic relationship with him. On this conception, theology does not seek to cut itself off from the rest of reality at the outset in a condemnatory judgement, but to achieve such a relationship with the world which will allow for its ethical transformation. It will be argued that such a model, which has been revived by the Liberation Theologians, is necessary for a satisfactory Christian social ethics.

## II. *Albrecht Ritschl*

Ritschl combined the affirmation of the transcendent God, which functions as the critical concept *par excellence*, with the attempt to provide a coherent framework for human behaviour. Whereas for many of his immediate successors, including most of the members of the *religionsgeschichtliche Schule*, the starting point of all theology was human religious experience,[6] and whereas for Barth the starting point was God, for Ritschl it was both God and the human being: God and the world had to be combined in an all-embracing system.[7] With his conviction that 'the pre-eminent excellence of Christianity' was 'its view of the world as a *well-rounded whole*'[8] Ritschl saw theology as centred on the combination of 'spiritual freedom and dominion over the world *and* labour for the Kingdom of God'.[9] Thus Barth's

[6]On the concept of religion in the *religionsgeschichtliche Schule*, see my essay, 'Religion and the History of Religion School' in the *Scottish Journal of Theology*, forthcoming.

[7]Cf. Hermann Timm (in *Theorie und Praxis in der Theologie Albrecht Ritschls und Wilhelm Herrmanns* (Gütersloh, 1967), esp. p. 24, p. 58) who maintains that Ritschl, although critical of Hegel, retained a quasi-Hegelian universal where both spiritual and natural phenomena were part of the same reality.

[8]*The Christian Doctrine of Justification and Reconciliation*, Pt. I: 'A Critical History of the Christian Doctrine of Justification and Reconciliation', tr. J. S. Black (Edinburgh, 1872), p. 188f.; (ET of *Rechtfertigung und Versöhnung²*, Bd.I, Bonn, 1882) Hereafter JR I.

[9]*Unterricht in der christlichen Religion* (Bonn, 1881). ET: 'Instruction in the Christian Religion' in Albrecht Ritschl, *Three Essays*, ed. Philip Hefner (Philadelphia, 1972), pp. 221-291, here §47 (hereafter *Instruction*).

insistence that Ritschl had completely ethicised the gospel[10] along Kantian lines is a misrepresentation since, for Ritschl, '[if] justification by faith is the basal conception of Christianity, it is impossible that it can express the relation of human beings to God and Christ without at the same time including a distinctive attitude of the believer to the world founded on that revelation'.[11] It was faith alone that gave meaning to any ethical activity.

Similarly faith itself was at the basis of any knowledge of God, which depended not on any metaphysics, but solely on the 'revelation through God's Son' (JR III p. 192). Thus, following Luther in 'his resolve to break with the scholastic methodology',[12] and against his own theological opponents who claimed a natural knowledge of God 'apart from some real revelation on his part' (TM p. 180), Ritschl asserted that knowledge exists only 'in its relationships and it is only in them that we can know the thing and only by them that we can name it' (TM p. 184). In the muddled epistemological sections of JR III (esp. §3, pp. 14-25), Ritschl points to Lotze as his philosophical mentor, for whom knowledge of the effects of a thing implied knowledge of the thing itself. Thus Kant's restriction of knowledge merely to phenomena was apparently overcome (p. 19f.) and the Kantian 'unknown=X' became for Ritschl the 'cause of its qualities operating upon us' (p. 20). For Ritschl, then, God was not 'wholly other', but was known

---

[10]*History of Protestant Thought in the Nineteenth Century*,(London, 1972), p. 655. Cf. Christian Walther, *Typen des Reich-Gottes-Verständnis*, Studien zur Eschatologie und Ethik im 19 Jahrhundert (München, 1961), p. 163.

[11]*The Christian Doctrine of Justification and Reconciliation: The Positive Development of the Doctrine*, tr. H. R. Mackintosh and A. B. Macaulay (reprint, New Jersey, 1966), p. 168 (hereafter JR III). All translations have been compared with *Rechtfertigung und Versöhnung*, Bd. III (Bonn, 1900⁴). Ritschl is critical of Kant precisely because of his ethicisation of the gospel (cf. JRI pp. 429-458, esp. p. 452f., ET pp. 387-415). Cf. David Lotz, *Ritschl and Luther*, Nashville, 1974, esp. pp. 144ff.

[12]Ritschl, *Theologie und Metaphysik. Zur Verständigung und Abwehr* (Bonn, 1881), (refs. are to the ET by Philip Hefner in Albrecht Ritschl, *Three Essays*, ed. Philip Hefner (Philadelphia, 1972), pp. 150-217) here p. 209 (hereafter TM). The translations have been amended where necessary.

through his actions towards us (cf. TM p. 194), which meant ultimately through the reconciliation effected by Christ.[13]

If God was known only through contact with the world, the Christian religion could not be simply indifferent to the world. The biblical and reformation doctrine of the forgiveness of sins through the justification of Christ meant that the Christian lived in a state of having been redeemed, which implied that the world did not constitute a lower reality from which the human was called upon to escape into a higher reality of faith, but had instead to be incorporated into an all-embracing system. Thus Ritschl asked:

> How can man, recognising himself as a part of the world and at the same time capable of a spiritual personality, attain to that dominion over the world, as opposed to limitation by it, which this capability gives him the right to claim? (*Instruction* §8)

Ritschl summarised his theology most clearly in JR I:

> Lordship over the world through trust in God, especially over the evils arising out of it, is the practical and purposeful correlate of justification, which Luther discovered in the footsteps of Paul and which Melanchthon was able to formulate in the classic documents of the Reformation. For whoever is reconciled with God is also reconciled with the course of the world which is conducted by God in one's best interest. (JR I p. 184f.)

However, all too often, according to Ritschl, the practical worldly aspects of the Reformation had been 'concealed' not least by the Reformers themselves.[14] 'Frankly it is shocking,' he maintained in his massive (and still definitive) history of pietism,[15]

[13]On Ritschl's epistemology, see esp. James Richmond, *Ritschl: A Reappraisal* (London, 1978), Chapter II, and J. Baillie, *The Interpretation of Religion* (Edinburgh, 1929), pp. 276-290.

[14]*Festrede* given at the University of Göttingen to celebrate the 400th birthday of Luther, in Lotz, *Ritschl and Luther*, pp. 187-202, p. 195.

[15]*Geschichte des Pietismus*, 3 vols. (Bonn, 1880-6, hereafter GP). ET of the Prolegomena in *Three Essays*.

that there is no mention of the practical aims of justification by faith in the Fourth Article of the Augsburg confession [i.e. justification by faith]. And if we explicate this aim in any other terms than blessedness, within present experience, and if we do not take the believer's attitude towards the world into consideration, how is it to be understood as distinctively Protestant? (GP p. 86, ET p. 128)

In contrast to this, Ritschl held that Protestantism had to centre on both religion and ethics without conflating the one with the other, and that a distinctive set of ideals (*Lebensideal*) had to lead to distinctive ways of behaviour (*Lebensführung*) if it was genuinely to be called Protestant. Thus he maintained that 'the object of transferring ascetic life outside the cloister walls to worldly society' was 'quite dissimilar from the endeavours of the Reformers' (GP I p. 15, ET p. 64). On the contrary, he wrote:

> Luther's distinctive view of the Christian life, as presented in *de libertate christiana*, is quite opposed to mysticism, and he confers the same value on the service of ethical activity towards other human beings as on those functions in which the character gains reconciliation with God. [Mysticism] teaches escape from the world and renunciation of the world and it places the value of the ethically good activity of human beings and of the formation of virtue, far beneath the ecstatic union with God. Luther taught that the Christian religion leads to spiritual dominion over the world. (GP I p. 28, ET p. 76)

The religious and the ethical, which Ritschl likened to two foci of an ellipse (JR III p. 11), were thus united in the whole which formed the Protestant religion: Christian perfection was not achieved in some other-worldly sphere, but in obedience to a 'worldly vocation (*Beruf*)' as the 'place for the practice of love' (GP p. 41, ET p. 86), which was the 'fundamental principle of Protestantism' (GP p. 41, ET p. 87). The true meaning of the Lutheran doctrine of vocation, according to Ritschl, was 'the practical expression for the fact that Christianity is not world-denying but world-fulfilling and world-pervading' (GP p. 41,

ET p. 87). Perfection was not to be found by Christians in some higher realm but precisely 'through continual intercourse with the world and within their distinctive vocations in worldly society' (GP p. 41; ET p. 86).

The objective redemption effected by Christ had the practical result of inspiring activity motivated by love which led to a new organisation of humanity, the Kingdom of God (JR III p. 12f.), as the earthly correlate of the love of God revealed for humankind in the reconciliation of Jesus Christ. Christianity was thus

> the perfected spiritual and ethical monotheistic religion, which, on the basis of the redeemed life and the kingdom of God established by its founder, consists in the freedom of divine adoption, and which includes the stimulus for activity for the motive of love which is directed to the ethical organisation of humanity and which establishes blessedness both in divine adoption and in the kingdom of God. (JR III p. 13f. (amended))

Divine purposes, however, could never be fully equated with worldly purposes; the motive of love would always 'reach out' beyond the world. 'It is an essential characteristic of the Kingdom of God,' Ritschl wrote, 'that the ultimate purpose in the world for created spirits reaches out beyond the world' (JR III p. 267 (amended)). All human activity pointed forwards to a future where reconciliation would be complete 'since the fullness of divine reward always reaches out beyond the measure of the presumed human achievement.'[16] The Church could never be wholly identified with the Kingdom of God but rather was a means to an end, representing the idea of the 'ethical unification of the human race through activity inspired by the motive of love' (JR III p. 267 (amended)). It thus fulfilled a function and was not an institution:

> those who believe in Christ are a church in so far as they acknowledge in prayer their faith in God the Father and present themselves as human beings well pleasing to him

---

[16] *Rechtfertigung und Versöhnung*, (Bonn, 1900⁴), Bd.Ii, p. 37 (hereafter JR II).

through Christ. Those who believe in Christ are a kingdom of God in so far as, without observing the differences of sex, class or nation, they act reciprocally towards one another out of love. (JR III p. 271 (amended))

Ritschl's idea of the Kingdom of God thus centres on a vocational ethic, on the need to live in a world which can be changed by the activity of love: it is consequently capable of profound world-transforming possibilities. However much Ritschl might have seen God as the Prussian paterfamilias, and however much he might have equated worldly vocation with the maintenance of the *status quo*, he nevertheless provided the basis for subsequent attempts to reform the present for the sake of the future, to bring love as the highest motivation for action to its concrete realisation. Against the other-worldly 'ascetic ethic' of the pietists who cut themselves off from the world, Ritschl's theology allowed for a shaping of the world around higher ends. As we will see, however, a new ascetic ethic emerged out of an over-zealous reaction to the most glaring defect of Ritschl's system.

## III. *Johannes Weiss*

The fatal weakness in Ritschl's theology lay in his reliance on untenable historical premises to establish his vocational ethic in the life and teachings of Jesus. The Kingdom of God, he contended, had been initiated by Jesus, who conceived of himself as Messiah (JR II p. 37), and in his person revealed the highest human capacity for obedience to a divine vocation. It was Jesus himself, Ritschl maintained, who had founded a community on earth directed to the realisation of the highest ethical good (JR II p. 40). In short:

> The realisation of the ultimate divine purpose in the world implies the messianic consciousness, and the success of education for the Kingdom of God is therefore dependent on the fact that the dominion of God which was to be realised ethically gained its archetype in [Christ's] person. (JR III p. 267 (amended))

It was Ritschl's own son-in-law, Johannes Weiss, who recognised the impossibility of this picture of the historical Jesus.[17] In his epoch-making *Jesus' Proclamation of the Kingdom of God*, Weiss sought to answer the questions, 'In what sense did Jesus speak of the *Basileia tou Theou*, and is this the sense in which the concept is normally used today?' (JP p. 68). Weiss maintained that Jesus saw the Kingdom of God as wholly future and as something which human beings could do nothing to bring about. There could 'be no talk of an inner-worldly development of the Kingdom of God in the understanding of Jesus' (JP p. 114). In the future reign of God, he went on, Jesus saw himself as the messianic ruler of the twelve tribes of Israel,[18] a consciousness that he adopted at his baptism. For Weiss, this wholly eschatological view had 'something strange about it for our modern way of thinking, but also for the religious imagination' (JP p. 128), and seemed to present an insurmountable gulf between Jesus' ideas and concepts of dogmatics. Thus Weiss wrote:

> Every dogmatics which employs biblical concepts is always in the more or less clearly perceived danger of stripping these concepts of their original historical character by reinterpreting or converting them to new purposes in accordance with new viewpoints. (JP p. 59)

This was particularly true with regard to the concepts of the Kingdom of God:

> Though in retrospect *we* certainly can say as a judgement of faith that Jesus established the Kingdom of God within his Church, it is just as certain that such a conception or expression is far-removed from the sphere of Jesus' ideas. (JP p. 79)

Weiss thus addressed the question of whether theology could still employ the concept of the Kingdom of God. Could it, he asked, 'issue the old coinage at a new rate of exchange?' (JP p.

---

[17]On Weiss and Ritschl, see Berthold Lannert, *Die Wiederentdeckung der neutestamentlichen Eschatologie durch Johannes Weiss* (Tübingen, 1989), esp. pp. 253ff.

[18]In the second edition Weiss had come to the view that Jesus felt another was to rule in the coming Kingdom.

60). The idea of the actualisation of the rule of God which dominated Ritschl's dogmatic concept seemed completely contrary to the transcendentalism of Jesus' original idea (JP p. 135). Weiss expressed this dilemma most poignantly in the much revised and lengthened second edition of his essay:

> In the school of Albrecht Ritschl I convinced myself of the incomparable importance of the systematic concept of the Kingdom of God which was the central organising theme of his theology. I am today still of the opinion that his system and just this central concept represent that form of Christian doctrine which is most likely to bring our race closer to the Christian religion and which, when it is correctly understood and correctly evaluated, is most likely to inspire and encourage the wholesome and robust life which we stand in need of today. But from the outset I was disturbed by the clear discovery that Ritschl's concept of the Kingdom of God and the idea of the same name in the proclamation of Jesus are two very different things... The modern theological concept has a completely different form and resonance from the concept in the faith of the early Church. Further studies have convinced me that the actual roots of Ritschl's idea were in Kant and the theology of the Enlightenment.[19]

In *Jesus' Proclamation* Weiss sought to unpack the modern concept of the Kingdom of God and connect it with ideas present under a different name in the preaching of Jesus. 'That which is universally valid in Jesus' preaching, which should form the kernel of our systematic theology,' he wrote, 'is not the idea of the Kingdom of God but that of the religious and ethical fellowship of the children of God' (JP p. 135).[20] It was thus quite possible, he concluded:

---

[19] Foreword to *Die Predigt Jesu vom Reiche Gottes* (Göttingen, 1900²), p.v.

[20] As Lannert (*Die Wiederentdeckung*, p. 263) makes clear, Weiss retained the practical emphasis of his father-in-law, even if this was often shrouded by his rediscovery of eschatology. In a letter to Martin Rade (12 May 1905, cited in Lannert, p. 264), Weiss believed the widespread misunderstanding of Ritschl as a Christocentric rather than practical theologian was at the heart of 'many of the calamities of the present'.

to approximate to Jesus' attitude, if only in a different sense . . . We do not await a Kingdom of God which is to come down from heaven to earth and abolish this world, but we do hope to be gathered with the church of Jesus Christ into the heavenly *Basileia*. In this sense we, too, can feel and say, as did Christians of old, 'Thy Kingdom Come'. (JP p. 136)

In *Die Idee des Reiches Gottes* Weiss traced the continual redefinition of the concept of the Kingdom of God through history, which had occurred from the very beginnings of Christianity. However, it was only with the elliptical theology of Ritschl, Weiss maintained, that the one-sided concentration on the individual or the Church was overcome.[21] He thus aimed to show how Ritschl concentrated increasingly on the religious side of the ellipse (DI §§23f.) and achieved, in the final edition of *Justification and Reconciliation*, a balanced theology where the ethical (or 'teleological') conception of the Kingdom of God was firmly grounded in faith (DI p. 112). According to Weiss, such a conception, although it was quite unhistorical, could still be of use for contemporary theology:

However modernising and dogmatising Ritschl's biblical–theological basis might be, the concept of the Kingdom of God as he formulated it is still not without its uses. For history shows that apart from in the very earliest times the idea of Jesus has never been unchanged and unaltered, but has always been redefined and altered. It was not possible to give it a value in any other way. And if it is otherwise useful and constructive then it seems to me that a difference from the biblical use is absolutely necessary. (DI p. 113)

Where Weiss parted company with Ritschl was in his insistence that the teleological or ethical side of the ellipse, the Kingdom of God, seemed to be irreconcilable with the objectivity of

---

[21]Indeed Weiss wrote his book to counter R. Wegener's charge in *Albrecht Ritschls Idee des Reiches Gottes* (Leipzig, 1897) that Ritschl had completely ethicised the concept of the Kingdom of God.

Christ's justification. The act of reconciliation in the past appeared disconnected to the goal of the future (DI p. 125). Instead of an ellipse there were two entirely different conceptions of Christianity which could be represented as two concentric circles — the one past and the other future. The universal world plan of God seemed to bear no relation to the specific foundation in Jesus Christ. Weiss' positive solution was to remove the historical sphere altogether in favour of a concentration on the future perfection of humanity on earth, something which was ultimately to be achieved only by God himself. The meaning of history could thus only be understood in the future, in the final consummation, and in no act of the past:

> The final results of history are as follows: God surrounds himself with a highly diverse horde of perfected spirits, who represent the human ideal in the most different forms, and who are all similarly perfected because they have become the most perfect they could be to the best of their capacities and strengths. It appears to us to be a fitting conclusion to history and also for God, whose highest and most beautiful creation is the human personality, because it is not merely the last generation of humanity which has climbed onto the shoulders of the previous generation which finds its joy, but all achieve the goal of their development, each in their own way, from the rich abundance of individuals from all times. It is within this context that the biblical idea of the perfected Kingdom of God has its place. (DI p. 155)

Although Weiss saw the importance of Ritschl's combination between faith and ethics, between the past and the future, he was forced by his dislocation of the dogmatic concept of the Kingdom of God from its rootedness in history into a one-sided concentration on the future, a future which appeared to lack any connection with the past and, more importantly, with the present. The study of history could provide no answers and appeared almost irrelevant for the dogmatic task. Consequently, if Christianity was to survive the onslaught of historical research, it had to be torn from its basis in history and in the teaching of

Jesus himself. All that was left for Weiss was what Ernst Troeltsch called an 'ecclesiastically "impotent"'[22] Christ-mysticism.

Weiss was quite unable to see Jesus as somehow shaping and directing the course of concrete history through an objective reconciliation. By showing Ritschl's historical Jesus to be incredible (on the basis of historical research), and in turn by dislocating dogmatics from history (on the basis of dogmatic need), Weiss managed to dislocate contemporary Christianity from all history, but in so doing he robbed it of its world-transforming power. He thus prepared the path for Bultmann's theology which developed this to brilliant yet ultimately ethically impotent conclusions.[23]

## IV. *Rudolf Bultmann*

In an article written in 1924,[24] Bultmann expressed his dissatisfaction with the prevailing liberal conception of religion which dominated biblical studies, which had sought refuge in a quasi-mystical experience of the cultic Christ who could alone overcome the vagaries of history.[25] This, for Bultmann, seemed nothing more than vain anthropocentrism and against it, he supported the position of the so-called 'most recent theological movement' which maintained that

> the object of theology is God and the objection of liberal
> theology is that it has dealt not with God but with the

[22]Ernst Troeltsch, *The Social Teaching of the Christian Churches* (London, 1931), p. 985 n. 504a.

[23]Cf. Gareth Jones, *Bultmann: Towards a Critical Theology* (Cambridge, 1991); Robert Morgan, 'Rudolf Bultmann' in *The Modern Theologians*, Vol. I, ed. David F. Ford (Oxford, 1989), pp. 109-133 and Ole Jensen, *Theologie zwischen Illusion und Restriktion*, (Beiträge zur evangelischen Theologie, Bd.71, München, 1975), pp. 163-208.

[24]'Die liberale Theologie und die jüngste theologische Bewegung' in *Glaube und Verstehen* I (Tübingen, 1964⁴), pp. 1-25 (hereafter GuV); ET: 'Liberal Theology and the latest theological movement' in *Faith and Understanding* I, ed. R. W. Funk, tr. L. P. Smith (London, 1969). (My translations.)

[25]Bultmann makes explicit reference to Weiss in GuV I p. 20, and finds him to be guilty of denying the cross in favour of ethical activity and the development of the personality. On Bultmann and Weiss see esp. J. C. O'Neill, *The Bible's Authority* (Edinburgh, 1991), p. 287f. and Lannert, *Die Wiederentdeckung*, p. 51.

human being. God means the radical negation and overcoming of everything human; a theology whose object is God can therefore only have the *logos tou staurou* for its content: but this is a *skandalon* for the human being. And so this is the objection to liberal theology: that it tries to remove this *skandalon* or to weaken it (GuV I, p. 2, ET p. 29).[26]

For Bultmann, the 'Jesus piety' of liberal theology was a 'self-deception' based upon an impossible historical picture. 'In my opinion,' he wrote, 'one has to free piety from the completely untenable bond with history which "liberal theology" wants to retain. In reality this was never anything more than a bond with historical knowledge and historical science',[27] which led to a 'pantheism of history' (GuV I p. 5, ET p. 32). All that remained in the pictures of Jesus of the liberal theologians were 'traces of religious moralism'. According to Bultmann, religion was something quite different, as had been most clearly recognised by Rudolf Otto who

> defined the reality of religion as the 'wholly other'. The world of the Good is not the 'wholly other' world, but is the creation of our own moral reason. The 'wholly other' spoken of by ethical religion is not the demand of the Good, but is God who meets the human being in his experience of obedience to the Good. Such a human being knows that if he feels himself to be a sinner he is judged in the deepest sense not by a law of the Good, that is, his own moral conscience, but he is impure in the face of the 'wholly other'. And he knows that if he feels pardoned it is not the dignity of moral thought that exalts him, but it is only in the stillness of the 'wholly other' that he can rediscover purity and himself. He knows that if, in work and struggle, his inner life increases he owes this not to the idea of the Good, but to the mysterious power of the

---

[26]Cf. 'Welchen Sinn hat es, von Gott zu reden?' in GuV I, pp. 26-37.

[27]Bultmann to Rade, 12 Dec. 1920 cited in Bernd Jaspert, 'Von der liberalen zur dialektischen Theologie', in *Rudolf Bultmanns Werk und Wirkung*, ed. Bernd Jaspert (Darmstadt, 1984), pp. 25-43 here p. 31.

'wholly other' which captures his destiny and supports his life.[28]

In short, Bultmann, wrote, '[the] greatest failing of "liberal theology" was, in my opinion, *its confusion of religiously coloured moralism with ethical religion*. Only in this way was it possible to ascribe such a meaning to the historical Jesus; because in what we have received from him the distinctively religious played a relatively minor role.'[29]

For Bultmann, God was 'the absolutely beyond' (GuV I p. 14, ET p. 41; p. 29, ET p. 55), a Judge who stood apart from the world and 'whose kingdom was not of this world' (p. 14, ET p. 41). The phrase '"For the sake of the Kingdom of God",' he wrote in *Jesus and the Word*, 'involves complete renunciation, brings every person face to face with the ultimate *Either-Or.*'[30] The Kingdom of God was 'that *eschatological* deliverance which ends everything earthly,' a deliverance that 'confronts man as an Either-Or'.[31] For Bultmann, it was meaningless to call the Kingdom of God the '"highest value", if by this is meant the culmination of all that human beings consider good . . . The Kingdom of God as eschatological deliverance is diametrically opposed to all relative values' (JW p. 35). Bultmann is thus unequivocal in removing any ethical dimension from the Kingdom of God: it has no connections whatsoever with anything in the world. 'Whoever seeks it,' he wrote, 'must realise that he cuts himself off from the world, otherwise he belongs to those who are not fit' (JW p. 37). Bultmann went on to show that in his message of the 'wholly other', Jesus succeeded in subverting Jewish eschatological hopes (which included all humanistic individualism and all mysticism). Unlike the Christ

[28]'Ethische und mystische Religion im Urchristentum' in *Anfänge der dialektischen Theologie* II, ed. J. Moltmann (München, 1977³), p. 45.

[29]Ibid. p. 44. Bultmann's italics.

[30]*Jesus and the Word* (New York, 1958), p. 31 (hereafter JW). Cf. GuV I p. 18. Cf. *Theology of the New Testament* I (London, 1952), p. 9.

[31]Later, as is well known, Bultmann advocated a de-mythologisation of the concept of the Kingdom of God. Nevertheless this did not rob it of what he considered its eschatological dimension. Cf. *Jesus Christ and Mythology* (New York, 1960), p. 13.

figure of his liberal predecessors, Bultmann's Christ did not preach 'a colourful realm of fancy to which the individual can flee for refreshment and escape from responsibility' (JW p. 50), but confronted the human being with a radical decision, the ultimate 'either/or'.

This interpretation of Jesus, however, completely removed his preaching on the Kingdom of God from the sphere of human history. 'The coming of the Kingdom of God,' Bultmann maintained, was 'therefore not really an event in the course of time)' (JW p. 51). Every hour was the last hour before God's future, which meant that the Kingdom of God was 'absolutely alien to the present-day conception of humanity' (JW p. 52). No achievement of the human personality could bring about this future, which rendered the human being worthless in the face of the wholly other. Similarly, any attempt to give a description of the Kingdom of God was futile since it

> would be possible only by projecting the demands and ideals of man or his spiritual experiences into the other world; and thereby the essential character of the beyond would be taken away. The Kingdom would be a creation of human desire and imagination; it would not be the Kingdom of *God*. (JW p. 56)

For Bultmann, God demands a wholesale rejection of all the products of human history. The biblical texts might open up new existential possibilities but such possibilities were located in a sphere quite out of touch with concrete history. He went as far as claiming that history could play no role in the individual's decision and that acts of love could never be learnt from history (cf. GuV I p. 11, ET p. 38). The critical principle taken to its extreme (which Bultmann equated with the scandal of the cross) robbed all human activity, even that inspired by the motive of love, of any positive meaning. In short, he asserted:

> The Sermon on the Mount demands the impossible and to make it into the norm for activity in the world is not only to do something futile but to deny its character as a *skandalon*. (GuV I p. 16f., ET p. 44)

## V. Liberation Theologies

In Bultmann's stark antithesis a combination of faith and
ethics along Ritschl's lines had been ruled out from the outset
since nothing human, not even a community inspired by love,
could ever make manifest the reign of God. All human goods
were relativised before the transcendent God, and constructive
human activity was robbed of all meaning. Despite the elegance
and power of its theological criticism, Bultmann's theology
seems to evade human social and political responsibility. This
has dangerous implications since, as will become apparent,
without the possibility of ethical construction history will be at
the mercy of the dominant ideology, however malignant, and
can easily become the unwitting tool for oppression. In short,
history goes on regardless: to remove God from it is to leave it
open for the devil.

At this point it is appropriate to introduce a 'hermeneutic of
suspicion' and to call into question the hidden motivation or
ideology of the theologian, since, as Segundo observed, the
very guise of academic neutrality can easily serve to obscure the
ethical and political implications of critical theology:

> Every theology is political, even one that does not speak
> or think in political terms. The influence of politics on
> theology and every other culture cannot be evaded any
> more than the influence of theology on politics and other
> spheres of human thinking. The worst politics of all would
> be to let theology perform this function unconsciously,
> for that brand of politics is always bound up with the status
> quo.[32]

Thus for the Liberation Theologians of Latin America any
theology must be tested by its practical implications. Its impact
on social and political reality must be brought into play, since
all too often theology has sided with those who would remove
religion from the political domain altogether, which amounts

---

[32]J. L. Segundo, *The Liberation of Theology* (Dublin, 1977), p. 74. Cf. Dorothee
Sölle, *Politische Theologie, Auseinandersetzung mit Rudolf Bultmann* (Berlin, 1971),
esp. pp. 49ff.

to nothing less than a tacit legitimation of the *status quo*. The real task of theology was thus 'to liberate the church from false theologies', to make it ever more aware of the political nature of all theologies, even those which purport to be above politics and in which 'the enemy remains hidden'. In this way 'the use of speech and God's word [might be restored to] the people of God'.[33] Theology must admittedly function to criticise all ideologies, but at the same time it must also attempt to discern those historical powers and ideologies which will bring liberation from oppression. Thus, according to Ched Myers, 'the proper vocation of theology is the practice of "ideological literacy", the critical discipline of political hermeneutics. It calls for discernment when liberating ideologies, including Christian theologies, become oppressively hegemonic.'[34]

From this perspective, Bultmann's question, 'What is the importance of the preaching of the New Testament as a whole for modern man?'[35] is to be approached, not in terms of its effect on the individual standing before God, but in terms of its concrete implications for social and political reality. Bultmann's removal of redemption from the sphere of concrete history is thus assessed from a practical viewpoint: praxis becomes the measure of theory.[36] The theologian who adopts this standpoint will look at the concrete implications of Bultmann's notion that the whole world of cause and effect is beyond redemption. From the practical perspective he or she might see Christianity as wholly immersed within the world of cause and effect. Forms of activity emerge from a theological critique but find their expression not apart from, but *within*, history. The criticism of all human institutions leads to constructive change (itself also open to continual criticism) *within* the world of cause and effect. Ultimately the theologian

---

[33]J. Comblin, 'What sort of service might theology render?' in *Frontiers of Theology in Latin America*, ed. Rosino Gibellini, tr. John Drury (New York, 1979), p. 63.

[34]Ched Myers, *Binding The Strong Man* (New York, 1988), p. 21.

[35]*Jesus Christ and Mythology*, p. 17. Cf. 'The Problem of Hermeneutics' in *Essays Philosophical and Theological* (London, 1955), pp. 234-261.

[36]Cf. Sölle, *Politische Theologie*, pp. 91ff.

is forced to judge for him- or herself between competing theological methods, but it seems clear that in any decision which seriously seeks to retain a connection between spirit and nature, between God and the world, there must be an account of the practical implications of any theological standpoint. A theology which takes history seriously, and which is concerned with the future of the concrete world, must inevitably become a political theology, since change is only possible through the often frustrating business of politics.

A post-Bultmannian theology must consequently reverse his vision[37] and become a theology of action, of world-transformation, escaping from the confines of being, to the liberation of becoming.[38] In short, according to Sobrino, God's very existence is defined in terms of his activity: 'the dynamic element should predominate over any static overtones'. 'God is insofar as he acts, insofar as he alters reality; and we must view the actions of Jesus in that light.'[39] Similarly, Fernando Belo's dense treatment of Mark[40] succeeds in pointing the interpreter to the character of the text as a 'narrative of power', to Jesus' *activity* of subversion, against exegetes like Bultmann who 'may talk about "the history of salvation",' but who in fact dissolve history 'into the timelessness of consciousness and interiority and its relationship to the "eternity" of God' (p. 284). Against this, Belo's materialist interpretation, whatever its faults, relates the gospel to its physical environment, to time and to concrete history.

A theology which takes account of its practical implications must thus set about recovering an authentic Christian expression of history which will prevent what Dorothee Sölle has called 'the bourgeois appropriation of the Bible',[41] where biblical faith is dislocated from its material context and thus removed from the social and political sphere. Such a theology

---

[37]Cf. Christopher Rowland and Mark Corner, *Liberating Exegesis* (London, 1990), esp. p. 71.

[38]Cf. Moltmann (ed.), *Anfänge* p. 45.

[39]Jon Sobrino, *Christology at the Crossroads* (London, 1978), pp. 43, 46.

[40]*A Materialist Reading of the Gospel of Mark* (New York, 1981).

[41]In *God of the Lowly*, ed. Willy Schottroff and Wolfgang Stegemann (New York, 1984), p. 92.

will seek to shape concrete history around an absolute goal by attempting to combine faith in the future with ethical activity in the present, which alone can liberate human history from the forces of oppression. On this model, sin is not reduced to the sphere of the individual, but is to be seen as a 'social, historical fact, the absence of brotherhood and love in relationships among men'[42] which 'can be tangibly verified in the oppression to which it gives rise.'[43] Faith in the future is not restricted to the hope for individual salvation, but is a faith in a future 'which we fashion with our own hands' (TL p. 238). The historical world is thus not a cage from which the human needs to escape in order to experience redemption, but is itself the arena for God's redemptive activity. The world of cause and effect can thus be transformed by human activity as the course of history is reincorporated into the purposes of God. This means that, for the Liberation Theologians, the vision of the future determines activity in the present: eschatology is realised by human beings acting in accord with divine ends. Fixing our eyes on the future, Gutierrez writes, determines our 'real action in the present' (TL p. 220) and becomes our 'effective commitment' (p. 237).

This vision has profound consequences for the understanding of the Kingdom of God, as is clear from J. L. Segundo's criticism of Bultmann's understanding of the Kingdom as 'a cosmic catastrophe which will do away with all conditions of the present world as it is'.[44] Instead, for Segundo, it can only be fully understood in terms of Jesus' relationship with the social and political forces of oppression. To suppose that everything could be explained as the assimilation of contemporary apocalyptic is seen by Segundo as a denial of the wider material context of the gospel message. 'I will not conceal my opinion,' he maintains:

> that one would have to erase practically the whole of the Gospel message to arrive at [Bultmann's] definition of

---

[42]G. Gutierrez, *A Theology of Liberation* (New York, 1973), p. 175 (hereafter TL).

[43]Sobrino, *Christology*, p. 54.

[44]*Theology of the New Testament* I (London, 1952), p. 4.

the coming of God's kingdom or reign. Everything we have seen so far shows Jesus, not only announcing its coming and preparing it in history, but also associating the group of disciples with this historical causality.[45]

The concept of history used in this model of theology is far broader than that used in the purely religious and philosophical categories of the history of religion. History here is not the object of a passive and academic study, but is the arena for activity and something open to change: '[the] whole of historical causality' has to be placed in the 'service of the Kingdom . . . Thus it is *from within* historical causality that human beings collaborate with the Kingdom.'[46] The religious vision is thus complemented by ethical activity.

The emphasis by the Liberation Theologians on the permeation of concrete history by religion is nothing less than a return to the union of the ethical and the religious, analogous to Ritschl's elliptical theology. For the Liberation Theologians, as for Ritschl, the meaning of human existence is not to be found in the isolated individual but only as he or she relates to society and to history. Revolutionary praxis is the dynamic equivalent to the Ritschlian concept of vocation and is demanded by a different concrete situation. What remains the same, however, is that Christian hope is combined with concrete history. In the words of Gutierrez: 'to hope in Christ is at the same time to believe in the adventure of history, which opens infinite vistas to the love and action of the Christian' (TL p. 238f.).

This model of theology takes the fullness of the incarnation seriously, in so far as it recognises that the spirit is as nothing without the body. And such a body is not a heavenly body, but a body that decays and dies within history. The alternative, which seeks to withdraw from the material world, is nothing less than a reversal of the incarnation: '[its] tendency is to exalt God more, to set him at a distance, to make the experience of God independent of the material, to separate it from popular

---

[45]J. L. Segundo, *Jesus of Nazareth Yesterday and Today* (New York, 1985), p. 149.
[46]Segundo, *Jesus*, pp. 149, 159.

piety and to spiritualise it.'[47] In a theology which takes the material world seriously, however, salvation cannot be found in some timeless reality of existential truth, in an 'eternal now', but within concrete history. Thus, in the words of Gutierrez 'the complete encounter with the Lord will mark an end to history, but will take place in history' (TL p. 168).

## VI.  *Back to Ritschl?*

It may be concluded that something analogous to Ritschl's elliptical theology has returned to the centre stage, at least in the Latin American reaction to the ahistorical critical theologies of the inter-war years. The need to free a continent from oppression has evidently forced theology back into history and ethics. Liberation Theologies are guided by the effort to incorporate human activity into theological reflection. This was also the distinctive characteristic of Ritschl's system. Bultmann's theology, with its 'ascetic' ethic of withdrawal, on the other hand, now looks like a distraction from the theological quest for a practical expression of redemption. Although Ritschl's theology may seem dated, and Liberation Theologies may date quickly, a theology which cannot date and which locates redemption in the *stasis* of being and not in the *dynamis* of events, cannot affect history, and ignores the material implications of the incarnation.

In an article written in 1935,[48] Horst Stephan called for a revitalisation of Ritschl's method to overcome the ethical impotence of the dialectical theology which dominated the theological faculties of his day. What was needed above all was a theology which at once says 'Yes' and 'No' to the world. The principles 'of diastasis and synthesis', he remarked, 'have to be inwardly combined if theology is really to continue to move forwards' (p. 42). Although Stephan's plea was in vain, it is still relevant, since, as part of the divine creation, human beings

---

[47]Sölle, *God of the Lowly*, p. 91.
[48]Horst Stephan, 'Albrecht Ritschl und die Gegenwart' in *ZThk* NF15: 1935, pp. 21-43.

have a vocation in the world and in history as builders of the kingdom.[49]

As we have seen, however, something similar to Ritschl's ellipse once again shapes theological reflection. Such a return of the spirit of Ritschl was predicted by his son, Otto:

> It seems in no way impossible that in the future the thoroughly activist theology of Albrecht Ritschl will once again play a leading role in the service of an energetic Christianity, since a fundamentally activist attitude is the distinctive possession [of theology].[50]

The alternative is a vision of Christianity which cuts itself off from this active immersion in the concrete historical world. Yet, as has become apparent all too often, a religion which separates itself from history loses its ethical potency and is soon replaced by all manner of malevolent competitors. As such it ought to take its proper place 'among the interesting occupants of that "Anchorage for Obsolete Vessels" which may be found marked in the Admiralty Charts of the Isle of Wight'.[51]

[49]On the ecological implications of an 'ascetic ethic' see my essay '"Theology within the walls": Wilhelm Herrmann's religious reality' in *NZSThRph* 33: 1992, pp. 69-84.

[50]Otto Ritschl, 'Albrecht Ritschl und die bisherige Schicksale' in *ZThk*: NF15, 1935, pp. 43-61, here p. 61.

[51]R. J. Collingwood, *Essay on Metaphysics* (reprint, Chicago, 1972), p. 246.

# 8

## Re-reading Schweitzer's *Quest*
### by Philip West

Albert Schweitzer's 1906 *The Quest of the Historical Jesus*[1] may seem an odd place to start looking for a modern Christian social ethic. Certainly it does not appear on any booklist that I have seen issued by the Christian ethics department of a British university. But it is a book that I have found peculiarly suggestive as a guide to the hinterland where ethics, doctrine and New Testament studies overlap, and therefore to the questions explored in this volume. It is the aim of this essay to explain why. I shall start by sketching the argument of the penultimate chapter of the book, where Schweitzer attempts to reconstruct the history of Jesus' own views about his role in the divine economy.

### Schweitzer's Jesus

Jesus, Schweitzer argues, expected the imminent inbreaking of the kingdom of God, accompanied by the revelation of himself as the promised Son of man (p. 384). More precisely, he thought this event so imminent that when one harvest time (Matt. 9.37f.) he sent the Twelve out on mission (Matt. 10), 'he did not expect to see them back in the present age'. The Kingdom would dawn 'before they shall have completed a hasty journey through the cities of Israel to announce it' (p. 357). The subsequent non-

---

[1]A. Schweitzer, *The Quest of the Historical Jesus: A Critical Study of its Progress from Reimarus to Wrede* (London: SCM, 1981).

164

appearance of the Kingdom, argued Schweitzer, 'was for Jesus
. . . the central event which closed the former period of his
activity and gave the coming period a new character' (ibid.). At
this point Jesus himself faced what was to later be the key
theological problem faced by the early Church: the delay of the
Parousia (p. 358). But whereas in the early Church this led to
'the abandonment of eschatology, the progress and completion
of the "de-eschatologising" of religion', for Jesus himself it was
different. Under the impact of the non-arrival of the Parousia
Jesus' own theology deepened and developed into a theology
of the cross.

According to the 'programme' of Jewish eschatology which
Jesus was heir to, argued Schweitzer, the inbreaking of the
Kingdom must be preceded by a period of woes and tribulation:
the *peirasmos* (p. 385). Jesus' purpose in sending out the Twelve
had been 'to hurl the firebrand into the world', 'to let loose the
final woes, the confusion and strife from which shall issue the
Parousia, and so to introduce the supra-mundane phase of the
eschatological drama' (p. 369). But he now came to see that 'it
was appointed for him to share the persecution and the
suffering' (p. 369) that was the essence of this period. Indeed,
'as the future bearer of the supreme rule he must go through
the deepest humiliation' (p. 370), followed by his disciples
who, to be saved, must take up their cross and follow him
(ibid.). Eventually, Jesus came to believe that the generalised
woes of the *peirasmos* had been replaced in God's purposes by
the event of his own death:

> In the secret of his passion which Jesus reveals to the
> disciples at Caesarea Philippi the pre-messianic tribulation
> is for others set aside, abolished, concentrated upon
> himself alone . . . That was the new conviction that had
> dawned upon him. He must suffer for others . . . that the
> Kingdom might come. (pp. 388f.)

Jesus thus went to Jerusalem to die, so as to 'at last compel the
coming of the Kingdom' (p. 388). Entering as the Messiah, he
deliberately provoked the authorities into action by attacking
the Pharisees and cleansing the Temple (p. 389), acts which
amounted to 'the deliberate bringing down of death upon

himself' (p. 390). And he died expecting his death to secure the establishment of God's Kingdom on earth — an expectation which was not fulfilled:

> Jesus . . . in the knowledge that he is the coming Son of Man lays hold of the wheel of the world to set it moving on that last revolution which is to bring all ordinary history to a close. It refuses to turn, and he throws himself upon it. Then it does turn; and crushes him. Instead of bringing in the eschatological conditions, he has destroyed them. The wheel rolls onward, and the mangled body of the one immeasurably great man who was strong enough to think of himself as the spiritual ruler of mankind and to bend history to his purpose, is hanging upon it still. That is his victory and his reign. (pp. 368f.)

*Significance*

There are at least four ways in which I find this Schweitzerian picture of Jesus suggestive for the constructive task of Christian social ethics, none of which stand or fall by the precise historical accuracy of Schweitzer's reconstruction.

(1) Much Christian social thought operates with a picture of Jesus that in effect if not in name, denies his humanity, and thereby renders him irrelevant as an example to be followed in the modern world. This figure, by virtue of being God, escapes from the contradictions of real worldly existence. He is able to predict the future with unerring accuracy, and his will is not thwarted by the vicissitude of events. He shares God's omnipotence and omniscience. Such a figure is of little use to us as an example, because he simply does not share our problems. Schweitzer's Jesus, however, is fully human. He can be wrong — and indeed is so over the timing of the parousia. He is embedded as we are in a particular social context with its constraints. He lives within the framework of his own thought-world as we do. This Jesus is a human being like us. He neither floats three feet above the ground, nor escapes the contradictions of real existence. He shares our problems. As such he can function as an example.

(2) Schweitzer presents us with a Jesus who starts off with a

fairly simple and uncluttered picture of what is needed to bring in the Kingdom, but who learns through the disappointment of events. No, it will not be as easy as simply sending out the Twelve on a preaching expedition; it will involve something far more messy, costly and involved. Schweitzer's Jesus reacts to his disappointment neither by retreating into quietism, nor by detaching the Kingdom from our world as a timeless realm attainable only after death. He remains committed to a programme of the establishment of the Kingdom of God in this world, but with a more mature realisation of the cost and conflict that such social transformation will require. Here there is a model for the simple revolutionary who is suffering from disillusionment. Utopia has proved to be more difficult to construct than he thought; the social material more intractable than he at first believed. Hurling the firebrand of his message into the world has failed to bring about the kingdom. Yet it is not necessary to yield to despair; and in fact to follow Jesus at this point is to refuse to yield to despair.

(3) Schweitzer presents us with a picture of Jesus reinterpreting the eschatological woes in terms of the need for his own martyrdom. This I find the most interesting part of his model. Realising that the Kingdom cannot come without suffering, Jesus takes upon himself the required suffering to bring it about. This is a compelling model of the atonement, which steers a middle course between mere exemplarism on the one hand and the metaphysical transaction of most 'objective' theories on the other. It is also a model for Christian discipleship and for the interpretation of the suffering and conflict that that involves. With the help of Schweitzer's Jesus we can make sense of the notion of *imitatio Christi* as the key moment in Christian ethics. God calls us to the way of the cross, which is suffering so that the Kingdom may come — suffering in the cause of social change. Like Jesus, we do not know (and may be wrong about) how near or how far that Kingdom is. Like him we may be (and are) thwarted by the intractability of the social material with which we deal. Yet we are called to share his hope in God's eventual triumph.

(4) Schweitzer's Jesus is often presented as being a deluded revolutionary who was simply proved wrong by events. But this

is too simple a reading either of *The Quest* itself or of the figure that it portrays. Consider that enigmatic passage from pp. 368f. quoted above (at the end of the section on *Schweitzer's Jesus*). Jesus is indeed crushed by events, and in that respect defeated. Yet Schweitzer can still say that he has a 'victory' and a 'reign' which consists in hanging still upon the wheel of the world. And that is surely the case. His life has inspired personal and social transformation from the very earliest Christian communities until the present day. His life and death have inaugurated, even if not yet brought to fulfilment, a new age in the history of the world. In this respect, even if in no other, the effects of his classic confrontation with the forces of evil are still reverberating in our own world. In his death, defeat and victory are paradoxically associated.

*This World and the World to Come*

The relationship between this world and the world to come has exercised a great deal of Christian thought. In recent writing (e.g. Michael Taylor's *Good for the Poor*) four possible models for the relationship have been sketched. It is interesting to note that Schweitzer's Jesus does not fit easily into any of them, although Schweitzer's theology has often been characterised as 'straight apocalypticism'.

The first view or model looks forward to the coming of God's future here on earth, an idea harking back in some ways to the old Jewish expectation. This is often characterised as too optimistic and bordering on Utopianism. It is said to be found in the nineteenth century liberal social gospel, in some secular theologies of the mid-twentieth century and in the writings of the Liberation Theologians.

Schweitzer's Jesus differs from this model because, despite the fact that he believes in the establishment of God's Kingdom here *on earth,* he cannot accurately be described as *optimistic.* The establishment of the Kingdom is not something that is already happening in the normal dynamic of human progress as nineteenth century evolutionary optimism and the twentieth century secular gospel believed; nor is it to spring *inevitably* from the contradictions of the present order as Marx (perhaps) held. The establishment of that Kingdom involves opposition to the current dynamic and power structures of society, and it requires (therefore) struggle and suffering to the point of death to bring it about.

(2) A second type of view sees no future for the world we know at all. It is destined to pass away after a spate of destruction of the sort described in apocalyptic visions found in biblical and intertestamental literature. This view involves hostility to the world; the world is a wicked place and our best hope is not to transform it but to survive it. Such views are found in the book of Revelation and in more recent revivals of apocalyptic pessimism.

Schweitzer's Jesus differs from this model in that his hope is this-worldly rather than other-worldly. Indeed, this world is in the grip of powers hostile to true human community; but these powers can be — and are to be — challenged in the hope that with God's help they may be overthrown. The hope is that the world may be transformed through sacrificial action, not merely survived in the hope of something better.

(3) The third model or view may be called 'transformationist'. It is usually rooted in convictions about the integral relationship between matter and spirit, and between human beings and the rest of creation. It sees a real future for the present world as it is taken up into the world to come in a process of transformation. The process theologians and the thought of Teilhard de Chardin may be instanced here. Romans 8 and 1 Corinthians 15 lie in the background.

Although Schweitzer's Jesus would accept the Jewish view of the integral relationship between matter and spirit, and would agree that the dawning of the kingdom is and would be a matter of transformation, he would not recognise the process theology of Teilhard de Chardin as convincing. In fact, Teilhard's optimistic evolutionism bears a closer resemblance to the optimism of our first model than to the picture in Romans 8 with its imagery of the birth-pangs of the new age drawn from apocalyptic.

(4) The fourth and last view is one which does not despise the present world or write it off, but sees it as 'a vale of soul-making'. God's plan is to make individual souls, and that is the

role for the present world. But one day its work will be done and then it will be forgotten and outgrown. Writers as diverse as Irenaeus, Rudolf Bultmann and John Hick have been seen as belonging here.

In clear opposition to this, Schweitzer's Jesus would deny that the kingdom can be a matter simply of individuals. 'Kingdom' is a social category, as human beings are essentially social and communal creatures. The idea that God's plan is to make individual souls is to be rejected in favour of the view that he aims to create a redeemed *community*.

### Hope, Kingdom and Creation

To take Schweitzer's Jesus as our model for Christian social ethics would be, as I have hinted already, to relate the themes of hope, Kingdom and creation in a particular way. It would be to insist that the reign of God is a project to be embodied in this world. It would be to insist that the category of Christian *hope* should steer a middle path between *optimism* on the one hand and *pessimism* on the other. And finally it would be to suggest that the suffering and setbacks that follow from the pursuit of that goal should be seen as the birth-pangs of the new age, as the inevitable price of the creative transformation that is to be brought about, rather than as meaningless or as cause for despair.

In closing, I would like to dwell briefly on each of these three points in turn.

(1) Any proposal which, openly or covertly, makes this world less than fully real must be rejected. The traditional Augustinian model of the earthly city and the heavenly is one such, but there are others still claiming attention. The struggles which we enter into in our present lives are, like the struggle of Schweitzer's Jesus, of final significance. In my opinion, the Christian doctrine of creation commits us to seeing *this* world as the arena of God's creative activity, and to insisting that the reign of God is an ideal to be established here through our activity that is at one and the same time God's own activity. We, like the Schweitzerian Jesus, are to be God's eschatological agents, striving for the establishment of his reign 'in earth as in heaven'.

(2) Optimism and pessimism I take to be attitudes that in essence 'close' the future. Thus evolutionary optimism assumes that a rosy future is secure whether we work for it or not, while pessimism assumes that the worst will happen whatever we do to try and avert it. Both have in common the belief that, in the long run, our actions do not matter, because history is predetermined. Hope, however, I take to be the attitude that is consistent with an 'open' future. It is the belief that the future *can* be different — indeed *better* — and that this difference depends upon human action. Hope is thus consistent with action, pessimism and optimism with paralysis.

A surprising amount of Christian writing seems unclear as to which of those three is the authentic Christian option. It is sometimes assumed that the general lot of humanity will remain constant, and that in overall terms history does not exhibit progress. Others (as we have seen) can argue that the goal of creation will be achieved; and yet genuine creativity must be a venture into the unknown in hope that what God has in store for us, and what we can achieve, will bring that hope to fulfilment. This hope is the authentic Christian position. Consider a specific contemporary issue by way of illustration (still contemporary even if it is fading from people's minds): the threat of nuclear holocaust. It is paralysing to assume either that nuclear catastrophe will certainly occur (pessimism), or that it certainly will not because God will not allow it (optimism). We need rather to act so as to avert what is a real, yet not inevitable, possible future. The future is open: Christian hope believes that a better future can be won. And if this is the case in the political and military spheres, then it is unduly pessimistic to assume that it is not the case in the economic sphere.

(3) It is important to stress that the Christian doctrine of creation can be combined fruitfully with a Schweitzerian view of the cross. Creation is to be seen as something closer to the Old Testament concept of *Chaoskampf* than to the mere effortless making of 'stuff'. It is a matter of imposing order on chaos — physical, personal and social chaos — so as to transform it into a peaceful universe ordered by love. Such work is demanding of sacrifice, and it takes place in the personal and social as well as in the natural dimensions. But if this is what creation means,

it is clear that the themes of creation and redemption are inextricably interwoven in God's action and our own, and that the crucifixion was a creative as well as a redemptive act. We are called to follow Jesus in costly action that is at once creative and redemptive — to wrestle with the chaos that is the present world so that it may be transformed into something that is a little closer to the world to come.

That too is to be our victory and our reign.

# 9

# Walter Rauschenbusch and the Coming of God's Kingdom

## by Mark Chapman

Walter Rauschenbusch (1861-1918),[1] who delivered 'the classic statement of American Social Christianity,'[2] has had a profound effect on American religious thought throughout this century.[3] Martin Luther King, for instance, remarked that he had left 'an indelible imprint' on his own thinking,[4] by making him aware 'that any religion which professes to be concerned about the souls of men and is not concerned about the social and economic conditions that scar the soul is a spiritually moribund religion'.[5] The Social Gospel, which was part of a 'social awakening that had got hold of the country'[6] where 'the social

---

[1] On Rauschenbusch's life see esp. Paul M. Minus, *Walter Rauschenbusch: American Reformer* (New York, 1988) which supersedes Dores R. Sharpe's *Walter Rauschenbusch* (New York, 1942). Cf. 'Edwin Dahlberg in Conversation: Memories of Walter Rauschenbusch' in *Foundations* XVIII: 1975, pp. 209-218. I wish to express my gratitude to Dr John Vincent of the Urban Theology Unit, Sheffield, for the opportunity of presenting an earlier version of this paper to a course on Radical Theology.

[2] Charles Howard Hopkins, *The Rise of the Social Gospel in American Protestantism, 1865-1915*, Yale Studies in Religious Education XIV (New Haven, 1940), p. 215f. Cf. Reinhold Niebuhr, *An Interpretation of Christian Ethics* (New York, 1935), preface.

[3] Cf. Paul A. Carter, *The Decline and Revival of the Social Gospel: Social and Political Liberalism in American Protestant Churches, 1920-1940* (Hamden, Connecticut, 1971²).

[4] 'Pilgrimage to Nonviolence' in *The Christian Century* LXXVII: 1960, p. 439.

[5] Idem. *Stride Toward Freedom*, New York, 1958, p. 91.

[6] Walter Rauschenbusch, *Selected Writings*, ed. Winthrop S. Hudson (New York and Mahwah, 1984), p. 4. Contains many previously unpublished essays and letters (hereafter SW).

ideal' was 'getting hot with life',[7] meant nothing less than an 'astonishing reversal in the position occupied by the churches'.[8] Indeed, Rauschenbusch felt himself to be living in

> the midst of a revolutionary epoch fully as thorough as that of the renaissance or the Reformation . . . We now see the struggle of the people to wrest a living from nature and to shake off their oppressors.[9]

What is clear, however, is that the 'contagious enthusiasm' which transformed American religion at the turn of the century 'had largely evaporated' by the 1920s.[10] Indeed 'the "crisis-theology" of Karl Barth could be taken, if one chose, as a rebuttal to Walter Rauschenbusch'.[11] By the 1940s with the growing pre-eminence of Reinhold Niebuhr,[12] 'the social gospel as a distinct, self-conscious movement with a clear sense of direction had largely disappeared'.[13] Even by his admirers, Rauschenbusch has thus long been regarded as having fallen 'victim to the "cult of inevitable progress" [where] he came perilously close to identifying the Kingdom of God with a particular social and economic system — a temptation which the church should never give in to'.[14] Similarly Reinhold Niebuhr remarked that it was astonishing that Rauschenbusch's epoch-making *Christianity and the Social Crisis* which 'meant so much to American religious life and to the older among us personally should be so obviously dated'.[15]

---

[7] *Christianising the Social Order* (New York, 1912), p. 69 (hereafter CSO).

[8] Winthrop S. Hudson *The Great Tradition of the American Churches* (New York, 1953), p. 196.

[9] *Christianity and the Social Crisis* (New York, 1907), p. 45 (hereafter CSC).

[10] Winthrop S. Hudson, *The Great Tradition*, p. 196.

[11] Paul A. Carter, op. cit., p. 61.

[12] Cf. Reinhold Niebuhr, 'Walter Rauschenbusch in Historical Perspective', *Religion in Life* 27: 1958, pp. 527-536.

[13] Robert T. Handy, *The Social Gospel in America* (New York, 1966), p. 15.

[14] Luther King, 'Pilgrimage to Nonviolence', p. 439. More recently this charge has been levelled by John C. Bennett. Cf. 'The Social Gospel Today' in Ronald C. White and C. Howard Hopkins, *The Social Gospel: Religion and Reform in Changing America* (Philadelphia, 1976), pp. 285-288.

[15] Reinhold Niebuhr, 'Walter Rauschenbusch in Historical Perspective', p. 527. Cf. *Moral Man and Immoral Society* (New York, 1932), p. 63.

Although it would be rash to deny that much of Rauschenbusch's thought is dated, this paper moves beyond these summary dismissals by reassessing his teaching on the Kingdom of God. It will become clear that the charge that he succumbed to the cult of inevitable progress cannot be substantiated. He never lost a very real sense of sin which tempered all his thinking, even if, in the circumstances in which he was writing, it was necessary to stress the social against the religious emphasis of the 'private Protestantism' of the time.[16] Both the religious and the social aspects of the Kingdom of God were integral to his system which formed

> a great synthesis in which the regeneration of the spirit, the enlightenment of the intellect, the development of the body, the reform of the political life, the sanctification of industrial life and all that concerns the redemption of humanity shall be embraced. (SW p. 76)

Rauschenbusch's theology turns out to be of great contemporary relevance: his fusion of the religious with the social helps restore the balance against theologies which emphasise either the purely religious or the purely social.[17]

## I

Rauschenbusch's interest in the Social Gospel was first aroused by his ministry in the second German Baptist Church in New

[16]Cf. Martin E. Marty, *Religious Empire: The Protestant Experience in America* (New York, 1970), pp. 177-187. Cf. SW p. 79: 'With most social reformers, it is the [religious] aspect which needs emphasis; with most religious people, it is the [social].'

[17]The rediscovery of Christian social thought by the Latin American Liberation Theologians displays a marked continuity with Rauschenbusch's method. Cf. T. Howland Shanks, S.J., 'Liberation Theology and the Social Gospel: Variations on a theme,' *Theologial Studies* 41: 1980, pp. 668-682. Cf. Roger Haight, 'The mission of the Church in the theology of the Social Gospel' in *Theological Studies* 49: 198, pp. 477-497. Cf. Alfred J. Ede, 'The social theologies of Walter Rauschenbusch and Vatican II in dialogue' in *Foundations* XVIII: 1975, pp. 198-208.

York's 'Hell's Kitchen' which he took up in 1886,[18] and he was soon contributing to the newspaper, *For The Right*, devoted to 'the interests of the working people'. He held that economic improvements alone would never be sufficient, since 'mankind rolling in material wealth with no moral earnestness and spiritual elevation would only be like swine champing in a full trough or maggots burrowing in a carcass' (SW p. 60). In its zeal for social reform the Church could not afford to ignore its 'distinctive spiritual work' (SW p. 65):

> Let us not be beguiled by that seductive devil who tells us that man will walk into the millennium . . . If he is to get in, he will have to be lifted in. There will have to be a force from above strong enough to overcome all the downward gravitation of flesh and world, and to conquer the devil in addition. (SW p. 68)

He later wrote: 'If the new interest in social questions crowds out the old interest in evangelistic work, it is a reaction from an old one-sidedness to a new one-sidedness' (SW p. 29; cf. CSO p. 103). God alone gave the human being the power to act morally and without him all social progress was as nothing. In short, if 'our personal religious life is likely to be sapped by our devotion to social work, it would be a calamity second to none' (CSO p. 104).

Rauschenbusch was 'inquiring for a religious ideal large enough to include social as well as individual salvation, and for ways and means of making the latent forces of religion operative in public life' (SW p. 123). He thus asked: 'What great idea has the Christian Church which will serve as the religious lever and fulcrum for the engineering task of the present generation?' (CSO p. 41). He was searching for

> a place, under the old religious conceptions, for this great task of changing the world and making it righteous . . . I

---

[18]On the origins of Rauschenbusch's Social Gospel see esp. Klaus Jürgen Jähn, 'The formation of Walter Rauschenbusch's social consciousness as reflected in his early life and writings' in *Foundations* XVI: 1973, pp. 294-326; 17: 1974, pp. 68-85.

had personal religion. I now had also that large social outlook, and how was I to combine these two things? I needed a unity of life — faith. A real religion always wanted unity. It wants to bring the whole world into one great conception that can inspire and fill the soul. It sees one God, it wants one world, and it wants one redemption. That is faith. No faith is really complete that cuts life up into sections, and applies only to a little bit of it. We want faith always as a whole thing.[19]

It was at this point that the Kingdom of God came

as a new revelation. Here was the idea and the purpose that had dominated the mind of the Master himself. All his teachings center about it. His life was given to it. His death was suffered for it . . . When the Kingdom of God dominated our landscape, the perspective of life shifted into a new alignment. I felt a new security in my social impulses. (CSO p. 93)

The concept of the Kingdom of God which had almost 'dropped out of the Christian vocabulary' (SW p. 72) was in fact 'the first and most essential dogma of the Christian Faith . . . the lost social ideal of Christendom' (CWO p. 49). It

was something so big that absolutely nothing . . . was excluded from it. It carries God into everything that you do, and there is nothing else that does it in the same way. (KG p. 267)

Just as 'in the first century the "Kingdom of God" meant a combination of the social and the religious hopes of the common people', so 'today the same elements are fusing once more under new conditions, and the same spirit has taken over possession of the ancient word' (CSO p. 92). From this moment 'all religious thinking' had 'to be done in a new synthesis' (CSO p. 94) and all religious issues had to be 'revalued . . . from the point of view of the Kingdom of God'.[20] The Kingdom of

---

[19]'The Kingdom of God' (1913) cited in Handy, op. cit., pp. 264-267, here p. 266 (hereafter KG).

[20]*The Social Principles of Jesus* (New York, 1916), p. 146 (hereafter SP).

God lent 'grandeur to the scattered and fragmentary purposes of life by gathering them in a single all-comprehending aim' (SW p. 132):

> The saving of the lost, the teaching of the young, the pastoral care of the poor and frail, the quickening of starved intellects, the study of the Bible, church union, political reform, the reorganisation of the industrial system, international peace — it was all covered by the one aim of the Reign of God on earth. That idea is necessarily as big as humanity, for it means the divine transformation of all human life. It alone can say without limitation, 'Nil humani a me alienum'. (CSO p. 93f.)[21]

As late as 1917 he still saw the Kingdom of God as 'absolutely necessary to establish that organic union between religion and morality, between theology and ethics'.[22] Without it theology would 'live like a negro servant family in a detached cabin back of the white man's house in the South' (TSG p. 131). In short:

> The Kingdom of God is to theology what outdoor colour and light are to art. It is impossible to estimate what inspirational impulses have been lost to theology and to the Church, because it did not develop the doctrine of the Kingdom of God and see the world and its redemption from that point of view. (TSG p. 137)

Having thus found a satisfactory concept to represent his synthesis of religion and ethics, Rauschenbusch sought a

---

[21]The return of the Kingdom of God to the centre of theology clearly points to the influence of Albrecht Ritschl, 'the great theologian, who has himself done more, perhaps, than any other man to rehabilitate the idea [of the Kingdom of God] in the theological thought of Germany' (SW p. 72). It was Ritschl who had 'put the idea to the front in German theology' even if it was his misfortune to have been 'born too early to get sociological ideas' (TSG p. 138f.). He dates his revelation of the Kingdom of God from the time of his visit to Germany in 1891 (CSO p. 93). He had earlier spent four years of his education in a conservative Gütersloh *gymnasium*. On his contacts with Germany see esp. Minus, op. cit., Ch. 5.

[22]*A Theology for the Social Gospel* (New York, 1917, reprint, Nashville, 1978) p. 140 (hereafter TSG).

practical expression of his vision of the Christian Faith, and with a few friends he set up the 'Brotherhood of the Kingdom' in 1893 to help 're-establish this thought in the thought of the Church, and to assist in its practical realisation in the life of the world' (SW p. 25; cf. CSO p. 94). The Kingdom of God was once again to become the 'great object of Christian preaching; the inspiration of Christian hymnology; the foundation of systematic theology; the enduring motive of evangelistic and missionary work; the religious inspiration of social work . . . the object to which a Christian man surrenders his life' (SW p. 25f.). In the close-knit circle of the Brotherhood, Rauschenbusch developed his most powerful ideas in fellowship with a group of men who gave him the power 'to draw back the bars and bolts of caution and distrust' (SW p. 27).

## II

Rauschenbusch sought a biblical basis for his theology and contended that by returning to the Bible, particularly to the Hebrew prophets, who, 'to speak frankly were revolutionists' (CSO p. 52; cf. CSC Ch.I) and to the Synoptic Gospels (CSC Ch.II), the union between the religious and the social could be recovered. Instead of reading into the Bible 'what we have been taught to see there' (CSC p. 45) we were to look at Jesus in his own 'historical environment' (CSC p. 46; cf. p. 49; cf. TSG p. 133) by opening 'our minds to the Spirit of Jesus in its primitive uncorrupted and still unexhausted power' (SW p. 143). Thus just as the Reformation went back to Paul's revolutionary teaching of justification by faith, so, today, we were forced to return to the 'revolutionary consciousness in Jesus' (CSC p. 85; TSG p. 161). This meant the original idea of the Kingdom of God, the 'center of all his teaching as recorded in the synoptic gospels' (CSC p. 54), 'the spiritual center on which he took his stand and from which he judged all things' (KG p. 143) would 'kindle anew into a blaze the now smouldering fires of Christendom' (SW p. 73; cf. p. 144).

Jesus himself announced the coming Kingdom but did not consciously adopt the 'exotic scheme' of apocalypticism (CSO p. 54; CSC p. 59). Instead he purified Hebrew prophetism which in turn gave us 'our warrant for modernising and purifying the inherited conceptions of the Kingdom' (CSO p. 56). Similarly he reached beyond the 'jingo patriotism' (CSO p. 60) of the prophets and the revolutionary fervour of his contemporaries (CSO p. 58; CSC p. 61), and, borrowing on his Jewish inheritance (CSO p. 70), democratised and universalised the concept of the Kingdom as 'the Commonwealth of God and Man' (CSO p. 61), which was 'a modification of immense importance' (CSC p. 62). Like the prophets, Jesus sided 'with the poor and the oppressed' (CSC p. 53)[23] announcing 'liberty to the bruised and crushed lives' (CSO p. 61), and, 'in his desire to create a true human society he encountered riches as a prime divisive force in actual life' (CSC p. 75). The real good was 'not dollars and cents, but the satisfaction of our craving for justice ... the gladness of unhindered brotherhood and humanity' (CSO p. 63). Rauschenbusch thus had a particular affection for Luke, 'the socialist among the evangelists', without whom 'our evangel would be immeasurably poorer' (CSC p. 82).

Jesus went further than the prophets with a 'vastly higher act of faith' (CSC p. 63) by announcing that the Kingdom was actually here: 'the future tense was changing to the present tense under the power of faith' (CSC p. 64; cf. TSG p. 141). Rauschenbusch's dismissal of apocalyptic is illuminating; although he was aware of the interpretations of Weiss and Schweitzer he found them singularly unconvincing:

> My own conviction is that the professional theologians of Europe, who all belong by kinship and sympathy to the bourgeois classes and are constitutionally incapacitated for understanding any revolutionary ideas, past or present, have over-emphasised the ascetic and eschatological ideas in the teaching of Jesus. (TSG p. 158)

---

[23]Rauschenbusch thus displays a clear option for the poor as he makes clear in one of his prayers: 'The wrongs and sufferings of the people and the vision of a righteous and brotherly social life awaken an almost painful compassion and longing, and these feelings are more essentially Christian than most of the fears and desires of religion in the past. Social Christianity is adding to the variety of religious experience, and is creating a new type of Christian man who bears a striking family likeness to Jesus of Galilee' (SW p. 209).

Those who held to apocalypticism were 'marking time on a set of ideas derived from pre-Christian Judaism and incompletely christianised' (CSO p. 65; TSG p. 157). Instead the Kingdom of God had to 'slough off apocalypticism if it is to become the religious property of the modern world' (CSO p. 56). It was the Lord's Prayer that provided 'the purest expression of the mind of Jesus' (SW p. 211), even if its dominating thought of 'the moral and religious transformation of mankind in all its social relations' had far too often been appropriated by people who had little sympathy with its spirit. Yet in 'looking up to God for our bread, everyone of us ought to feel the sin and shame of it if he habitually takes more than his fair share and leaves others hungry that he may surfeit. It is inhuman, irreligious and indecent' (SW p. 213).

## III

Building on this biblical basis Rauschenbusch aimed to rid the concept of the Kingdom of God of its subsequent distortions:

1. Other-worldliness. The Kingdom of the Heavens had become the Kingdom of Heaven, an idea which was 'not Hebrew, but Greek' (CSO p. 73; cf. CSC p. 55; cf. TSG p. 147). This other-worldly concentration 'practically constitutes the gospel now preached in a majority of American churches' (CSO p. 75), but was also characteristic of the 'tranquillity and forgetfulness of mystic absorption' (TSG p. 155). Against this, Rauschenbusch asserted that the 'earth is even now the habitation of God, and it is ours to make it wholly so ... The hope of the Kingdom of God makes this earth the theatre of action, and turns the full force of the religious will and daring towards the present tasks' (CSO p. 97; cf. SW p. 223). In short: 'The Kingdom is here and at work. The Kingdom means individual men and women who freely do the will of God, and who therefore live rightly with their fellowmen' (SW p. 79; cf. TSG p. 141).

2. This-worldliness. According to Rauschenbusch, socialism[24] retained a vision of the ideal but lacked the religious basis for

[24]Rauschenbusch had studied socialism at length on his visit to Europe in 1891 and was particularly impressed with Joseph Chamberlain's 'municipal socialism' in Birmingham, but was critical both of Booth's failure to address the causes of poverty and of Maurice's ecclesiocentrism (Cf. *Minus*, op. cit., p. 72).

the attainment of this ideal; it had the Kingdom of God with God left out (SW p. 73). Socialists were 'right in emphasising the economic ends of human society; but Jesus is also right in emphasising its spiritual ends' (CSO p. 63). The mark 'of the distinctively Christian conception of the Kingdom of God [is] that the spiritual values of human life are set above all economic aids to life as the real end to be sought' (CSO p. 64). Nevertheless, socialism often united with religion to produce the most formidable force. For instance, 'the Frenchmen lost all their bearings when they heard Keir Hardie . . . declaring that it was Christianity that made a socialist of him' (CSO p. 109). The need to alleviate hardship naturally drove people towards a form of socialism, but infinitely more powerful was

> where the new social spirit combines harmoniously with the inherited Christian life [where] a new type of personal religion is produced which has at least as good a right to existence as any other type. Jesus was not a theological Christian, nor a churchman, nor an emotionalist, nor an ascetic, nor a contemplative mystic. A mature social Christian comes closer to the likeness of Jesus Christ than any other type. (CSO p. 111; cf. CSC p. 92)

3. Individualism. The designation of the Kingdom of God as individualist was the favourite of 'men of a mystical mind' who loved to cite the passage, 'The Kingdom of God is within you' (Luke 17.21). This was, however, a fundamental distortion of Jesus' preaching:

> If he did not mean the consummation of the theocratic hope, but merely an internal blessedness for individuals with the hope of getting to heaven, why did he use the words around which all the collective hopes clustered? In that case it was not only a misleading but a dangerous phrase. It unfettered the political hopes of the crowd; it drew down on him the suspicion of the government; it actually led to his death. (CSC p. 57)

The 'most devastating sins of our age' (CSO p. 112) always displayed a social character and the Kingdom of God was essentially a 'collective conception involving the whole social life of man ... it is not a matter of getting individuals to heaven, but of transforming the life on earth into a harmony of heaven ...[Jesus] never forgot the gregarious nature of man' (CSC p. 65f. cf. CSO p. 96). The 'power of the individual rests on the social cohesion of mankind' (CSO p. 461) and 'salvation is always a social process' (CSO p. 114; cf. CSC p. 67). For both the 'poor "bum"' who had been rescued from drink, and for the millionaire 'who had caught a new vision of business', the temptations of society would cause them to backslide since 'sin is a social force. It runs from man to man along the lines of social contact' (CSO p. 116). Salvation implied a 'saved environment' (CSO p. 117) and had to 'come out of its spiritual isolation' (CSO p. 464). Indeed the failure to concentrate on the stewardship of the world created terrible waste: 'We have long wasted our forests ... we pour the precious sewage of our cities into our rivers ... We waste the splendid strength of manhood by industrial accidents and tuberculosis' (CSO p. 97f.).[25] Moreover, 'those Christian men who are the outstanding and bold friends of the people's cause are today the most effective apologists of Christianity' (CSO p. 119). Christ was nothing less than the 'great emancipator', an emancipator at work in history (TSG p. 165), the 'sacred workshop' (CSO p. 119) of a God who 'thinks in acts' (SW p. 135) and 'the full greatness of the problem of Jesus strikes us when we see him in his connection with human history' (TSG p. 166).

4. The Church. Especially after Augustine 'the Kingdom ceased to be the dominating religious reality [and] the Church moved up into the position of the supreme good' (TSG p. 143; cf. CSO pp. 79ff.). Religion could easily become 'a conservative clog, and a real hindrance of social progress' (SP p. 143) and thus, although 'the church is indispensable to the religious education of humanity and to the conservation of religion ... the greatest future awaits religion in the public life of humanity'

[25]Some of Rauschenbusch's prayers similarly display a remarkable ecological awareness: 'We remember with shame that in the past we have exercised the high dominion of man with ruthless cruelty, so that the voice of the Earth, which should have gone up to thee in song, has been a groan of travail' (SW p. 223).

(TSG p. 146). The call 'to the emancipation of our personalities' (TSG p. 162) had little to do with institutional religion and 'the Kingdom of God wastes no time on religious paraphernalia, but concentrates it all on the real task of sin' (CSO p. 97). 'Is it not true', Rauschenbusch asked, 'that Jesus has been experienced as a Liberator more frequently apart from theology than within it? If so; why?' (TSG p. 163).

5. Millenarianism. The millenarian sects, although retaining a vision of the Kingdom of God had 'restricted the term of the reign of Christ to be established after his return' (SW p. 77; cf. CSC p. 412). Rauschenbusch addressed himself at length to the issue,

> because so many of our brethren have an intense but one-sided interest in eschatology. They try to round this Cape Horn of theology with all sails set, but with little of the ballast of historical knowledge in the hold. And so they often run into vagaries that lame their practical usefulness, or into fantacism which does damage to their Christian character and to the cause of Christ. (SW p. 80)

Nonetheless he did not dismiss millenarianism 'with a sneer' (SW p. 84) but sought to learn from its positive aspects: it 'bids us lift up our eyes and behold the coming Christ' and preserved the collective ideal of the Church so often lost in individualisations of the gospel. Similarly it revitalised the sweet hope of Israel and kept alive the revolutionary spirit of Christianity (SW p. 87). Nevertheless it was guilty of dangerous distortions: its pessimism led to a wholesale refusal to believe that things could improve. This was a 'practical abdication' from the task of conquering the world for Christ which was essentially no different from 'monkishness':

> We should have no quarrel with Millenarianism if it held that the world, *minus* the redemptive forces of Christianity, sags downward instead of rising upward, that society naturally decays, that the increase in material wealth only hastens the rotting, and that the spread of intelligence makes evil even more malignant. But when Millenarianism asserts the same things concerning humanity, *plus* the redemptive forces of Christ, we feel in our hearts an

impassioned protest, and that protest issues, not from unsanctified optimism, but from sanctified faith in Jesus Christ. (SW p. 91)

Similarly the faith in catastrophes led to the 'disjointing of faith and action' (p. 93) and a refusal to work for the abolition of child-labour, or even to endow public parks. For Rauschenbusch, on the other hand, 'the best method of keeping ourselves intact from the Devil is to keep charging down on him' (SW p. 92):

Which will do more to make our lives spiritual and to release us from the tyranny of the world, the thought that we may at any moment enter into the presence of the Lord, or the thought that every moment we are in the presence of the Lord? (SW p. 94)

IV

After outlining the concept of the Kingdom of God, Rauschenbusch applied it to an analysis of capitalism where 'a small group of great wealth and power is set over against a large group of propertyless men' which enabled 'the greedy and cunning to set the pace for the rest . . . The charge of Christianity against competitive capitalism is that it is unfraternal, the opposite of co-operation and teamwork'. Capitalism was not Christian but 'tribute collected by power from the helpless, a form of legalised graft, and a contradiction of Christian relations'. (CSO p. 311f.)

If the Kingdom of God is the true human society, it is a fellowship of justice, equality and love. But it is hard to get riches with justice, to keep them with equality, and to spend them with love. The Kingdom of God means normal human relations to others, and it is exceedingly hard for a rich man to be in normal human relations to others, as many a man has discovered who has honestly tried. It can be done only by an act of renunciation in some form. (CSC p. 77)

Indeed, 'to set Mammon before God is the only idolatry against which Jesus warned us' (CSO p. 315).

A new apostolate was required 'to meet the new needs in the harvest time of history' (CSC p. 415):

> The championship of social justice is almost the only way left open to the Christian nowadays to gain the crown of martyrdom. Theological heretics are rarely persecuted now. The only rival to God is mammon, and it is only when his sacred name is blasphemed that men throw the Christians to the lions. (CSC p. 418)

Against the inequalities of capitalism (CSO p. 31), Christianity taught 'the unity and solidarity of men' (CSC p. 412). Thus 'when the Christian business man is presented as a model Christian, working people are coming to look with suspicion on these examples of Christianity' (SW p. 142). Indeed 'no social group or organisation can claim to be clearly within the Kingdom of God which drains others for its own ease, and resists the effort to abate this fundamental evil' (TSG p. 143). Both the poor and the wealthy thus required 'sanitation', the former literally and the latter metaphorically:

> The most comprehensive and intensive act of love in which we could share would be a collective action of the community to change the present organisation of the economic life into a new order that would rest on the Christian principles of equal rights, democratic distribution of economic power, the supremacy of the common good, the law of mutual independence and service, and the uninterrupted flow of good will throughout the human family. (CSO p. 323)

In short: 'People sneer at communism, but I bless God for every fractional bit of communism we have, and pray for more' (SW p. 105).

Rauschenbusch made no apologies for the fact that all this sounded like a pipe dream since he would rather 'meet God in a dream than not at all' (CSO p. 325). Nevertheless there were 'channel buoys' to guide our way — history was littered with experiments in visions and 'every approximation is worthwhile' (CSC p. 421). Christian people were 'to use the prophetic insight and moral determination which their Christian discipleship ought to give them in order to speed and direct' the transformation of society (CSO p. 331). This call was not just to reform society but to repent and believe in the gospel: the Kingdom of God was at hand. Rauschenbusch thus regarded his classic *Christianising the Social Order*[26] as 'a religious book from beginning to end. Its sole concern is for the Kingdom of God and the salvation of men. But the Kingdom of God includes the economic life' (p. 458). The mammonism that was debilitating economic life could only be overcome by 'a new mind and heart, a new conception of the way we ought to live together,' in short, by a revival of religion (p. 459). Without religious inspiration capitalism would triumph and 'all capitalistic governments would combine to trip and cripple the first Socialist Republic' (CSO p. 471). He concluded by pointing to the examples of St Martin who clothed a beggar, and to St George who conquered the dragon. 'Every Christian man should embody both kinds of sainthood in one life' (p. 476). *Christianity and the Social Crisis* finishes on a similar note:

> If at this juncture we can rally sufficient religious faith and moral strength to snap the bonds of evil and turn the present unparalleled economic and intellectual resources of humanity to the harmonious development of a true social life, the generations yet unborn will mark this as that great day of the Lord for which ages waited, and count us blessed for sharing in the apostolate that proclaimed it. (CSC p. 422)

## V

It should now be clear that Rauschenbusch maintained a very clear picture of the need for religion to empower any reform of the social world: 'Men do not become more moral by saying: "Go to, let us be more moral". Instinctively men turn to religion

---

[26]For a brilliant account of the continued relevance of this book see Charles R. Strain, 'Toward a Generic Analysis of a Classic of the Social Gospel' in *JAAR* XLVI: 1978, pp. 525-543.

as the generator of moral force' (SW p. 123). Without a religious input, society was doomed to the survival of the fittest:

> The social efficiency of religion — what call is there in that to the college men and women of this generation? Shall they cease to worship and pray, seek the salvation of society in ethics and sociology, and abandon religion to stagnation? Or shall they seek a new experience of religion in full sight of the modern world, and work by faith toward that reign of God in which his will shall be done? (SP, p. 146)[27]

With this overpowering conviction that only religion could conquer sin Rauschenbusch was heir to the tradition of the Reformers. Indeed, it was precisely *because* he recognised God as sovereign, as present in his life, that Rauschenbusch was called to the Social Gospel:

> In my efforts to secure more freedom and justice for men I acted under religious impulses. I realised that God hates injustices and that I would be quenching the life of God within me if I kept silent with all this social iniquity around me. (SW p. 45)[28]

Rauschenbusch also saw the deficiencies of 'private Protestantism'. Not merely had he rediscovered the social

---

[27]Cf. H. Richard Niebuhr, *The Kingdom of God in America* (New York, 1959), p. 194. 'In Rauschenbusch the reign of Christ required conversion and the coming Kingdom was crisis, judgment as well as promise. Though his theory of the relation of God and man often seemed liberal he continued to speak the language of the prophets and St Paul.' Rauschenbusch, who was almost completely deaf, was acutely aware of his own frailty as is clear from the author's prayer in *For God and People*: 'O thou who art the light of my soul, I thank thee for the incomparable joy of listening to thy voice within . . . I pray thee to over-rule my sin and turn aside its force before it harm thy cause. Pardon the frailty of thy servant, and look upon him only as he sinks his life in Jesus, his Master and Saviour. Amen' (SW p. 239).

[28]H. Richard Niebuhr, *The Kingdom of God*, p. 163: 'Rauschenbusch was directed to march . . . toward the coming kingdom not by a rationalism which regarded cross and resurrection, redemption and atonement as ancient superstitions, or by liberalism that denied the divine sovereignty, but by [his] loyalty to the kingdom of God which has not been ashamed of the Gospel.'

teaching of Jesus, he had also shown that the human being, by the grace of God, was given the power to improve social conditions:

> Even when our strength is broken, when our hopes are frustrated and nature seeks to cast us aside, a brother to the shrivelling worm, we can trust and wait. By holding up the will of the Holy One as the norm of action and character religion spurs us on to endless growth. (SW p. 132)

His recognition of an objective justification in which Christians had been liberated from sin, together with a belief that the Kingdom of God had dawned, allowed him to see his own social conditions as capable of transformation and not merely as oppressive structures from which one had to flee to a higher timeless world. Instead of dividing reality into two, the higher reality of God and the lower reality of the world, he maintained faith in a unified conception of reality expressed most clearly in the Kingdom of God. Without such a synthesis between the religious and the social, there seems little possibility for a coherent ethics capable of empowering a transformation of the world, a fact which points to Rauschenbusch's continued relevance: the choice for Christians today still remains that between unity and ethics, or dualism and flight from the world, either to be in the world which has been redeemed or to be apart from a world beyond redemption.[29]

[29]Cf. Carl E. Johnson, 'The new present and the new past: Some timely reflections on the Rauschenbusch legacy' in *Perspectives in Religious Studies* 14: 1987, pp. 131-145.

# 10

# Signs of the Kingdom — a Reflection on Motivation

(A Consideration of the Possible Relationship Between the Ancient Doctrine of the Kingdom of God and Contemporary Political and Ethical Decision-Making.)

## by John McGuckin

*Preliminary Remarks*

To ask of the relationship between the biblical teaching on the Kingdom of God and contemporary political decision-making, is a question beautifully simple in its directness and eminently reasonable in its expectations, but it has the simplicity of the blade-edge. Even more troublingly the field before us is strewn with the battle detritus of many attempts by the great to identify the essential nature of the biblical doctrine of God's kingdom so that it could be unfastened from the grip of antiquity and do service again in the domain of human decisions and social orientations. While the issue can hardly be said to be resolved, nonetheless (as befits a major concept of the preaching of Jesus) neither can one plead shortage of reading matter on the subject, ancient or modern. What makes the terms of the present essay particularly difficult is the invitation to the theologian to set aside a comfortable tradition of academic neutrality in the face of differing interpretative emphases, and not only to elect or synthesize a biblical position but even to go on to harness it to the ethico-political issue of the nature of decision making. Surely a simple and reasonable request?

It is certainly a necessary request, unless one is to consign, *a priori*, the entire theological endeavour to the simple-minded or the antiquarian. To that extent it is also a reasonable request. The biblical doctrine of the Kingdom, and the nature of human decision making are certainly legitimate and tractable areas of study. But it is by no means a simple request considering the vast complexity of both areas. To answer such a question with any claim to systematic completeness it would be necessary to consider the philosophical and theological intractables involved in correlating an ancient philosophy of history (the eschatological) with wide-ranging contemporary interpretations of existence, and, what is more, to consider the economic and psychological labyrinths that form the pathway to an understanding of human decision making. It is this very complexity that must make anyone pause before the great suppositions that must be made before even beginning a tentative assault. For the very small-scale study that follows even 'tentative assault' may be too grandiose a title, but perhaps even a single roof tile deftly whizzed over the battlements of the ivory tower may be considered an honourable engagement, if not quite a systematic offensive.

## Characteristics of Jesus' Ministry

If we were to abstract from the old and the more recent 'Jesus of History' movements, and try to take into account the sharpening up of focus that has taken place in the last fifty years through the achievements of Form, Redaction, and Tradition Criticism, with regard to the nature of Jesus' preaching and its deployment in the first phases of the Church's life up to the time of the composition of the Gospels,[1] then what would be unarguably agreed as a scholarly consensus concerning the ministry of Jesus? What firm ground could we find, as befits the wise man, to build up a house of conclusions? Rather than beginning with the Kingdom sayings, parables, or the wider logia tradition, where redactive work on individual pericopai

---

[1]See, for example, E.P. Sanders & M. Davies, *The Study of the Synoptic Gospels* (SCM, London, 1989).

still needs to go on apace before one could rightly claim a sufficient body of evidence to justify synthesis, perhaps we may posit instead three dynamic characteristics of Jesus' ministry; namely the urgent energy that describes it, the engagement with exorcisms that highlights it, and the recurring fact (and image) of feasting that illuminates it.

## *The Urgency of the Proclamation*

One part of the urgent, almost breathless, pace of the ministry of Jesus is given to us in what are undoubtedly redactive devices, such as Mark's breakneck speed of narrative and his abrupt conjunctions between text units, or in Luke's journeying motif which increasingly accelerates Jesus' progress to Jerusalem and death. Above and beyond these narrative devices, however, and prescinding from questions as to how long the actual preaching ministry lasted, one may still sense the urgency of the motivation of Jesus' preaching. The root of this urgency may be posited as Jesus' own sense of what we might call his prophetic commissioning[2] or, alternatively, the faith Jesus had in the authenticity of his mission, a faith based ultimately on the quality of his faith in the God he perceived to have inspired him. Not only does the essence of the doctrine of the Kingdom lie here, but in the end the heart of Christology and all that is specifically 'Christian' about our doctrine of God and God's providence. Brief illustrative examples must suffice to indicate the ramifications of this. Urgency of motivation is itself no guarantee of authenticity of vision, and in the long term both society and church may prove to have suffered more from the urgencies of the fanatic than they have from the impotence of the unconvinced and unconvincing. Nonetheless a 'qualified urgency', an energy, that is, for a vision of the good and the true, is at the heart of all that one means by 'inspiration' and 'hope', and 'development'. In this light we may posit the quality of Jesus' urgency as of great interest and import despite

[2]For a fuller elaboration see my: 'Jesus' self-designation as a prophet'. *Scripture Bulletin*, 19, 1, 1988, 2-11.

the oft-heard claims that the 'consciousness of Jesus' lies outside the range of the New Testament texts. E. Stauffer may serve as a typical example when he says: 'No serious historian can, or would wish to, penetrate into Jesus' mental processes.'[3] This is either the truism that the Gospels are not psychological biographies, or a dubious historical axiom to the effect that the Gospels suffer from a unique dislocation of the standard premiss that one may legitimately correlate motives and actions within the domain of historical enquiry. If what I take to be Stauffer's understandable diffidence about the reliability of psychological deductions about Jesus is pushed to becoming an axiom of the latter type, then it would have disastrous effects on dogmatics generally, not only in the general terms of bankrupting the 'Scripture principle' within an understanding of revelation, but even in terms of denying the legitimacy of the Church looking to the continuing inspiration of its Lord. Be that as it may, what is the concern of the moment is neither to argue the ecclesiological point, nor to speculate in the domain of Jesus' psychology, except in so far as one may look at motives and deeds in terms of cause and effect in an area which for the ancients was primarily a theological/metaphysical locus but which has come in our time to be far more personalistically interpreted — the area, that is, of Jesus' faith in God. And so, we return to the claim that the kind of 'urgency' witnessed in Jesus is quite legitimately a matter of historical interest and import.

Some graphic examples might serve best to illustrate the import of such an enquiry. The three test cases, which I am selecting largely at random as examples of logion, parable, and miracle story gobbets, suggest that the equation of eschatological urgency in Jesus' kingdom preaching with a kind of 'wild-eyed enthusiasm' may be a particularly misleading stereo-type. These three are: The Sparrows Logion, Matt. 10.29; Luke 12.6; The Parable of the Sower, Mark 4.1-9; Matt. 13.1-9; Luke 8.4-8; Gospel of Thomas 9; and The Calming of the Sea, Mark 4.35-41; Matt. 8.18, 23-27; Luke 8.22-25.

---

[3] E Stauffer, 'Jesus and History', p. 124 of *In Search of the Historical Jesus*, Ed. H.K. McArthur (London, 1970).

I would suggest that the Sparrows Logion gains its force not in the generic dictum (as if it were a Qal Wahomer Rabbinism) that Providence embraces all things, and if sparrows, then how much more so human beings,[4] but rather from the wryness of a highly particular observation, for the birds were brought down for food, and carted into the alleys for plucking, roasting, and sale as snacks. What sparked off the dictum about God's care, therefore, was in all likelihood the sight of blackened, brazier-roasted birds skewered in groups on a stick. In this context Jesus' doctrine, that God's care of the disciples in Jerusalem will exceed that which he so assiduously gave to the sparrows under his protection, is not a great comfort. On the contrary it is a sharp challenge to face realities from a mind which was by no means optimistically oblivious to the problems of suffering and evil in a providential theodicy.[5]

That the dry realism of such a religious view, spoken over red-hot coals, as it were, is none the less committed to hopefulness may be further borne out in a second illustration drawn from the Parable of the Sower, and an interpretation of the same which following Jeremias[6] reads it as originally expressing Jesus' eschatological hope in the authenticity of his vision, and his faith in the God who inspired it in him, despite all the contrasting evidence of failures accumulating against such a hope. We might take this, again, as suggesting something of the quality of Jesus' urgency which has the calibre to take the long view and sing harvest songs in fields that are locked in the checkless grip of winter. His doctrine of the inevitability of the Kingdom's coming is one that takes full cognisance of all the evidence that cries out that the Kingdom has not come, but still insists on the irreversibility of the providential working of God for salvation. And in the force of his own belief in the message

---

[4] Pesikta of Rab Kahana 10: 'If the bird is not captured without the will of heaven, how much less we.'

[5] For a fuller elaboration see my: 'Sacrifice and atonement: an investigation into the attitudes of Jesus of Nazareth towards cultic sacrifice', pp 648-661 in *Remembering for the Future* (Pergamon Press, Oxford, 1988).

[6] cf. J. Jeremias, *The Parables of Jesus* (London 1963).

he eases the way for others, though by no means all, to share in that belief by association, to be convinced of his doctrine, and thus, by implication, to come to trust in the authenticity of Jesus' inspired view of God and life in a way analogous to Jesus' own trust in that inspiration.

A third and final test-case example of what we mean by 'urgency' could be taken from the story of the Calming of the Sea. Being neither logion nor parable this example more than the others needs some redactive justification — but presented here as a brief illustration it will have to suffice merely to note the Marcan redaction in Mark 4.40, introducing a series of rebukes of the disciples,[7] and the (probably pre-Marcan) Heggadic remnants in verse 36b, denoting the influence of Psalm 107.23f. in the hermeneutical shaping of the pericope and its growth through the kerygmatic tradition to the full stature of a 'Nature Miracle'. Prescinding from all this detailed exposition by pleading economy, we could perhaps turn our attention to what kind of historical event could have given rise to such a kerygmatic memory, and with not too much fear of going astray we can posit one of a number of lake crossings that Jesus made with the disciples around the Sea of Galilee, in the course of preaching his message, as the historical root of the story. To this day boats will not set out on Kinneret if the wind funnels down from the East, and even on a calm day there is a sense of a dark abyss of water under the gloomy massif of the Golan, and a few fragile planks separating danger from disaster. Mark's regular theophanic theme of awe (*thauma, Phobos*) as a revelatory moment in the gradual disclosure of the identity of Jesus marks this motif out as clearly a central redactive device. But in the present pericope the story begins with simple fear — fear of the natural events, and only then is this fear subsumed by the evangelist into the theological notion of religious awe (the transition from the faintheartedness (*Deilos*) of Mark 4.40 to the great awe (*Phobos*) of 4.41). As is the case with the momentum of the narrative, is not such a physical fear the primary datum for the subsequent reflections that inspired the biblical haggadah of the episode in the pre-Marcan Palestinian

[7.]Mark 4.40; 7.18; 8.17; 8.21; 9.19.

tradition? And cannot such a fear, growing into awe, not be readily understood as a genuine wonder at the strangeness of a man who was not afraid of drowning in a situation that called even for practised sailors to indulge in panic? If this is a correct scenario, it again sends us back to Jesus' attitude to Providence. In the fixed determination of trust in the authenticity of his vision, there followed an implicit obedience in the working out of that vision's demands. In other words if, for Jesus, God has inspired him to proclaim the message around the Sea of Galilee then *de facto* God wishes him to cross the lake to the villages and towns on the far shore. If this is God's will, which to doubt would mean for him to doubt in the self-evident authenticity of his inspiration, then the boat simply cannot sink, despite all and every indication to the contrary. In such a case it seems to him that he might as well try to take as much rest as he can on an uncomfortable journey, at least until it becomes necessary to rebuke his companions whose mounting panic he sees as evidence of their poor trust in the validity of his mission. Not only would such a rebuke have all the calming effect of a slap for the hysterical, we might go further to suggest that it would carry with it the sense of an awe-inspiring epiphany of the character of this man's faith, and the consistency and totality of his submission to it — an awesome unveiling of the quality of Jesus' inspiration that the disciples did not forget and interpreted later as part of the Jesus Kerygma with the help of Psalm 107.

All three examples which we have briefly set out above suggest that the character of urgency that runs throughout the ministry, and is in a sense the existential power behind Jesus' preaching of the Kingdom, was a 'costed' urgency, one born from the realistic acknowledgement of, even submission to, difficulties, frustrations and oppositions, but an urgency that gives witness to the quality of a faith in the overarching progress of the good and the true in a world replete with the evil and the false.

### The Act of Exorcism

Our second characteristic of the Kingdom ministry was posited as exorcisms. The Gospels clearly have a fascination for such stories and while that fascination, both for writer and reader, might have accounted for a higher profile for such things in the text than in the historical ministry, nonetheless the practice of exorcism is unquestionably to be associated with Jesus. Even if the early Christian preachers did use exorcisms as a continuing part of their kerygmatic strategy[8] this is not of sufficient force in itself to account for the fathering of such a tradition, unwarrantably, upon Jesus. Josephus' important account, before it was doctored, saw him primarily in this light, and we might 'restore' his text somewhat as follows: 'About this time there was a certain Jesus, a Magus and doer of wonders, a teacher for those who eagerly welcomed that sort of thing. He drew over many Jews and gentiles to himself. Pilate, at the instigation of the Chief Priests, had him crucified, and the tribe of so-called 'Christians' is not extinct to this day. Another sad calamity that happened around this time was. . . .'[9]

If we avoid the anachronism of distinguishing sharply between exorcisms proper and healing narratives in the Gospels, then the genre grows by coalition. A brief example, if any should be needed, that healing acts and exorcisms are of one family may be afforded by the 'demonic' explanation of the old woman's illness (Luke 13.16) or by the motif of the pneumatic rebuke of sickness (as in Mark 1.41). We may posit, therefore, that both healings and exorcisms proceeded from the same motive in Jesus' case, and served as signs of the Kingdom, symbolic actions to underline graphically the implications of his preached message. It is this subordination of the phenomenal signs to the preaching they are designed to signify that marks off Jesus from other examples of Levantine Magi. The developing tradition tended to elaborate the signs into epiphanies of Jesus' own status, which was yet another element of a wider tendency to transmute the theology of Jesus into a Christology. The proper interpretative context for the significance of the phenomenal deeds is, however, the kingdom

---

[8] Mark 6.13; 16.17, 20; Acts 4. 30-31; 19. 11-12.
[9] Josephus, *Antiquities* 18.3.3. (my emendation).

doctrine they are meant to illustrate.[10] In this case, like the parables that call for an immediate, present-term response to the implications of the eschatological message, the signs and wonders are localised expressions of a liberating release from bondage that is unwaveringly expected to generalise itself. The energy of Jesus' faith in the inevitability of the great liberation of all from the bondage of sin and Satan's oppression leads to that personal vision communicating itself actively to liberate individuals symbolising that oppression.

In an analogous way when the power and administration of the armies of the Third Reich had already begun to collapse, local resistance movements across France could seize towns and local areas in an armed rebellion that only months earlier would have been impossible and suicidal. These are examples of the despoiling of powerful overlords whose force is largely spent, where each act of despoiling and liberation cumulatively mounts up to a definitive collapse of the opposing power. Only in the context of a faith in the authenticity of the news of liberation would there be either the courage to wish the venture of rebellion, or the energy to trust in its success. In the case of Jesus, as it was with his preaching, and his reorganisation of his personal life, so it was with the phenomenal signs he did — he attempted to lay hold of a greater reality by means of smaller symbols of the same. In the way he offered exorcisms as evidence of a wide-scale change in the deployment of the cosmic forces of good and evil, rather than as isolated instances of a charismatic's success against tractable demons, we have another example of the faith of Jesus conditioning the form of the ministry, and there are indications that these 'offensive sallies' (for such they become when set in the theological context of a claim of imminent, large-scale redemption) soon became major points of controversy within his own time.

### Jesus' Doctrine of Meals

The doctrine of meals was posited as the third of our particular

---

[10] cf. Mark 3.27; Luke 11.20 (+ Exod. 8.19); Matt. 12.28.

characteristics of the kingdom ministry.[11] This is not as remote as may at first appear from our preceding example if we approach it from the perspective of prophetic signs. When Isaiah calls his child by a strange name (Isa. 8.1-3), Hosea takes home a faithless wife (Hos. 1.2f., 3.1f.) and Ezekiel is found digging a hole under the city walls (Ezek. 12.1-16), we find prophets acting out in the present the future implications of their doctrine. While for the gospel reader of every age the exorcism stories seize a certain priority of attention in the narrative, perhaps for Jesus' own contemporaries these phenomenal events were less unusual as a characteristic of his ministry, being part of an expected behaviour pattern for a wandering sage/holy man, and certainly not a proprium of Jesus' activity. One logion draws direct attention to the success of other contemporary workers in the field (Luke 11.19). If we were to look for a distinctive 'prophetic sign' for Jesus as we could, perhaps, encapsulate Ezekiel's political judgement in his sign of escape, or epitomise John's ministry in its great sign of baptism, then we can note that Jesus makes a key change after his departure from John and clearly abandons the symbol of repentance through purification, fittingly emanating from the wilderness and so concretely realised in the cleansing waters of the river, and turns instead to a symbol of reconciliation celebrated in an intimately communal context — the sign of meals.

Apart from the act of celebrating meals, the image of the feast runs like a leitmotiv through many of the parables and logia and if we add to this the corollary observation that Jesus seems to have set his face decidedly against the established Jewish practice of fasting (despite the early Church's subsequent rehabilitation of the practice)[12] then we see some of the force that originally lay behind the anti-Jesus polemic: 'Here is a glutton and a drunkard, a friend of tax collectors and sinners' (Luke 7.34; Matt. 11.19). The symbolic purpose of fasting in

[11]For a fuller elaboration of the argument of this section and more detailed redactive evidence see my: 'The significance of meals in the doctrine of Jesus', *Scripture Bulletin*, 16,2, 1986, 36-38.

[12] *Scripture Bulletin*, 16,2, 1986, 36-38.

Second Temple Judaism was to express mourning. Religiously it extended its significance to become a demonstrative way of adding force to prayer, to invoke the pitiful mercy of the Most High who would look upon the self-humbling lamentation of his servants in need. This was exactly why stress was placed on the need for externally observable signs of distress when fasting.[13] In simple terms fasting forced God's hand, as it were, and was a fitting prelude if one expected a reconciliation with God. It is reminiscent of the ingratiating techniques of the bazaar trader who wishes to persuade a reluctant customer. Jesus' theological economy was altogether different. If we are right in our analysis that the original form of the logion on fasting which Matthew edits in 6.2-8 emerges as: 'Do not fast like the hypocrites', it is a call to end the practice not to interiorise it. In Jesus' understanding of the covenant, fasting served the purpose of lamenting the absence of God and pleading for his return to his people in living experience. *If he has returned*, then fasting no longer has a place, and the wedding feast must surely be the more appropriate spiritual exercise. Such appears to be the logic behind Jesus' controversial rejection of the practice of the fast. In this context the feast becomes the hopeful celebration of God's reconciliation with his chosen people, and a way of entering into the experience of faith in his return, especially if those meals were themselves designed as possible occasions of effecting reconciliations within the village, in so far as the celebrating rabbi unexpectedly insisted on inviting the alienated. But the presence of sinners and marginal, unpurified, people at Jesus' religious feasts surely made doubly offensive to his contemporaries, what must have appeared blasphemous from the outset. The call to celebrate the feast for God's return must have seemed premature and presumptuous to many. The invitation to that feast of habitual law-breakers must have seemed dangerously lax in that it appears to dispense with repentance as a necessary preliminary of seeking God's mercy. What Jesus' doctrine of

---

[13.]That is… dirt, sackcloth, ashes, torn clothes and unkempt hair: the signs of mourning. See Matt. 6.16.

meals symbolises, therefore, is firstly that the age of lament for the absence of God has passed, for God has returned to his people in living experience making it a time of rejoicing, and secondly that the presence of the Holy One has reconciled his people by liberally, prodigally, bestowing his graceful forgiveness. In other words the God of Jesus Christ is not a God who needs to be persuaded like a reluctant buyer, but on the contrary he himself has initiated the reconciliation of an alienated people and brought about that reconciliation with an unexpectedly magnificent generosity.

To many this must have seemed a lax doctrine of cheap grace, and like the elder brother (Luke 15.28) they were too incensed to enter into the celebration on such terms. But those who did enter into Jesus' peculiar enthusiasm for the feast of reconciliation discovered in the doctrine of prodigal forgiveness not an easy option but rather the heart-rending demands of a divine mercy which in embracing the sinner called out to the sinner himself to embrace and reconcile all others in an equally generous mercifulness. This, we suggest, was how Jesus' faith in the return of God in mercy to his people was communicated to those among whom he preached. By the sign of the meal where village tensions and enmities were exposed, the challenge of reconciliation was first posed, and those who believed Jesus' vision of the primacy of mercy discovered reconciliation with one another and with a God who had earlier been distant to them. Incidentally this use of the meal as an acted-out parable of reconciliation perhaps gives a special edge to one of his last preaching efforts — the attempt to reconcile the divisions he recognised among his disciples by a meal in the old city on the night of his arrest.

## Conclusion

These three aspects, briefly outlined, we may offer as three substantial tokens of Jesus' historical ministry, and to that extent as three defining characters of the biblical doctrine of the Kingdom of God: that is
— the urgency of the proclamation,
— the act of exorcism,
— the doctrine of meals.

If we were to seek to realise their central attributes in such a way that they could be applied in a contemporary environment, we could, perhaps, call such a correlation 'Kingdom Ethics', and ask how they could have political relevance.

The first of our 'tokens' depicted Jesus' own faith in the rightness and the trueness of his vision; it focused on his energy in pursuing that vision and his simple consistency in performing the perceived good. This amounted to an urgency and direction to his life. His was also a qualified eagerness that embraced the realities, not an optimism that had to feed on fantasy if it were to survive at all. It was sometimes a grim wryness, words of hope spoken over the coals, harvest songs sung in winter fields; but it was an optimism that was indefatigable and communicated itself all the more powerfully because of its realism and determination. Such a spirit of faith, hopefulness and loving charity is still touchable and communicable, but those who would seek to live by such a vision would be well-served by mutual support. To keep such a flame of inspiration for the good alive, without recourse to naïvety or institutionalised dishonesty, needs honest dialogue, joint efforts and mutual encouragement. The Church could be a fitting locus for this if it were to be really a place of communion. Efforts at development inspired by such a vision would need first of all to upbuild the trust that draws one to such hope; to offer encouraging persuasion that the good and the true are one with the beautiful and as such inherently desirable; to proclaim that such a vision is possible, self-authenticating and realisable. In short this would amount to the rehabilitation of the principle of hope. It would be the unsealing of the wells of authentic living. If we were to abstract a dictum from our first token then we might say that political decisions which were correlated to the biblical doctrine of the Kingdom of God would be proleptically hopeful and expressive of the commonweal's constructive aspirations for higher goals not dictated by appeals to its baser instincts of immediate self-interest. While the Kingdom doctrine might not have direct continuity with the present age, given the size of the metaphysical problems and the fact that the eschatological no longer holds sway as a general matrix for coherent decision-making, nonetheless such an initial premiss as outlined in our dictum can claim to have some contiguity with the eschatological matrix which first inspired Jesus.

In the second instance we outlined how the exorcisms of Jesus could be seen to symbolise in a concrete way (whatever our contemporary metaphysical attitude to them) the energy and vigour with which Jesus applied his urgently perceived mission. To use the biblical phrase, they represent the *exousia* — the spiritual and moral authority that was generated by his faith in the rightness of his vision. Later, in the age of the Desert Fathers the exorcising charism was still related to the spiritual stature and vigour of the *abba*. The words of the desert *abba* were pointed and authoritative. He was the seer of the truth in a tradition carrying on from New Testament archetypes, and the exorcisms that still fill the pages of Christian texts in the fourth century continue to be regarded as merely preludes to the reorientation of the whole person, with far-reaching religious, moral, political and financial implications.[14] The questing vacillators who took the first pilgrim routes through the Thebaid or Syria, who wanted to come to faith, or seek healing, or find reconciliation, were told in uncompromising terms to perform hundreds of metanies, or eat beans, or stand on one leg for a month — or whatever! The detail of the initial act was, in many cases, utterly pointless, it served only to offer an easy and readily attainable example of the Christian principle that the grace of truth is perceived by obedience and celebrated by deed — a simple insight that is still at the forefront of the Eastern ascetical tradition, but has been horribly muddled by post-Augustinian Western controversies on grace and merit. The point is that the urgency of the vision both for the seer and the seeker perforce expresses itself in communicative action. The pilgrims could not match the ascesis or the vision of the *abba*, but that was not the point either; they were definitively set upon an ever-unfolding process of personal involvement and costed action, and just as definitively turned away from their

[14]See e.g. B. Ward, *The Wisdom of the Desert Fathers* (SLG Press, Oxford, 1986); Athanasius of Alexandria, *Life of Antony*, 88 (London 1950).

passive intentions of admiring their heroic role models from a safe distance.

For individuals and societies paralysed by self-interest and uncertainty, who have lost the urgent vision in varying measures, the prestigious acts of liberation are arguably beyond their grasp. Totally considered, the ascesis involved in moving from a life funded by and founded on inequitable distributions of human resources, to a life governed by justice, is so great that those who are in the comfortable bondage of oppressions usually cannot find the will to respond. But the principle of ascesis does not begin with the totality, it slowly moves to the truth through an economy that starts with people where they are, and if the great acts of liberation are beyond the reach of most, then there is ever an act of liberation which is at hand: a first instalment which extends to countless acts of liberation. The obedience and the act are always within range, and with each obedient act that range always extends. In other words, those in society who retain a greater sense of the urgency of the true and the beautiful (in which category we look hopefully to find the presence of the Church) can extend the range of others by acting in their spiritual power as the agents of release, and suggesting what is possible to do in the case of liberation by those who themselves are locked in the bondage of self-interest. This suggests that if the Church is to remain in the truth of the Kingdom it must not only be characterised by its radical orientation to liberation in fact and deed, but must be ready to take up the office of guide and interpreter of what liberation and liberating entail, and perform that office with sufficient wit and grace to make it clear that the initial asceticism of engaging in such a life-course is compensated abundantly by the joy of engagement with the true and the beautiful. This office of *paideia* seems, at least to me, to have been greatly neglected, and to look at the spreading tonnage of Christian books about 'spirituality' currently in print which seem to have no awareness of the dimensions of social and political ethics is to be made aware of the extent of the problem facing even the explicit Christian community.

The lethargy of Western society for the business of justice, and the unwillingness of leaders to pursue policies that even remotely threaten the immediate self-interest of their people is not a rational thing, or even a realistic base-fact of political life. It is part of a bondage; it is the lunatic rationality of the demoniac; it is the passivity of the paralysed body. And so, if we could abstract another dictum from our second token we might argue that even to allow for the correlation of political decision-making and Kingdom-ethic demands prior exercise of the skills of our exorcists. We ought to value the role of the exorcist understood in this way as much now as the ancients did in the first preaching of the Kerygma, and even now their necessary role will be to pronounce the proper word, in the power of their vision — the proper word for the right occasion — and to suggest what true deeds of liberation are within the scope and range of which classes of people at what time. The central role of asceticism and its economic application must be kept clearly in mind. Individuals within the Churches who have experienced something of the 'divine urgency' are frequently outstanding both in terms of the commitment to action they manifest and in terms of the power of their voice of protest and warning. Frequently, however, this strategy is not enough. The voice of the prophet needs to be supplemented by the skill of the *abba/*exorcist who practically and immediately can help the great range of ordinary, good-willed people to move from that state of anxious inability to face reality (the fearfulness of generally good people who will walk over or through the poor in the streets as if they were non-existent, or who send a regular payment to relief agencies to discharge, partially, an accumulation of the consumer's oppressive guilt) — to move them, that is, into a condition of 'willingness to learn', even to an eagerness to be advanced in the cause of creating a more just social condition. Such a fusion of the roles of prophet and exorcist was certainly manifested by Jesus, and it gave his prophetic urgency the fitting didactic medium that accounted for its successful diffusion. A great part of the answer to that practical question originally posed in this essay's title will, I suspect, be provided in the elaboration of such strategies of communication. And such strategies are greatly needed: in the Churches, in the educational system, and in the political mechanisms that form the substructure of policy-making in the consciousness of the nation.

It stands as a minor corollary of all this that the Church's own record in the work of liberating the oppressed, and the cost it has been willing to bear in effecting this work, will come under close scrutiny. In the act alone, whatever its initial size or scope according to an all-encompassing but ever-challenging economy, can the force of the vision of God's Kingdom be experienced, witnessed, fostered.

The doctrine of meals was seen as a proprium of Jesus' ministry and as a token of the Kingdom summarised the heart of his preaching as the glorious celebration of reconciliation. The 'politics of reconciliation' is a phrase that has earned bad associations for certain past usages where it signified scaling down to a common agreement or compromising to the point of uncontroversial blandness. Such a political outlook could rightly be dismissed as weakness. If contemporary decision making is to be in line with the doctrine of the Kingdom of God, however, then it too would have to reflect the central character of the Kingdom promise, and be designed to reconcile not to alienate or antagonise. If political choices were to be judged against this criterion of the restoration of communion, then no-one could cherish for long any notion that such choices as would have to be made would be the 'politics of weakness'. Rather they would be the politics of a courage that at present seems all too elusive. The minor corollary of this is again that the Church needs to gain confidence in its role of a prophet of reconciliation. Its track record in reconciling its own will be examined before it has credibility in acting as a messenger of national let alone global reconciliation. It will need to pursue reconciliation joyfully even against the opposition of those of lesser vision who regard such a path as laxity or spinelessness, in order to allow the force of reconciliation to speak for itself, and to hold fast itself to the gospel of the primacy of mercy.

Each of these areas represents a massive undertaking. Each one demonstrates the integral relationship of Christian theology and the domain of human decisions, where the vision and the act are held in an inseparable union and each one rebuffs the old and the good lie that religion and politics should be divorced. To experience the wonder of the good and the true

as the guiding vision of life, to gravitate by instinct to the
liberation of the oppressed, to facilitate and insist on the
primacy of mercifulness and reconciliation — these things
would not only signal the spiritual renewal of the one, but in all
truth the political regeneration of nations. These things must,
at least implicitly, be involved in that prayer which should
never be said lightly:

May your kingdom come,
May your will be done on the earth as it is in heaven.

# 11

# The Resurrection of Jesus as the Coming of the Kingdom — the Basis of Hope for the Transformation of the World

## by John Muddiman

The essays in this volume are bound together by a common concern to understand the biblical image of the Kingdom of God and its contemporary implications for Christian social ethics. The relation between ethics and eschatology is a highly controversial topic. For example, eschatological hope for the Kingdom may be understood to induce human passivity in face of the social evils of the present age, in the conviction that they are soon to be removed by an irresistible intervention of God: 'It is well to remain as one is . . . For the form of this world is passing away' (1 Cor. 7. 26 and 31). But alternatively, eschatology can equally be interpreted as inducing greater human effort and activity, realising already in the present conditions that will prevail universally in the imminently expected future: 'You are all children of light and of the day; we are not of the night or of darkness. So then let us keep awake . . .' (1 Thess. 5.5f.).

When the first Christians proclaimed that 'God had raised Jesus from the dead', they were making an eschatological assertion in eschatological language. They were not simply referring to a miraculous event, peculiar to Jesus, which had happened within the ordinary course of history, like his walking on water or Transfiguration. They were referring to an event which properly belonged to all the redeemed at the End-time and which had been uniquely anticipated in Jesus' case. This proclamation had immediate and distinctive consequences for Christian ethics. Since resurrection life is already available to those who are 'in Christ', it precedes and nullifies the fear of death and judgement to come; it represents, then, the priority of grace over demand; but at the same time, since the End has already begun, the present is not just a time for patient expectation, it is also a time of liberation from slavery and active cooperation with the Spirit of the risen Christ. God's prerogative to initiate the End is safeguarded, since it has already been exercised in raising Jesus from the dead; thus action towards the realisation of the Kingdom of God can now be seen as legitimate human response to the divine initiative.

The purpose of this essay is to explore more fully this approach to the Resurrection of Jesus, seeing it against its indispensable eschatological background, and relating it to its ethical consequences; and to answer the main objections that can or have been raised against talk of the Resurrection as a form of, and the beginning of, the coming of the Kingdom of God.

Although the title and stated purpose of this essay may sound innocent enough, several serious objections must be acknowledged to the formula 'The Resurrection of Jesus as the Coming of the Kingdom', and the attempt to answer these objections will provide the structure of our argument.

1. Kingdom language is only rarely associated with resurrection language in the New Testament itself. The biblical image of the Kingdom of God appears prominently in the synoptic tradition of Jesus' teaching, but hardly at all in the post-Easter proclamation of the Church. If the early Christians believed that Jesus' Resurrection was the coming of the Kingdom, would they not have expressly identified it as such?

2. The early Church would not have continued to expect an imminent End and second advent of Christ, if it had understood Jesus' Resurrection as fulfilment of the hope for the coming of the Kingdom which he preached.

3. The essentially corporate, public and social dimension of biblical hope for God's Kingdom would be lost, if that hope were to be seen as 'realised' in the individual instance of Jesus.

For faith in the Resurrection of Jesus, and in the person of the risen Christ, although it may have dramatic effects for the believer, leaves the external conditions of this present age largely unaffected. To interpret Jesus' Resurrection as the coming of the Kingdom would be to narrow the breadth of that vision and privatise it within the circle of believers, and in consequence transpose it from the realm of ethics into that of dogma and personal faith.

4. In our modern ideologically and religiously plural society, it is bad tactics to appeal to an article of faith so exclusivist and internal to Christianity as that of Jesus' Resurrection, if one wishes either to provide a broadly based and widely acceptable ground for social ethics, or to provide a platform for the critique, and alternative vision, of society which will gain a hearing beyond the confines of the Church.

5. Even if we were to grant that the Resurrection of Jesus was one and indeed the chief form in which hope for the coming of God's Kingdom came to *expression* for early Christians, it could not for that very reason have been the *basis* of that hope. For, as St Paul says (Romans 8.24) 'Hope that is seen is not hope. For who hopes for what he sees?'

I do not want to underestimate the force of these objections, or to understate the case against the sort of position to be adopted in this essay. The radical character of the biblical image of the Kingdom has often been 'neutralised' and 'domesticated', by reinterpretations of it in terms of the Resurrection and Christology. One popular motive for this domestication is that it provides a ready-made solution to the problem of the non-arrival of the Kingdom within the one generation time-limit envisaged by Jesus and his first followers. To identify the coming Kingdom with something that did arrive on time, whether the historic ministry of Jesus, the Resurrection, the Church, the gift of the Spirit, the universal preaching of the gospel, or even the political events that led to the destruction of the Jerusalem Temple, offers an easy escape route out of an apologetic difficulty, but at the cost of emasculating the original idea. There is, however, another tradition that identifies the Kingdom with the completed work of Christ, which is motivated more by systematic than by apologetic considerations. This is the tradition that stretches from Origen, who defined Christ as the '*autobasileia*' of God, to Karl Barth who spoke of 'Jesus Christ as the established Kingdom of God'; and is best represented among contemporary theologians by Wolfhart Pannenberg.[1] It is imperative that those who wish to advocate this position should take due note of the obstacles in its way which we have listed above.

1. The first problem we have to consider is the rarity of explicit connection between the Resurrection and the coming of the Kingdom in the New Testament. By far the majority of references to the Kingdom of God occur in the Synoptic Gospels, in the pre-Easter teaching of Jesus. It is a notorious problem of synoptic studies[2] that they appear uncoordinated with the Son of Man sayings and the predictions of his resurrection. Without entering the minefield of that debate, we could fairly say that the most common solution to this problem is to attribute the Kingdom material firmly to the historical Jesus, and to refer the predictions of the resurrection of the Son of Man to the post-Easter theology of the Church. If so, it is noteworthy that, even when reading back Easter faith into the story of Jesus, the synoptic tradition resists the temptation to identify the coming of the Kingdom with the Resurrection. When such an identification appears in the post-apostolic writings, it is commonly explained as the result of disappointed hopes for the coming of the Kingdom. For example, the Lucan redactor attempts to correlate Kingdom and Resurrection language in passages like: Luke 23.42 'And he said: Jesus, remember me when you come in your kingdom. And he said to him: Truly I say to you, today you will be with me in Paradise' and Acts 1.3 'To them he presented himself alive after his passion by many proofs, appearing to them during forty days and *speaking of the kingdom of God*.' The deduction is drawn that it is in response to the failure of hope for the Parousia that the redactor has attempted to replace the

[1] See W. Pannenberg *Jesus God and Man* (SCM, 1968) esp. ch. 3 & 10. Pannenberg gives the references to Origen and Barth on p. 369.

[2] See P. Vielhauer 'Gottesreich und Menschensohn in der Verkündigung Jesu' in his *Aufsätze zum Neuen Testament* (Munich 1965); and H. E. Tödt *The Son of Man in the Synoptic Tradition* (London 1965) Excursus VI.

emphasis, away from the future Kingdom and onto the already achieved experience of the risen Christ. The effect of this apologetically motivated change on social ethics is then seen in an alleged posture of political compromise and social conservatism adopted by the author of Luke-Acts. Whether this is a fair assessment, we shall consider in a moment, after taking another example. The Fourth Gospel also associates the Kingdom and the Resurrection. Some Johannine scholars see the hope for the Parousia of Christ as already exhaustively fulfilled in the Resurrection and coming of the Paraclete.[3] The only element of future eschatology retained is a vestige, the exercise on the last day of Jesus' already demonstrated power to raise from the dead. The actual phrase, the Kingdom of God, has all but completely disappeared from the teaching of Jesus in John,[4] but we find instead, especially in the Passion, the idea of the kingship of Christ, which is specifically dissociated from any involvement with 'the world'; thus John 18.36 'Jesus answered: My kingship is not of this world; if my kingship were of this world, my servants would fight, that I might not be handed over to the Jews; but my kingship is not from the world.' So, as with Luke-Acts, the effect of this change on social ethics is allegedly disastrous, in John's case not so much compromise as passivity and retreat into a pure otherworldliness.

In short, this reconstruction sees the identification of Jesus' Resurrection with the coming of the Kingdom as an apologetic manoeuvre, precipitated by disappointed eschatology and having largely negative and undesirable consequences for Christian social ethics and involvement with the world.

There are, however, several good reasons for rejecting this view. It is not at all clear to recent scholarship on Luke-Acts that the political stance of the author is one of acquiescence and compromise.[5] Nor, in the light of the sociological approach to

[3]As R. Bultmann, *The Gospel of John* (Oxford 1971), p. 581: 'By combining the terminology of Easter and the Parousia, the Evangelist shows that for him they mean the same thing.'

[4]Only 3.3 and 3.5 remain and they have been 'individualised' in relation to baptism and rebirth in the Spirit.

[5]See R. Maddox, *The Purpose of Luke-Acts* (Edinburgh 1982); P. Esler, *Community and Gospel in Luke-Acts* (Cambridge 1987); and L. Johnson, *The Literary Function of Possessions in Luke-Acts* (Missoula 1977).

the Fourth Gospel, that the Johannine community was one that willingly took refuge in a religious ghetto; on the contrary, it seems to have tried for longer than most Christian communities to maintain wider links within Judaism.[6] Although both Luke-Acts and the Fourth Gospel imply an awareness of delay in the eschatological timetable up to their time of writing, neither of them has eliminated future hope altogether. Even more importantly and contrary to what one might have expected from this reconstruction, it is not just the latest writings in the New Testament that exhibit this change of emphasis from the Kingdom to the Resurrection. The genuine letters of Paul share the same feature. Here there is unqualified imminent End expectation, yet also subordination of Kingdom language to Resurrection language. Here also we find elements of resignation in face of insoluble social evils, and of practical compromise with prevailing authority, and retreat into the realm of the Spirit, and yet also elements of radical social critique, in for example the rejection of the distinctions of race, gender, wealth, education etc. within the Christian community itself (Gal. 3. 28; 1 Cor 11.22 etc.). In Paul the focus of attention rests decisively on the present lordship of the risen Christ, rather than the future coming of the Kingdom. But the subversive elements in Paul's ethics derive from the former, rather than the latter. Thus Paul's infrequent references to the Kingdom of God (e.g. 1 Cor. 6.9) are more concerned with individual, personal morality; while his comment on the kingship of the risen Christ at 1 Cor. 15.24 is much more radical; Christ will 'deliver the kingdom to God the Father after destroying every rule and every authority and power'.

Taken in its temporal development, then, the evidence of the main writings of the New Testament does not imply that an original millenialist hope for the coming Kingdom of God, inherited from the teaching of Jesus, was gradually subordinated to a realised focus on Jesus' Resurrection, and that this coincided with the toning down of the earlier radical vision of social change. Rather, from the very beginning of Christianity, the image of the Kingdom was reinterpreted christologically in the

[6]See e.g. R. Brown, *The Community of the Beloved Disciple* (London 1979).

light of the Easter faith; and tendencies towards spiritual escapism or practical compromise, when they do occur — and they are never wholly unqualified — have more to do with the peculiar circumstances facing different communities, than with a gradual turning away from hope for this world, born of disappointment.

The apparent separation of Kingdom language and Resurrection language in the synoptic tradition, nevertheless, remains a problem. There are sayings of Jesus which imply the coming of the Kingdom, with consequences of a public and indeed political upheaval, within the lifetime of his hearers. Mark 9.1 'There are some standing here who will not taste death before they see the kingdom of God established in power.' In this perspective, the resurrection of the dead is no more than a marginal feature. The long-dead Ninevites or Queen of Sheba will arise, presumably by resurrection, at the End, but only so that they may function as witnesses to condemn the still living people of this generation (Matthew 12.41f.). In the same way, the redeemed are those who survive the final tribulation at Mark 13.20; they do not pass through death to resurrection life, but are saved precisely from death, and therefore from any need of resurrection.

This picture is confused, however, by the presence in the tradition of other sayings which imply the opposite, i.e. that the redeemed themselves suffer, that they lose their lives in order to save them, that death and resurrection are necessary for the 'Son of Man'. To achieve consistency, we might simply dismiss the latter type of saying as read back from later reflection on the fate of Jesus. But equally, we could argue that inconsistency on such a question as this is a characteristic feature of Jewish apocalyptic thought, where we find both conviction of survival and heroic disregard for survival. Thus Daniel 3.16b-18: 'O Nebuchadnezzar, we have no need to answer you in this matter. If it be so, our God whom we serve is able to deliver us from the burning fiery furnace: and he will deliver us out of your hand. O King! But if not, be it known to you, O King, that we will not serve your gods, or worship the golden image which you have set up.'[7]

---

[7]For further discussion of the question of the involvement of the elect in the Great Tribulation, see D. Allison *The End of the Ages Has Come* (T. & T. Clark, 1985), ch. 2.

Whatever solution we adopt for this problem as regards the teaching of the historical Jesus — and it may after all be incapable of solution at this remove — it would not be justifiable to extract the Kingdom image from the New Testament and use it as the basis of a Christian social ethic in isolation from the Resurrection faith. For it is beyond question that the choice of resurrection language to describe the destiny of Jesus and the continuing effect of his person and message derives from the apocalyptic world-view in which the age to come, or Kingdom of God, is the central focus. The apocalyptic metaphor of rising from the dead is chosen in preference, say, to that of exaltation to the side of God, because the events of Jesus' death and Resurrection were understood from the beginning as eschatological. His rising from the dead to a new form of life beyond the limits of mortality was proof of the presence of the Kingdom and a significant anticipation of the imminent End. 'Christ is raised as the first fruits of them that sleep' according to 1 Cor. 15.20. And the identification of Jesus' Resurrection with the realisation of hope for the coming Kingdom must therefore be seen as an unstated axiom for the transmitters of the gospel tradition. And they do not identify the coming of the Kingdom with the resurrection and coming of the Son of Man, precisely because these are alternative ways of speaking about the same thing.

2. The Resurrection of Jesus was interpreted from the beginning as a unique realisation of hope, and the vindication of his teaching about the coming of the Kingdom. If this is so, we have to ask why early Christianity resisted a complete and full identification of the Resurrection with the Kingdom; in other words, why it still persisted in speaking of something still to hope for in the future. In one sense, the christological revolution was indeed complete, since that future hope was now expressed in terms not of the coming of the Kingdom, but of the second coming of the glorified Christ. But in another sense elements of the original Kingdom hope remained as yet unfulfilled by the Resurrection.

In Jewish apocalyptic, the age to come would see a public and universal demonstration of divine sovereignty, putting an end to the kingdoms of this world and ushering in the reign of the saints, the redeemed community. The Resurrection of Jesus was not a public event in the same way; he appeared to disciples, and occasionally to opponents like Paul and James his brother; but he had not yet revealed himself to the world. The Resurrection was not itself a universal event, even if it issued in a universal missionary imperative, for physical death still held sway, even among believers. The Resurrection was not the end of worldly kingdoms, except in part within the limited sphere of the Church. In each aspect, there is significant but as yet incomplete realisation, and room therefore is left for pre-Easter traditions to be retained and reapplied with only slight editorial adjustments for the interpretation of the events of continuing history. Thus, for example, the destruction of Jerusalem is explained as the result of Jewish rejection of the Messiah in the parable of the Wicked Tenants, Mark 12.1-9, with only an appended and oblique allusion to the fundamental alteration of the apocalyptic scheme effected by the Resurrection of Jesus, in v. 10f.: 'Have you not read this scripture: The very stone which the builders rejected has become the head of the corner; this was the Lord's doing and it is marvellous in our eyes?'

It is a mistake, then, to assert baldly that early Christian hope for the end of the world was falsified in the course of time. It was rather immediately, and significantly, verified in the Resurrection of Jesus. This is surely the reason why Christianity did not suffer any fundamental crisis of credibility when the age of the apostles came to its close.[8] There was no sudden change in orientation from the future to the past, or from the material to the spiritual. Since its eschatological hope had already, to an important degree, come to fulfilment, it was able to treat the delay, more or less, with equanimity.

We have argued so far that the New Testament everywhere assumes that the Resurrection of Jesus and the Kingdom of God are intimately connected, that the former is the anticipation and guarantee of the latter, and that without belief in his Resurrection, Jesus' message of the Kingdom would not have survived the crisis of his crucifixion, quite apart from the so-

---

[8]See O. Cullmann, *Salvation in History* (London 1967), pp. 30ff. and *passim.*

called crisis of the delay of his Parousia. Thus, we are not entitled to ignore the impact of Jesus' Resurrection, when we attempt to use the Kingdom motif for the construction of a Christian social ethic. Nor are we entitled to extract Jesus' vision of the Kingdom and isolate it from the all-pervasive context for its preservation and interpretation constituted by faith in his Resurrection.

3. We turn now to the objection that the christological interpretation of the Kingdom imagery which results from seeing it as fulfilled in the Resurrection of Jesus, inevitably narrows its scope and reduces its usefulness for ethics. Faith in the Resurrection can, of course, be presented in such a way that it appears to be a matter of personal salvation in the present and reassurance of survival and a future beyond this world, with no implications for the survival or future *of* the world. But this impoverished interpretation results precisely from detaching the Resurrection from its original apocalyptic context. It can even find some aspects of belief in the Resurrection rather puzzling: from a completely privatised and spiritualised viewpoint, all that is really required to assure personal salvation is some proof of the immortality of the soul; bodily resurrection introduces a quite unnecessary and disruptive element.

I want to argue at this point that the gospel narratives of the empty tomb and Resurrection appearances retain this connection with the wider apocalyptic context, and are therefore relevant to social as well as personal ethics.

The normal critical interpretation of the empty tomb story is to see it as a late addition to the Passion narrative, arising in response to the requirements of Christian apologetics;[9] faith being propped up with factual proof. This is not the place to rehearse all the difficulties with this view. There are in fact two quite different and independent traditions of the discovery of the tomb (Mark 16.1-8 and John 20.1-10), which disagree on almost every point of detail. There must then have been an early tradition, which has been developed in different ways and not, therefore, from late, apologetic motives but from

[9]See R. Bultmann *The History of the Synoptic Tradition* (Blackwells 1963), p. 287.

theological and literary ones. The basic intention of the empty tomb stories is to represent Jesus' eschatological victory over death, symbolised in different ways, whether as the great stone blocking the mouth of the grave, or the winding cloths restraining the corpse. They are, as it were, illustrative sermons on the apocalyptic theme: 'Death is swallowed up in victory.' The story was not, then, intended to be taken individualistically, as the paradigm for the fate of the individual believer after death. It is not just modern theologians who feel uncomfortable with the idea of a general resurrection to bodily, fleshly existence; Paul already senses it: 'I tell you this, brethren, flesh and blood cannot inherit the kingdom of God, nor does the perishable inherit the imperishable' (1 Cor. 15.50). It is possible to believe that Paul knew of and accepted the traditions concerning Jesus' tomb and its discovery empty on the third day; but if so, he must have understood it differently, not as a pardigm for the fate of the individual, but as exceptional and unique to the case of Jesus.[10] The meaning of what happened to him was corporate rather than individual. His raising from the tomb was the symbol, planted in history, of the eschatological transformation of the world. The theme of incorporation into Christ's Body, pervasive in Paul, surely finds its starting point here.[11] Certainly Paul refers to the risen Christ in 1 Cor. 15 not merely as the first example of a resurrected individual, the first recipient of eternal life, but corporately, as a new raised humanity and the source which dispenses resurrection life to others (cf. 1 Cor. 15.45). In the same way, the Resurrection discourse in the Fourth Gospel identifies Jesus not as the risen one simply but as the source of 'resurrection and life' to others: (John 11.25 cf. 5.21).

We turn next to the appearance narratives. In Matthew's short completion to the text of Mark, 28.16-20, the risen Christ does not appear in order to confirm private faith, but to announce his cosmic lordship: 'All authority in heaven *and on*

---

[10]I am not convinced that even at Phil. 3. 21 Paul uses the Resurrection of Jesus as the paradigm for the future resurrection of the individual believer. Notice that Paul speaks of 'our lowly body' in the singular, which could have a corporate sense in parallel to the evidently corporate 'our commonwealth' of the preceding verse.

[11]See J. A. T. Robinson, *The Body* (London 1952), pp. 55ff.

*earth* has been given to me', whose earthly manifestation is the ubiquitous presence of Jesus in the worldwide mission of the Church.

The appearances in Luke and John are different in many respects, and are, like the empty tomb, commonly said to be constructed for apologetic purposes. This again seems unlikely, since the evangelists themselves are not concerned with the provision of physical proof of the reality of Jesus' Resurrection. Luke is chiefly interested in proof from Scripture (see 24.27 and 44 and cf. 16.31); and John with the superiority of a faith that does not require sight (20.28). Perhaps therefore the most striking feature of these stories, the still remaining marks of crucifixion on Jesus' body, should not be understood as an apologetic device, but in a more strictly theological sense. The fact that the risen one is represented as not yet healed from the wounds of his suffering indicates that his appearance does not symbolise the pure blessedness of the life to come, but the more ambiguous combination of necessary suffering and future hope which corresponds to the present life of Christians in the world.

In short, Jesus' Resurrection does not narrow the vision of God's Kingdom to an individual instance of redemption; on the contrary the risen Christ, the last Adam, remains like the Kingdom of God, a corporate vision of the redemption of humanity as a whole. Furthermore, it is impossible to take the Kingdom of God in a restricted sense, as the vindication of righteous Israel, when that symbol is interpreted with reference to the cross and Resurrection of Jesus. The christological concentration on Jesus, far from individualising the hope, genuinely universalises it, and extends it decisively to non-Jews, breaking out of the boundaries constituted by obedience to the Law.

4. When we appeal to the Resurrection of Jesus as the beginning of the realisation in history of hope for the Kingdom of God, are we thereby restricting ourselves to an ecclesiastical audience and effectively ignoring the pluralist context in which Christian social ethics has to operate? In answer to this, it may be worth pointing out that the Kingdom of God is itself an image of limited appeal; it works better in certain societies,

like that of contemporary Britain, with a surviving vague theism and a constitutional monarchy, than it does in others.

Christian faith in Jesus' Resurrection is, as we have just argued, the starting point for its sense of universal mission, and mission inevitably involves dialogue. But dialogue should be distinguished from the search for neutral common denominators. It is rather predicated on a measure of mutual tolerance and respect for differences of view. There are, in other words, limits to pluralism that arise from genuine conviction. It is incumbent, however, on those who propose from within any particular religious tradition a vision of hope for the whole world, to 'translate' the symbols they are using, as far as possible, into terms understandable to those outside it. 'Translated' then, what does it mean to see the Resurrection of Jesus as the coming of God's Kingdom? Two points are particularly clear: that hope is personal and is involved with ongoing history. In the biblical tradition, the idea of resurrection is introduced when the survival of the nation comes to be thought of as a somehow insufficient hope, and a limitation on the sovereignty of God. It is introduced also to protect the insight that history is the locus of divine self-revelation, against mounting contrary evidence. Because hope is personal, focussed for Christians on the person of the risen Christ, the well-being of persons cannot then be sacrificed to remoter gains in the social order. Because hope is historical, focussed for Christians on the life and continuing risen life of Jesus, the option of writing off the future of the world has to be rejected. Even when 'translated' in this way, there will be points of conflict and challenge in the dialogue. Impersonal and atemporal accounts of hope, whether secular or religious, which block the way to any kind of social change, have also to be resisted. Christians share their 'translated' hopes and values with others; what differentiates Christians from others is their conviction that they have in Jesus' Resurrection a good reason for hope.

5. Can hope by its very nature only ever be grounded on itself? Is it a protest against present reality which may inspire or debilitate but cannot point to any basis except the negativity against which it protests? This was not the view taken by the first Christians. Paul may speak of Abraham's attitude as 'hope

against hope' but it was grounded in the promise of God (Rom. 4.18 cf. v. 13). When Paul speaks of hoping for what is unseen (Rom. 8.24), namely the revealing of the sons of God (v. 19), he bases this on something which is already seen and given, the Spirit that raised Jesus from the dead (v. 11) and cries 'Abba, Father' in those who are heirs of God, and fellow heirs with Christ (v. 17). At 1 Cor. 15.19, he is most outspoken: 'If for this life only we have hoped in Christ, we are of all men most to be pitied. But,' he continues, 'in fact Christ has been raised from the dead.'

To reach such a level of conviction about the contingent historical truth of Jesus' Resurrection appears to most modern theologians highly problematic. The difficulties raised by historical criticism of the New Testament evidence are well known. But if we stand back from these difficulties and speak in general terms we can at least say something: that the first Christians did believe in Jesus' Resurrection as an actual event that had occurred in their recent history; that explanations of the origin of Easter faith that depend on knowing fabrication or deliberate falsification on the part of witnesses are incompatible with the moral character of the movement that found its inspiration in Jesus; and that some kind of sufficient historical cause must be posited to account for the perceived historical effect of the continuation and expansion of the Church. The claim that the eschatological Kingdom of God had already arrived, uniquely and dramatically in the case of Jesus, is so peculiar and unprecedented that we have to posit something which externally compelled that conclusion. When all the necessary criticism of the Resurrection narratives is done, we are still confronted with named historical witnesses: Joseph of Arimathea who buried Jesus; Mary of Magdala who discovered his tomb empty; and a whole series of individual and group visions in different places and at different times of the risen Christ.

The view that takes Easter faith to be only an expression of realised hope and not the realised basis for continuing hope has to deal satisfactorily with some hard and resistent fragments of counter-evidence.

*Concluding Remarks*

The general discussions of the biblical image of the Kingdom of God which the contributors to this volume and others have had over recent years, under the auspices of the Foundation for the Study of Christianity and Society, have revealed a whole series of unresolved tensions in the material — tensions between the present and the future, the individual and the corporate, the local and the global, spirit and matter, divine initiative and human effort. This is not at all surprising, for there is no such thing as *the* biblical image of the Kingdom of God. It has to be approached, as it is in the other essays of this volume, in relation to particular bodies of literature. Some of these tensions have also been detected in the teaching of the historical Jesus; that is not surprising either, for we do not have access to the teaching of Jesus except insofar as that is mediated to us through the Easter faith of the Church, and if we try to by-pass that fact, his teaching is bound to appear incoherent.

When however the image of the Kingdom is focussed, as it was for all the writers of the New Testament, through the Resurrection of Christ, these tensions, I would claim, begin to be brought into balance. Christ is risen and therefore the Kingdom is present, in so far as we are already raised from sin and the fear of death. But in so far as humanity suffers still with Christ, and Christ still suffers with us, its resurrection and transformation remain a future hope and the Kingdom is still to come. The christological focus of Christian hope ensures both concern for individual persons and for the social context of human personality, for the Resurrection is the source of a new understanding of corporate personhood in Christ. The presence of the risen Christ is experienced by the worshipping community and is therefore local, but that experience impels them to a universal mission and vision. The Resurrection of the body of Christ from the grave is a unique symbol both of the power of the Spirit and of the value of the material in the purposes of God. And finally, divine initiative in establishing the Kingdom is safeguarded in the act of raising Jesus from the dead; thereafter, in the building up of the Kingdom already inaugurated, appeal is made to human co-operation in faith and hope.

There is one final, practical result of our study: the proposal that a Christian social ethic, using the symbol of the Kingdom, should properly have 'stereoscopic' vision; it should be constructed around the motif of the biblical Kingdom of God focussed and realised by the Resurrection of Jesus, or in other words the motif of the present kingly rule of the one whom God raised from the dead, as a pledge and promise of the future transformation and recreation of the world.

# 12

# Reflections on the Politics of the Gospels

## by Christopher Rowland

In this essay I want to consider three related issues which have had important implications for the discussion of Christianity and politics: the character of the Kingdom of God, the relationship between history and eschatology and the appropriateness of speaking of the political involvement of Jesus in the accounts as we have them of Jesus' activity in the New Testament.

I

Eschatology achieved prominence in modern theology because exegetes of the New Testament became convinced that the best way to understand one of its key concepts was in the light of future hopes of Judaism. So, from being something of an after-thought in Christian theology nineteenth century New Testament scholarship began to demand that eschatology be placed at the centre. At the heart of this view of eschatology is the notion of the imminent irruption of God into the old order and the establishment of a new creation. On the basis of his exegesis of the New Testament Johannes Weiss concluded that Jesus expected the coming of the kingdom in the near future, a cataclysmic event in which humanity had little or no part to play. He recognised that such a view, rooted in first century eschatological beliefs, was unpalatable to the theological humanism of his day. Weiss (and Schweitzer after him) placed eschatology at the centre of the New Testament message. In the work of both Jesus was portrayed as a proclaimer of the imminence of God's transcendent Kingdom. Their picture of Jesus was of the single-minded apocalyptic zealot whose whole outlook was dominated by the coming of this future new age. They argued that this fervent belief dominated the outlook of the first Christians too. To a significant degree the story of the emergence of early Christianity involved coming to terms with frustrated and disappointed hopes. New Testament theology in the twentieth century has involved attempts to come to terms with these theories.

It is a mark of the greatness of Albert Schweitzer's creative genius that I like many others find myself interacting with his portrait of Jesus. Schweitzer argued that Jesus expected the imminent inbreaking of God's Kingdom. When he sent out the Twelve on their missionary enterprise, he did not expect them back in the present age for he expected the Kingdom of God to come before their return (*Quest* p. 357). When they did return, however, Jesus came to see that it was necessary for him to share the suffering which would have to precede the coming of the Kingdom. That meant a journey to Jerusalem to die, the necessary prelude to the glorious reign of God, according to the eschatological hopes of ancient Judaism.

For all its shortcomings this portrait has the merit of taking seriously those twin themes of the Gospels: the cross and the Kingdom. It portrays Jesus as one who wrestles with the circumstances confronting him so that eschatological beliefs he inherited and was convinced were realised in his activity were refracted through the lens of the social realities which confronted him. Jesus is presented as one committed to the Kingdom but recognising the cost to himself that this realisation involved, faced as he was with opposition and rejection of his message. There is an acceptance of the reality of the struggle and turmoil which must be gone through. In it there is little disillusionment (until the very end) and certainly no easy optimism. Jesus may, in Schweitzer's words, be crushed by the wheel of the world which he seeks to move in order to bring this age to its close (p. 368f.). Yet the costly commitment to a different vision and the hope that the brutality of the reality of opposition need not always be so is an inspiration for faith. Schweitzer asserts that the continued relevance of Jesus lies in the espousal of hope which enables a critical distance from the institutions of the present and at the same time a universal applicability of the 'one great man'. Paradoxically, in Schweitzer's view, the hope for the future guarantees that this message will go on challenging every generation:

> Men [and women] feared that to admit the claims of eschatology would abolish the significance of His words for our times; and hence there was a feverish eagerness to discover in them any elements that might be considered not eschatologically conditioned. When any sayings were found of which the wording did not absolutely imply an eschatological connection, there was great jubilation — these at least had been saved from the coming debacle. But in reality that which is eternal in the words of Jesus is due to the very fact that they are based on an eschatological world-view, and contain the expression of a mind for which the contemporary world with its historical and social circumstances no longer had any existence. They are appropriate, therefore, to any world for in every world they raise the man [and woman] who dares to meet their challenge, and does not turn and twist them into meaninglessness, above [their] world and time, making [them] inwardly free, so that [they are] fitted to be, in [their] own world and time, a simple channel of the power of Jesus. (op. cit. p. 400)

Schweitzer's portrayal of Jesus is provocative and perhaps even alarming. It prompts the question: if Jesus was so misguided about his expectations, how can Christians go on having faith in such a figure or even make much sense of a life which was so determined by such an unswerving, perhaps fanatical, expectation? There are obviously passages (though few in number) which indicate a hope that the coming Kingdom of God would not be long delayed. Mark 9.1 (cf. 13.30) is a good example of this kind of passage. It seems to indicate that at some point in his career Jesus seriously anticipated a manifestation of the hoped-for age of perfection either in his lifetime or that of his followers. While it seems to me important to recognise this probability, this should not necessarily lead us to the dramatic conclusion that Jesus was utterly mistaken. The presentation of that hope in the New Testament demands of us a more nuanced approach.

The way in which New Testament eschatology is formulated in the Pauline letters may help the way in which we approach the material in the gospels. The difference in the intensity of eschatological expectation and the extent of its coverage in the letters have long been a matter for comment. The diminution of the raw expectation of the Thessalonian letters led to the view that there was an evolution in Paul's eschatological beliefs from the Jewish apocalypticism of his early career to a less sectarian and warmer universalism later in life. In occasional pieces the specific circumstances determined the extent and shape of the eschatological language used. The (probably early) Galatians has little reference to the future hope mainly because the concern is to stress what believers already possess. In the later Philippians a conventional expectation is to be found alongside a more individual offer of communion with the Messiah continuing after death. The variety of eschatological formulations is the result of the influence of circumstances on eschatological terms (see C. F. D. Moule, *Essays on New Testament Interpretation*, Cambridge 1982).

The important insight that circumstances determine ideas is a salutary reminder when we turn to the eschatological expectation of the Gospels. Here, of course, we are faced with a problem. The presentation of the life of Jesus may itself in each particular case reflect the circumstances of each evangelist. Thus, it is something of a commonplace in New Testament studies that the Fourth Evangelist has a diminished sense of the cosmic eschatological cataclysm and replaces it by the present crisis confronting the world in the Word become flesh (see now J. Ashton *Understanding the Fourth Gospel*). In a different way Luke diminishes preoccupation with the end of the age by the insertion of the study of the Church into the saga he wishes to tell, thus enabling concentration on the present task. Also, despite its increased incidence of eschatological material the Gospel of Matthew combats complacency and demands recognition of the apocalyptic Son of man in the mundane and insignificant person of the poor (Matt. 25.31ff.). Mark too refuses to allow the satisfaction of a consolatory eschatology in which imminent expectation removes the need for the difficulties and complexities of the response in present circumstances.

The need for sensitivity to the context in which we find eschatological material in the Gospels is an essential prerequisite for interpreting the eschatological discourses in the Synoptic Gospels. They must not be separated from the narrative of Jesus' proclamation and inauguration of the reign of God. It is that context which is necessary to prevent the discourse about the future becoming the goal of the narrative. Discipleship involves sharing the way of the cross of the Son of man as he goes up to Jerusalem. What is offered the disciple is the sharing of the cup of suffering of the Son of man rather than the promise of sitting at his right hand and his left when he reigns on earth. It is not that this request is repudiated but, as the eschatological discourse makes plain, there can be no escape from the painful reality of the present witness with its need to endure the tribulations which precede the vindication. That is the challenge which faces those who wish to live out the messianic narrative in their own lives; no short cuts to the messianic reign are to be found here. It is easy to see how the discourse materials in the Gospels can be extracted from their narrative context and function as instructions which abstract the reader from the challenge of facing the cost of the shadow of suffering and martyrdom.

The narrative framework of the Gospels is a necessary medium for understanding the eschatology. In taking sayings of Jesus out of context we risk being left with no setting other than that offered by the reconstruction of the exegete. The task of getting back to the original historical setting of a saying may be an appropriate one, but can it really be allowed to override the guidance for a Christian interpretation given by the narrative contexts of the Gospels? In saying this I realise that I am in some respects turning my back on the hermeneutics of suspicion of nearly two hundred years of exegesis which refuses to remain content with the ideological distortions which the original process of production brought about. I do not want to return to a simplistic acceptance of the text as sole determinant. Nevertheless suspicion about the fragmentary character of our information about the original settings of Jesus' sayings places inevitable limits on the amount of reliance we can place on our critical reconstructions.

We would all like to know exactly in what situation Mark 9.1 or Luke 11.20 were uttered or whether Jesus ever uttered anything like the discourse now found in Mark 13 and parallels. Amidst such uncertainty the resort to speculative alternative contexts tends to displace the narrative context of the sayings which offers crucial guidance for interpretation. The circumstances in which a particular saying is imbedded do matter. Not that this will always facilitate precise exegesis: Mark 9.1 remains as much of an enigma in its context as it does when treated in isolation. What the narrative framework does demand of us, however, is a recognition that the setting of a saying in the presentation of Jesus' short career changed dramatically. The situation in the last days in Jerusalem was very different from the heady optimism of the signs and wonders which accompanied the proclamation of the good news in Galilee. The triply attested eschatological discourse with its dark prognostications is to be read in the light of the failure to win over Jerusalem and its hierarchy and the enigmatic but emphatic denunciation of the Temple. Mark 13 does not offer general predictions about the end of the world nor is it full of glib promises (Jesus had already refused to grant these in Mark 10.38ff. cf. Luke 22.24ff.). In the wake of the 'failure' in Jerusalem to win over the city the mood changes, and so does the character of the eschatology. That is not to deny the hints of a less happy outcome before this. It has been a realistic possibility as far back as Mark 3.6.

In the synoptic discourses there is in fact very little attempt made to sketch the ideal society, a mark of either a lack of any political realism or of a merely Utopian outlook. One of the problems of Utopianism is that it can lead the reader into construction of ideal worlds which distract him or her from the demands of the present. Utopianism can lead to an escape from reality however much its attempts betoken that yearning for something better. Writers who resort to Utopianism do so as a compensation for the inability to do anything about the world as it is. Early Christian writers prefer to hint at their conviction that one is coming without being too precise about what it will involve. It is the language of myth and metaphor which is to the fore rather than the offering of any detailed political manifesto. It is about the beyond in the sense that it is both future and different from the patterns of society currently on offer. To speak of it, therefore, demands a language which is both less precise and yet more potent and suggestive, a language which after all is what is appropriate when one sets out to speak of that which is still to come.

The book of Revelation offers us a timely reminder in its own form about supposing that its preoccupation with eschatological matters offers an opportunity to avoid the more challenging preoccupations of the present. Thus, the vision of hope inaugurated by the exaltation of the Lamb is set within the framework of the Letters to the Seven Churches. Even if we can discern a preponderance of 'religious' issues in these letters (warnings against false teaching, suspicion of false prophecy, loss of an initial religious enthusiasm), we should probably regard the issues being touched on here as typical of a complacent second generation religious movement. Christianity appears to be making too many accommodations with the surrounding culture and it needs to be brought back once again to its counter-cultural affirmation in the light of its witness to the new age. Thus the promise of a part in the New Jerusalem is linked with present behaviour. The readers of the Apocalypse are not allowed to dream about millenial bliss without being brought face to face with the obstacles which stand in the way of its fulfilment and the costly part to be played by them in that process.

What the narrative of the Gospels demands of us is the recognition that the circumstances changed rapidly. The message of the Kingdom of God in deed and word met by a popular response contrasts with the very different reality confronting Jesus in the hostility, attempts on his life, and perceived disaffection among members of his circle. That change conditions the character of the eschatological pronouncement. Judgement, doom, pain and the need to endure take the place of practical demonstrations of divine sovereignty in the present. Of course, the two are not mutually exclusive. It is not the case of realism displacing a naïve belief in human perfectibility. The extent of the need and the resources of divine healing of the God who reigns do not disappear merely because they are confronted by the recalcitrance of the politically powerful. The agent of God's reign meets the apparently immovable force of the *status quo*. Something has to give: it appears to be the former rather than the latter, though the final verses of Mark's Gospel suggest another ending (15.38). In the changed circumstances of reduced opportunities and lack of faith other priorities take their place. The commitments and opportunities of Galilee remain, the programme of God's reign is one to be entered into by all who will. Yet consistent refusal to do so does not mean the extinction of its influence. As Amos put it centuries before, to those who refused to accept the Lord who came, the Day of the Lord was gloom and judgement not joy and bliss.

## II

The importance of Schweitzer's presentation is that he exploits to the full that contrast between the early and late parts of the narrative of Jesus' life in the Gospels. He looks for an explanation of the journey to Jerusalem and the suffering in a changed eschatological perspective. In Schweitzer's presentation Jesus' outlook is still dominated by an eschatological programme, so that one still has to reckon with the problem of Jesus being mistaken in his expectation. While I think that there are enough indications to suggest that Jesus' expectation about the coming of the Kingdom of God may have at certain stages of his career been over-optimistic, it seems to me that it is too simple to describe Jesus' outlook as false or mistaken merely on the basis of two or three sayings. In suggesting this I do not want to be seen as trying to protect Jesus from error. I am quite prepared to believe that Jesus entertained expectations which may have been mistaken. Rather I think that we should follow the directions given to us by Schweitzer and engage with the complexities of the narrative presentation which indicate subtle shifts in the presentation of Jesus' eschatology.

What is most striking about the New Testament is that the present is seen as a time of fulfilment. The significance of the present is so integral to the understanding of God's propitious time that history is the arena for eschatologically significant actions. In the New Testament the present becomes a moment of opportunity for transforming the imperfect into the perfect; history and eschatology become inextricably intertwined, and the elect stand on the brink of the new age itself. A feature of New Testament study has been the way in which the stress there on the fulfilment of the ultimate purposes of God has reduced interest in present history. Given that the age to come was near then there seemed, so the argument runs, little point in trying to change society as it was. When the kingdoms of this world would shortly become the kingdom under the lordship of Christ then human endeavour to wrest them from the grip of the ruler of the present evil age seemed either presumptuous or unnecessary. Political activity on the part of those committed to the coming of the Kingdom is at best limited. Radical change is in the hands of the God who will supernaturally intervene to establish the Kingdom. Humankind is merely a passive spectator of a vast divine drama with the cosmos as its stage. With their eyes so firmly fixed on what is to come the early Christians had little concern for ordinary human history.

Such a dichotomy between history and eschatology is not entirely borne out by the ancient documents themselves. It was certainly a matter of debate between the first Christians and their Jewish contemporaries whether the promises were near to fulfilment. This was a basic issue which separated them. But it is important that we be clear that *this* was the issue. The Christians did not abandon a hope for this world. Early Christian and Jewish writings offer a this-worldly hope which did not consist only of a cataclysmic irruption from the world beyond and the destruction of the present world for the manifestation of the divine righteousness. When we recognise that the teaching in the New Testament, particularly that attributed to Jesus, is about the ideals applicable to God's reign *on earth*, the New Testament writings can certainly be seen as the struggles of those who looked forward to a new age but also recognised the obligation to live in the present *as if* they were living in the age to come.

In this, human beings thought of themselves as the agents of God's eschatological purposes. We can see this in the story of Jesus of Nazareth and he proclaims the present as decisive in God's purposes and himself as the messianic agent for change. The carefully constructed entry into Jerusalem signifies the risk of deeming the present moment in history as ultimately significant. Similarly Paul of Tarsus took upon himself as the result of his deep-seated convictions the role of the divine agent through whom the eschatological act of offering the gospel to the nations could be completed. The central theme of the New Testament, therefore, is of human agency as a central means of eschatological fulfilment.

As harbingers of God's propitious moment, the New Testament actors are hardly ideal role models for Christians who seek to muddle along trying to make the best of the old aeon. One can understand why reserve is expressed towards a close alignment with historical projects which take sides in contemporary political struggles. After all, how can one be sure that they are of God rather than marked with the sign of the Beast? We may be less troubled if we retain a clear contrast between history and eschatology, the latter being conceived as something totally *beyond* history. Such a view is one that all too easily bolsters conservatism in church and academy. If we can only see life as consisting of different shades of grey, we may well be reluctant to take sides in struggles for justice, thereby helping to support those structures of society and patterns of relating more or less as they are.

There may be a way of dealing with this dilemma. The question is whether there is a comprehensive enough hermeneutic of suspicion which recognises that those who profess themselves to be children of light cannot but be infected with the reign of darkness, living as they do in the midst of the old order. The reign of God has not come in all its fullness. To behave as if it had is itself a denial of the reality of evil and the extent of the struggle. Confronting the powers of the old order in the name of the new and naming the Antichrist necessarily involves the potential, indeed the reality, of the demonic within ourselves. Merely 'demonising' one's opponents can be accompanied by a self-righteous attitude which lapses into perfectionism. That itself can lead to destruction rather than the restoration which comes from God. The children of light can see themselves as the appointed agents of the divine will; matters begin to be sharply defined and the division between good and evil clearly seen. But there is no guarantee of clarity this side of the millennium. Yet the difficulty of certainty and the risk of a nostalgia for a past where greater clarity seems to be found than is actually the case should not prevent action. Jeremiah's words about the deceitfulness of the human heart (Jer. 17.9) are particularly apposite for those who espouse righteous causes. Confronting the powers and the demons in others and in the institutions of church and state must be accompanied by the co-operative task of confronting them and struggling with them in ourselves. That will be a co-operative and communal task in which critical testing will help to prevent brutal short-cuts to perfection. Individual champions of sacred causes who feel the need to leave behind the critical support of the people of God are particularly vulnerable to self-deception. But to be honest about that does not diminish the importance of the task of the Church to confront the powers in conformity with the ministry of Jesus.

In the old order Christianity must be a religion constantly dissatisfied with its attempts to realise the Kingdom. The problem with any kind of realised eschatology (and also revolutionary activity, as Barth pointed out) is that it misses the central point that we live still in the midst of the old aeon. We need to give an account of our hope but recognise that our articulation of it in word and deed is necessarily fragmentary and partial. Study of the chiliastic tradition in all its dimensions illustrates the perpetual danger that it encourages naïve optimism. As Engels rightly pointed out with regard to the religious revolutionaries of the sixteenth and seventeenth centuries, they had the right ideas but wrongly believed that they could actualise them at the wrong time. The activities of those like Münzer, who were confident in the rectitude of their ideas but ignorant of the political possibilities, were in fact profoundly reactionary. They offer a salutary message to all those who believe that activism in itself will guarantee eschatological success. To be aware of the dangers, however, is not the same as relegating such views to the mistakes of Christian discipleship, simply because of the breadth of their vision and the earnestness of their hope.

The New Testament seems to speak of a cataclysmic 'irruption' from heaven, a supernatural intervention. But we need to beware of an over-literal interpretation of this in the Gospels and elsewhere. There are questions to be asked about the legacy of an interpretation of eschatology which is so pervasive in twentieth century New Testament study. Is it really appropriate to speak of Jesus expecting some 'supernatural' intervention? Indeed, how far is talk of 'direct intervention' and supernatural occurrence part of the way in which we have sought to make sense of the metaphorical language of Jewish and Christian eschatological discourse? This kind of separation between present history and future eschatology is not borne out by the ancient texts themselves. Life in heaven is the ultimate destiny of the cosmos when God will be all in all. The evocation of this demands the colourful, the spectacular and the bizarre, in order to convey the tremendous character of that which is hoped for. There is at times a woodenness about our treatment of eschatological language. Nowhere in the interpretation of the New Testament are we more guilty of a simplistic literalism. The language of myth and parable can have a historical referent but remain allusive in precisely what it specifies. That is appropriate for that which is to come, which defies our feeble attempts to encapsulate it.

There is a wider issue here which has been touched on in recent theology but has received too little attention in twentieth century exegesis. There has been a growing criticism of the dualistic notions which undergird post-Enlightenment philosophy and theology. That critique applies to questions of biblical exegesis also. The discussion of eschatology by Weiss makes a clear distinction between God's work and human activity. We are told that there was an ancient Jewish view of the Kingdom of God. We are told it is entirely transcendent; its coming is God's task alone. Here there are two histories: salvation history and secular history which only partially overlap. The reconstruction of ancient Jewish and early Christian eschatology took place in an intellectual climate where the contrast between God and the world, the sacred and the secular, was a typical way of viewing reality and God's relationship to history. The other-worldly imminent expectation has seemed to be an unchallengeable 'scientific' finding of modern critical exegesis. Yet the texts themselves as well as the attention given to the philosophical context in the history of interpretation demand that we think again. The inbreaking of what appears to be 'beyond' into history is at the heart of what traditional theology asserts about the resurrection of Jesus and the experience of the Spirit. The intertwining of history and eschatology is at the heart of what is distinctive about the first Christians' interpretation of the Jewish tradition and their attachment to the story of Jesus. The modern tendency to polarise history and eschatology, the transcendent and the material, God and humanity, ignores the stubborn refusal of the Bible to draw such hard and fast lines between them. The expression of the Christian hope in the form of the tension between the now and the not yet refuses to push eschatology and the transcendent into some other realm but demands that the present is seen as a time of eschatological significance.

Liberation Theologians like Gustavo Gutierrez have added their voices in rejecting the dualism which subtly distances God from the world and salvation from human liberation and the sacred from the secular. For them there is *one* history, and the desire to speak of God in relationship to some special sphere of existence is a product of a philosophical era where such dualism pervades our thought. That insistence on present history as the arena of the manifestation of the reign of God in the needs of the poor and the vulnerable is their distinctive contribution. That emphasis on history and the eschatological significance of the present has meant that leading Liberation Theologians are sometimes charged with naïve optimism in their hopes for humanity. There is, however, a consistent renunciation of projects which are unrelated to political circumstances. There is little in Liberation Theology to suggest that their links with the reality which surrounds them are in fact so tenuous that a fantasy of a grassroots revolution, a modern-day holy war, could ever be nurtured uncritically. They have seen the human cost of so-called sacred causes and are in the business of mitigating their effects. Most are engaged in costly small-scale protests and programmes at the grassroots to offer glimpses of God's eschatological Kingdom amidst the injustices of the old order. The centrality of the portrait of the synoptic Jesus in the theology of liberation places a clear constraint on the fantastic and unreal and demands of those who believe that the Kingdom impinges on the life of the present the recognition that such commitment usually ends up with a cross rather than the millennium.

In recognising the eschatological tension, however, we must not subordinate the story and practice of our hope, admittedly mind-blowing in its extent and quality, to a secular realism which is reductionist in character. The central parts of the story we tell raise questions about a version of history which maintains the *status quo* by closing off the possibilities which the inauguration of the Kingdom of God opened up. History is always, of course, a problematic term; it presupposes a view and a particular narrative. The Christian narrative of the past does not render the arena of history unnecessary. It offers a perspective for making sense of the world, its past, present and future, in the light of a particular set of memories focussed on the life, death and resurrection of Jesus. The answer is not to look merely beyond history to some transcendental world. Rather, it demands that we remain ever open to possibilities for change, however dramatic and beyond our comprehension they may be, in accord with the spirit of the justice and mercy of God which indeed pass our understanding. Above all at the heart of the story is one who suffered at the hands of those who sought to maintain conventional political activity in their own interest. The commemoration of Jesus involves continued identification with those in whom the risen Christ meets us in his real presence in our day: the despised, the needy and the vulnerable.

III

The politics of the New Testament have been a subject of intense debate in the last thirty years or so, as political theology has been very much in vogue. It is impossible to abstract the story of Jesus from a political framework without irredeemably reducing its significance. The use of phrases like social activist and political campaigner to describe Jesus in the gospel narratives is misleading without a word of qualification. The character of political life in Judaea and Galilee in Jesus' day was neither political in the entirely secular sense of modern political life nor was it in any sense open or democratic. The framework provided for political activity in the time of Jesus was a despotic royal court (that of Herod Antipas) and a colonial power in Judaea (Rome). There was little room for formal political activity for an artisan like Jesus.

Yet Jesus' mission is thoroughly imbued with an understanding of polity which was rooted in a theocratic tradition derived from the Bible. To claim to be messiah, to promote that claim actively as he did when he entered Jerusalem and the Temple, and to conduct himself in the way in which he is described in the Gospels are political in the broadest sense of that word and constitute a campaign which may have been vague in detail but not without premeditation. Thus we are presented with narratives of one who deliberately 'set his face to go to Jerusalem' (as the Gospel of Luke puts it). In the Gospel of John Jesus is portrayed as choosing his own moment for the decisive visit to Jerusalem (7.1ff.). His was a deliberate act, provocative and risky, something which the Jesus of the gospels is presented as recognising in the predictions of suffering. The activity may not be the conventional politics of Sanhedrin, hierarchy or Roman imperium. But Jesus is portrayed as bursting in on the cosy arrangements of Jerusalem and shattering the fragile peace which existed.

The fact that Jesus does not speak in overtly political ways and address what would be for us obvious political issues does not constitute a lack of political content in Jesus' message. Jesus addressed the people of God and their way of relating and interacting. There is hardly enough detail to construct a political programme, but there is enough evidence to discern the contours of a different kind of polity which differed sufficiently to lead to a challenge to current arrangements and which consisted of the controversial assertion on his part of the right to articulate that difference. We might feel that a more obviously political Jesus might have addressed himself to Roman occupation, the reasons for poverty, and the existence of slavery. Also, he might have constructed his parables with stories which were less accepting of the *status quo* than he did. To stand before the Sanhedrin and assert his messianic status, however, is to lay claim to a different pattern of human relationships, to be political, within the framework of late Second Temple Judaism. We can only guess at what that might have involved if Jesus had had the chance to activate a different kind of polity. The memory of him is of one whose career was cut off with little opportunity for the measured preparation of a political legacy. We have no ground for assuming that this would have excluded the construction of a polity on the grounds that his kingdom would not have been in this world (cf. John 18.36).

So far I have concentrated on the narrative of Jesus' relationship with formal political processes. It is a measure of the way in which we have reduced the nature of the political that we should conceive of it solely in terms of a programme for action in society. For most of us the political is of little direct impact in the way in which we conduct ourselves. But those interactions between individuals and in small groups, remote as they might often seem from formal political processes, deserve the description political. Not only are they shot through with the influences of the wider social setting, but in themselves they manifest the exercises of power, the subordination and the impoverishment of human beings in the struggle for the maintenance and extension of individual interests.

The political character of the actions of Jesus in the Gospels deserves more attention than it has received. By 'political' in this context I mean their relationship to conventional patterns of human interaction and organisation, whether formal (like a Sanhedrin or a local body of elders) or informal and traditional (like widely established practices). The political challenge posed by Jesus involved departures from norms of behaviour, status, attitude and access to social intercourse which are typical of a particular society. The narratives of Jesus' action portray a challenge to convention and imply different standards of human relating. The touching of lepers and of 'unclean' women, the restoration of those excluded as 'mad', the healing of paralytics and blind, whose disabilities inevitably caused impoverishment, signify sitting loose to boundaries of conviction and a preparedness to countenance in human action something different which claims to be more restorative. There is, of course, nothing that is unconventional in healing the sick but the challenge and perhaps even the breaking of 'taboos' represent a shake-up of the personal relationships which constitute the fabric of human relating, the very stuff of politics. The disturbing of what counts as normal and acceptable is also evident in the reaction to Jesus. The surprise is that those who are abnormal recognise Jesus, whereas those who are supposedly normal are suspicious and hostile. The former are 'blessed' with an insight which seems to be denied to 'normality'. But here too there is resistance to change. Jesus has come to torment. The stability or equilibrium of impoverishment and spiritual disintegration is suspicious when the possibility of temporary dislocation confronts it. How true is the maxim 'better the devil you know' when it comes to being confronted with change brought about by the new and disturbing.

The wider perspective reminds us that in many of the reports concerning Jesus there is a process described which only tangentially relates to the formal political processes. But as the narratives themselves often indicate there is an exercise of power in particular, and frequently controversial, ways. In understanding the politics of the Gospels we do well to note the politics of individual interaction as exemplifying patterns of relating which may offer significant steps forward in the betterment of human relations, applicable even in those situations where access to formal political power is limited. In such situations the experience of the first Christians proves invaluable. They understood the mechanics of change within situations where the levers of political power seemed to be denied to them. Perhaps that is a lesson we have to learn once more even in societies where access to political power appears to be quite open. A political theology which takes seriously the gospel narratives will not concentrate only on gaining the levers of power. They too need to be transformed but not at the expense of the transforming politics of personal relationships, the impact of which helped send Jesus to his death.

## BIBLIOGRAPHY

J. Ashton, *Understanding the Fourth Gospel* (1991).

E. Bammel and C. F. D. Moule, *Jesus and the Politics of His Day* (1984).

F. Engels, 'The Peasant War in Germany' in *Marx and Engels on Religion*, pp. 87ff. (1972).

G. Gutierrez, *A Theology of Liberation* (1974).

R. A. Horsley, *Jesus and the Spiral of Violence.*

N. Lash, *Easter in Ordinary* (1988).

C. Rowland, *Radical Christianity* (1988).

C. Rowland and M. Corner, *Liberating Exegesis* (1990).

A. Schweitzer *The Quest of the Historical Jesus* (1931).

J. Weiss, *Jesus' Proclamation of the Kingdom of God* (1971).

# 13

---

# Paul and the Kingdom of God

## by Frances Young

The earliest Christian writings known are the Epistles of Paul. Furthermore, Paul and his associates may claim to dominate the literature of the New Testament, in sheer length if nothing else. Yet many find Paul problematic. It has been claimed that Paul in one way or another distorts the teaching of Jesus and complicates the simple Gospel. For those concerned with social action, Paul seems particularly awkward because of his pessimism about human nature and this world, his apparent 'otherworldliness'. So do we need to pay attention to Paul? To what extent is Paul responsible for projecting the kingdom of God onto the heavens? To what extent does he or does he not reflect similar patterns of thought to those we find in the Gospels? Does Paul have any sense of social responsibility?

## I. *The Kingdom of God*

It is often suggested that whereas the idea of God's kingdom predominates in the teaching of the Synoptic Gospels, it is not for Paul a primary category of thought. Yet the phrase 'kingdom of God' is used by Paul, and certain key things are said about it.

## (i) The Thessalonian Letters

The present writer accepts the authenticity of 1 Thessalonians, together with the view that it is the first of Paul's letters and therefore quite possibly the earliest Christian writing that we have. 2 Thessalonians is more problematic, but reflects a similar world of discourse.

In 1 Thessalonians Paul's remarks presuppose that his Gospel has been presented to Gentiles who have turned from idols to serve a living and true God, and that apart from accepting the God of the Jewish Scriptures, who is also the God of Paul and his compatriots, they are 'awaiting his Son from heaven, whom he raised from the dead, Jesus who delivers us from the wrath to come' (1.9-10). The converts are also exhorted and encouraged to 'lead a life worthy of God who calls you into his own kingdom and glory' (2.12). The same idea is found in 2 Thessalonians — they are to be made worthy of the kingdom of God (1.5). This worthiness involves being holy, and holiness means being blameless when facing God's judgement.

These references to the kingdom read in the total context of Paul's writing here, suggest that it is understood entirely in eschatological terms: the elect will inhabit the kingdom of God when Christ returns in glory, when the old order is finally wound up. Meanwhile those who respond to the Gospel are a kind of 'nucleus' of the future, a holy remnant which will escape the wrath and inherit the kingdom when it comes.

## (ii) Galatians

Galatians was clearly written in the midst of profound controversy over the terms on which Gentiles were to be admitted to the community of the elect. So there is a significant shift from a primary focus on the future, to the situation in the present.

The one reference to the kingdom of God occurs in a passage concerned with contrasting the fruits of the Spirit (love, joy, peace, patience, kindness, goodness, etc.) and the works of the flesh (fornication, impurity, idolatry, enmity, etc.): 'those who do such things will not inherit the kingdom of God' (5.21).

The kingdom of God clearly belongs to the future, and those who belong to the elect community and live a life of holiness will be in a position to enjoy the benefits of that future kingdom. There is perhaps a hint that the Spirit produces a kind of anticipation of that future, a hint confirmed in Paul's later epistles.

### (iii) The Corinthian Correspondence

The phrase 'kingdom of God' occurs more frequently in 1 Corinthians than any other letter of Paul's, and in a greater variety of contexts. But most usages confirm what has already been noted. The unrighteous will not inherit the kingdom, nor those who are immoral, idolaters, adulterers, thieves, etc. (1 Cor. 6.9-10); here Paul echoes the need for purity and holiness already noticed in the earlier epistles. Then in chapter 15, Paul speaks of all being made alive in Christ, in the appropriate order, Christ being the first-fruits, and then those in Christ at his coming: 'then comes the End, when he delivers the kingdom to God the Father, after destroying every rule and every authority and power' (v. 24). The kingdom again belongs to the future, to the events that wind up the old order. Those in Christ, it seems, will inherit the kingdom. This impression is confirmed by the statement: 'Flesh and blood cannot inherit the kingdom of God, nor does the perishable inherit the imperishable' (v. 50). Entry to the kingdom implies a transformation, a transfer from one *aeon* (world, age) to another by a process parallel to the death and resurrection of Christ.

On the other hand, 'the kingdom of God does not consist in talk but in power,' says Paul (1 Cor. 4.20), in a context where he is threatening recalcitrant church members with a rod: judgement has become present, and the same threat is made at the end of 2 Corinthians (ch. 13), though without reference to the kingdom. This is perhaps an important hint that Paul does think of the kingdom being already operative, and has significant 'equivalents' to the phrase 'kingdom of God', which must be explored if his full position is to be understood.

### (iv) Romans

'The kingdom of God is not food and drink,' claims Paul in Romans 14.17, 'but righteousness and peace and joy in the

Holy Spirit; he who thus serves Christ is acceptable to God and approved by men.' The principal focus here is clearly present rather than future, and the statement relates to controversy over Christian practice. The fruits of the Spirit (cf. Galatians), rather than dietary scruples, clearly constitute in some sense the kingdom of God. Yet the focus of much of Romans (e.g. ch. 8) remains future: the whole creation groans and travails awaiting its redemption, and 'we who have the first-fruits of the Spirit groan inwardly as we wait for adoption as sons, the redemption of our bodies'.

Clearly the phrase 'kingdom of God' is not Paul's most characteristic (any more than it is for the author(s) of the Johannine literature). Yet it occurs in such a way as to link the promise of the future reign of God with present experience of the Spirit, with present lifestyles and priorities. The kingdom appears to be present in embryo in the elect who have the gift of the Spirit, who constitute the new covenant community and are the Body of Christ. Whether Pauline or not, Colossians 1.13 sums up Paul's view: 'He has delivered us from the dominion of darkness and transferred us to the kingdom of his beloved Son.'

It cannot therefore be said that Paul's view of the kingdom is simply a projection onto the heavens: it is not simply otherworldly or spiritual or gnostic, and it does not imply a simple rejection of material existence, despite the suggestion that flesh and blood cannot inherit it. It is eschatological in the sense that it is effected by God when the old order is brought to an end and the new order created. It is certainly not to be 'achieved' by human effort. But there is a continuity between the body of flesh and blood and the spiritual body like the continuity between seed and plant, and there is a continuity between the old world and the new, the new being anticipated in the midst of the old. The kingdom means the redemption and transformation of the kind of existence known already. It has an ethical dimension in that it is anticipated in the Christian way of life, in obedience to the will of God through the Spirit which has created new hearts and minds in believers, so producing love, joy, peace and righteousness.

## II.  *Becoming What You Are*

In fact Paul's use of the phrase 'kingdom of God' appears to cohere with that frequently observed feature of his understanding, the 'overlapping of the ages'. It seems that Paul, in common with many others at the time, expected the fulfilment of the prophecies to mean God's final intervention to wind up the present evil age and bring in the new, and what he believed to have happened with the coming of Christ was the initiation of that process. God's wrath and righteousness were alike being revealed: the cross marked the beginning of the final woes, and the Spirit the beginning of the new creation. Yet the present evil age was not yet over, and the final consummation still belonged to the future.

So there is a tension in Paul's language between the 'now' and the 'not yet': on the one hand, believers are already justified, sanctified, adopted as sons of God and heirs of the kingdom; on the other hand they have to become what they already are, and there is plenty of advice about what that means in terms of personal purity, relationships in the church community, etc. They cannot live in sin so that grace may abound. The tenses in Romans 6 are instructive: having died with Christ they will rise with him. Christian believers will be saved, they are awaiting their redemption; yet that future has to be lived in the present.

What is striking is that an exactly parallel tension between the 'now' and the 'not yet' is particularly associated with the kingdom in the Synoptic Gospels, and with 'eternal life' in the Johannine literature. The problems of relating future eschatology and realised eschatology constitute a long-standing area of discussion in New Testament scholarship, and need not be considered in detail here. Suffice it to say that the imminence of the kingdom appears to be the burden of Jesus' message in the Synoptic Gospels, and sometimes it appears to be present in his activity, especially his confrontation with the powers of evil. His proclamation is the fulfilment of the prophecies and of all the hopes of Israel for God's reign on earth; yet his life is not 'messianic' in the accepted sense, and there is a constant note of looking forward to the consummation of God's kingdom, a tension between the 'now' and the 'not yet'.

Similarly in John's Gospel, 'eternal life' is sometimes spoken of as a present possession, sometimes as a future reward; it appears to mean the 'life of the age to come' rather than simply life that goes on for ever, in other words it is the kind of life to be lived in God's kingdom, which is in a sense already available. The phrase 'eternal life', like 'kingdom of God', does not seem particularly characteristic of Paul, and yet is found as a kind of 'formula' in a number of places, and its usage parallels that of the 'kingdom language' in such a way that it seems to be for Paul another way of speaking of the inheritance of the kingdom (see e.g. Gal. 6.8; Rom. 2.7; 5.21; 6.22-3). The crucial point is that despite different characteristic emphases, Paul's usage mirrors the fundamental patterns and tensions found elsewhere in the New Testament, even though his favourite expressions are different.

In fact, where the Gospels seem to identify the coming of the kingdom, which is nevertheless still to come, with the appearance of the Christ, Paul seems to focus the anticipation of the kingdom in the gift of the Spirit and the life of the Church. The kingdom is present in embryo in the 'body of Christ' which is the new covenant community. Yet Paul has no illusions about the realities of life in those communities: his letters are an appeal to work out their salvation with fear and trembling, to become what they are.

But what does this mean in practical terms? Traditional Protestant exegesis of Paul would emphasise his perception of the sin and corruption of humanity and the need for divine grace: there is a sense in which he despairs of the present evil age and all its works. Humanity can do nothing to save itself. The present evil age is under judgement, and redemption involves a kind of 'abstraction' from it. So it might seem that what Paul seeks to achieve is a network of elect communities withdrawn from the world in which the love, joy, peace and goodness of the kingdom may be anticipated, that he has no ambition to change the world, at least not while this present evil age persists. It is as much as he can do (if not more than he can achieve in a place like Corinth!) to foster the unity of the little 'nuclei' of the kingdom he has brought into being. This picture might seem to be encouraged by Romans 15: Paul seems to claim that the foundation of churches from Jerusalem to Illyricum has completed the work there, and it is not an implausible suggestion that he thought the End would come when a representative group from every nation had responded to the Gospel. So does the anticipation of the kingdom in the 'body of Christ' through the down payment of the Spirit mean that the kingdom is for the moment confined to the Church and contained in 'cells' which are the seeds of the future but 'withdrawn' from the realities of this present evil age?

Certainly the temptation is to think that Paul's concern is limited to the personal holiness of his converts and their inter-relationships within the communities he is founding. Undoubtedly he is concerned with that, and he does not seem anxious to work out even there the social implications of his statement that in Christ there is neither slave nor free, male nor female (see 1 Cor. 11 and Philemon). Furthermore, his attitude to the powers that be (Rom. 13) betrays no sense of urgency to reform the social and political realities of his time. No doubt, it is said, his expectation of the End led to a somewhat 'quietist' response.

But to leap to that conclusion is probably to do less than justice to Paul's perspective. If he accepted the *status quo* where women and slaves were concerned, he certainly did not in the case of that other great divide between Jew and Gentile. He realised that the unity of Jew and Gentile in Christ had to be expressed in the actual relationships that appertained in the day-to-day life of the Church, and he fought long and hard for his views to prevail. The fact that history shows he was ultimately unsuccessful does not mean he did not try. Here was a profound social and political division that could not be acceptable within the 'nuclei' of the kingdom.

Nor should we underestimate the ultimate 'universalism' of his perspective. The kingdom meant God's reign over the whole of his creation, it was clearly to come, and to come quickly. In Colossians fellow-workers could be described as fellow-workers for the kingdom. The kingdom was certainly to be God's doing, but meanwhile God called ambassadors and 'ministers' to create the 'nuclei' of the kingdom, and the way God called people related to his ultimate plan for the whole of his creation: notice the importance of 'call' in Romans 9 — God might 'call' people or 'harden' people, in order that his ultimate design be accomplished, and that ultimate design involved the salvation even of those hardened (11.25-32). However mysterious (or perhaps from our perspective, however arbitrary) the process of election, Paul allows for some human participation in God's plan. He can hardly be said to envisage a social or political revolution, but he does see that somehow the purposes of God to bring about the transformation of all things at the End are served by the creation of these new covenant communities, and he presumably saw the fruits of the Spirit at work there as the fundamental qualities of the universal kingdom soon to come. The struggle to create a new societal relationship between Jew and Gentile within the Church was a practical outworking or anticipation of a totally new kind of society.

To 'become what you already are' is Paul's exhortation to those who have responded to God's call to live in anticipation of the kingdom. To a large extent the implications of this are spelt out in terms of individual holiness and personal relationships, but these communities of the elect also have potential significance in terms of the kingdom as a social reality.

## III. *The Cross and the Kingdom*

If the language of 'kingdom' is not particularly characteristic of Paul, what might be the principal focus of his theology? It would seem that it could be characterised as increasingly cross-centred. How then does his understanding of the kingdom relate to this prominent streak in his theology?

### (i) The Thessalonian Letters

At this stage, where Paul seems to be summarising the content of the Gospel he preached, the cross is less prominent than the resurrection. Yet suffering, affliction and persecution are taken to be the marks of the Christian who is subject to the same hostility as Christ, and reading what Paul says in the light of the apocalyptic tradition that wars and rumours of wars, earthquakes, travail and woes would precede the coming of the End, we may discern something of how Paul understood the place of the cross in the story of salvation. Far from being merely the prelude to the resurrection, it was the beginning of the judgement process marking the 'turning of the ages', the destruction of the old order into which Christ had come, so that its re-creation by resurrection could happen. The cross belongs to the process whereby the kingdom comes into being.

### (ii) Galatians

The shift already noted away from the future to present issues produces greater focus on the cross and its significance. It was not just the Christ who died, but Paul's old self: I have been crucified with Christ. New life has been made available through faith, and Paul is presumably not merely giving personal testimony, but saying something about what has happened in principle for the whole human race. He is concerned in this letter to press home the practical consequences of this in relation to the validity of Law, and the detail of that argument cannot be examined here. Suffice it to say that the cross is again related to the winding up of the old order, the bearing of the curse and its annulling, so that the promise of the new can be realised. Because of the particular controversy behind this letter, this is now focussed less on external struggles with evil typified in persecution and more on the renewal of human motivation. Thus it relates to the fruits of the Spirit and the inheritance of the kingdom discussed earlier.

### (iii) The Corinthian Correspondence

It is in the letters to Corinth that the foolishness of the cross becomes most prominent in Paul's argument. From the first chapter of the first letter, it seems apparent that Paul is faced with people making claims about spiritual powers, intellectual, moral, visionary, miraculous, or whatever, which imply their superiority, and by the time we reach the second letter, Paul's own apostleship is clearly being subject to adverse comparisons.

In this context, conformity to the cross becomes more and more evidently the mark of the true apostle.

Coupled with this there seems to emerge a resistance to the kind of talk which suggests that the resurrection has already happened, or the kingdom has already come: for this is a refusal to grapple with the realities of this world. The acceptance of Christ involves acceptance of the cross, of weakness and contempt, persecution and suffering. Yet the foolishness of God is wiser than men. The dishonoured are to be honoured in the Body of Christ. A reversal of normal human values and priorities is involved simply because the cross is a nonsense in human terms. It demands total reliance on God and God alone. The tension between the 'now' and the 'not yet' is perhaps most marked in these letters, where Paul is struggling with a triumphalism which for him threatens the very nature of the Gospel. The cross cannot be circumvented in the process which brings the kingdom into being.

## (iv) Romans

It is through Romans that we can see how these developments and themes knit together. It is not the place here to grapple with the complex argument of Romans, much of which is an outworking of the meaning of the cross by implication if not primarily and explicitly. Suffice it to draw attention to Romans 8 with its image of the creation in labour to bring forth the new, of believers being involved in the struggle, groaning as they wait for their redemption, of the Spirit's involvement through intercession.

It is but a short step to the idea that sufferings are a matter for rejoicing in that they fill up what is lacking in the sufferings of Christ (Col. 1.24). It is also natural that the mind of Christ who humbled himself and became obedient to the cross should become the ideal to be worked out in relationships within the Church (Phil. 2.1-18). Thus Paul's theology holds together the 'kingdom' and its equivalents and the centrality of the cross. It could be said that the Gospels, by the very way in which they tell the story with its culmination in the Passion, have a similar perspective, though it is worked out in different ways in different circumstances.

## IV.  *Do We Need to Attend to Paul?*

The present writer would answer that question in the affirmative. Like Paul we live in a pluralistic society in which Christians are a minority, yet there appears to be a new kind of seductive triumphalism emerging in a number of different movements within the life of the Church, and Paul's resistance to first century forms of Christian triumphalism becomes apposite in this context. There is also widespread pessimism about the future, not unlike the fatalistic mood of the Hellenistic age which is the wider context to which Paul belonged, and within which he preached 'Good News'. Even if Paul's 'world-view', deeply imbued as it is with apocalyptic perspectives, seems utterly foreign, much of what he says 'rings true' to our human experience. Let me spell this out more fully.

First some comments on triumphalism: on the one hand, idealistic claims are found among many Christian activists, whether for development, for peace or for political liberation; on the other hand, in the charismatic movement, groups and individuals promise health, wealth and success if you only let God into your life. Despite the declining influence of the Churches, there is an unrealistic and uncharacteristic spirit of 'optimism' around, an optimism that speaks of the present reality of the kingdom as if all the problems of the world could be wafted away if we only found the right 'formula', whether it be 'the power of prayer' or 'the revolution' or the scrapping of nuclear weapons. This attitude is at variance with experience, with one's reading of history and one's reading of the Scriptures. One cannot help wondering whether it may not be basically a 'sell-out' to the spirit of the age — the optimistic Utopianism created by the real, though temporal, successes of science, medicine and technology.

But speaking of the spirit of the age, alongside this tendency to an unrealistic optimism about the future, we also commonly observe both inside and outside the Church a profound pessimism, a sense that things are not what they used to be —

memories are short, and the social conditions of Victorian England, or the time of war and depression are forgotten; the scenes on the television screens make bad news all too present and contemporary. There is a massive discontent and despair about society, about violence, about economic forces — there seems something inevitable about the passing on of social inadequacy or communal conflict from one generation to another. Such pessimism is also misplaced and unrealistic: surely nothing quite compares to the institutionalised violence of discipline in the English navy when able-bodied men were liable to be pressed into service, and suffered little better conditions than those carted off in the slave trade. There are ways in which things have improved and our moral sensibilities have developed: genocide may still go on, but at least it is no longer something to boast about.

In this kind of way, perspectives may be shifted by taking a longer view of things, but also by respecting the tension and balance within the Christian tradition, the tension between the 'now' and the 'not yet' observed in the very earliest Christian writings. Over the centuries, Christianity has had a variety of views concerning the future to be expected, whether concerning the final outcome of history or the destiny of the human individual. Most expositions have involved abandoning one or other of the poles of this tension.

The present writer, in struggling to come to terms both with the proclamation of the kingdom as a present reality and with the tragic intractability of human vulnerability and mortality ('personified' in a profoundly handicapped son), has found this tension instructive and helpful. Naturally, simple adoption of the eschatological views of the New Testament period in all their strangeness is difficult if not unreasonable, but whatever one makes of it theoretically or philosophically, the realities of our existence seem well characterised by the tension inherent in New Testament thinking in general and in Paul in particular.

For whether we like it or not, there are things we cannot change; there are handicaps we cannot overcome, and old age eventually gets us all; and what is the point of delaying death when we shall in fact all die? We cannot now un-invent nuclear weapons, so there can be no long term security. There is no hope of an earthly Utopia, and human attempts to create a perfect world nearly always go bad on us — one only has to think of the disturbing results of the grand programme of slum clearance: intentions good, outcome socially disastrous. Much of the problems of famine and underdevelopment is the inadvertent result of 'progress' and over-population. Over so many areas of life, the very effort to do good seems to end up going wrong, and this applies on a corporate scale, not only in the case of the proverbial Pharisee who in seeking moral uprightness commits the sin of pride and self-righteousness. Human life is subject to bondage and corruption, however unfashionable it may be to suggest this.

And yet this is not the whole story: human life is shot through with a kind of magic, miracles of grace, genuine change, real hope at the penultimate level. Against all the odds, the slave trade was abolished. There are little anticipations of the kingdom in Christian communities, if only we have the eyes to discern them, and we look in the right places. And those anticipations embody values which often seem at variance with the dreams of humanity in general, values informed by conformity to the cross of Christ. The over-optimism and over-pessimism characteristic of contemporary attitudes is to some extent born out of ever-increasing expectations, and those expectations need to be put into the right perspective.

So Paul gives us a perspective on things, a perspective in which we cannot escape both the 'now' and the 'not yet': for

(1) human nature and human society, even within the Church, is corrupted but redeemable;

(2) the present evil age is a reality but it is not the whole of reality;

(3) God is trustworthy and is at work in the world, despite appearances;

(4) human effort cannot produce the kingdom, but we may be called to be fellow-workers for the kingdom and to participate in effecting God's plan of redemption;

(5) we can experience now what life in the kingdom of God is to be, and yet we cannot take it for granted — it is always under threat and always has to be struggled for;

(6) individuals need to be changed, but that change is only evident in the resulting community of relationships — neither personal salvation alone, nor structural change alone, can bring kingdom values into effect;

(7) neither optimism nor pessimism is appropriate — the Christian virtues are faith, hope and love; these transcend the present, and yet are anticipated within the present order;

(8) the pattern of Christ's death and resurrection means that Christian hope is never a bland confidence — for Christian faith is in a God who can bring life out of death, and death has to be accepted for the transformation to take place.

In other words, while there is a relationship between the values and hopes of the world and those of the kingdom, there is also a fundamental critique of a worldly Utopia effected by worldly programmes of reform.

Maybe we should attend to Paul.

# 14

## Biblical Theology and the Pressing Concerns of the Church

### by John Riches

The biblical scholar whose concerns are more than purely antiquarian faces a dilemma. If the earlier part of the century saw the development of biblical theologies which the Church could understand and act on, the last two decades have seen their collapse; New Testament studies, on the other hand, not least in the fields of history of religion, sociological and literary critical studies, are alive and well, but becoming increasingly the preserve of the specialist. At the same time the Church is faced with an epochal crisis in its life, as it attempts to find its way and understand its heritage in a world caught up in a bewildering process of change and revolution. In this it rightly turns to the Bible as its primary source of guidance — but in so doing it rarely consults the biblical scholar. Has critical, historical study of the Bible nothing to offer the Church at this time?

Some analysis of actual uses of the Bible in this context might help to suggest ways in which such new approaches could indeed prove fruitful and to open up the prospect for a rather different kind of relationship between the scholar and the Church than was formerly achieved. I choose by way of example an essay from Latin America.

In his essay entitled 'Christ's liberation via oppression' [1] Leonardo Boff asks: 'What meaning does Christ's liberation

---

[1] In R. Gibellini, ed. *Frontiers of Theology in Latin America* (London SCM, 1979), pp. 100-132.

have in a context where people are yearning for liberation and suffering from oppression?' (p. 101). Such a question, as Boff is fully aware, is not a straightforwardly historical question. Boff wants to discover those elements in Jesus' life, death and resurrection which transcend the particular circumstances of his time and can be worked out anew at other times and in other places. In another sense it is precisely historical: in that he seeks concrete answers to his question which will 'flesh out his (Jesus') liberation in history' (p. 101).

Boff attempts to get at the answers to this question via an account of Jesus' life and death viewed in the socio-political context of his times which presents 'striking parallels to the situation that gave rise to liberation theology in Latin America' (p. 103). Here some strange things occur. Boff starts by describing the long standing political dependence of Palestine on its neighbours, leading to its domination by Rome in the first century. He further offers some account of the socio-economic oppression which was to be found in first century Galilee. All this is fair enough so far as it goes. What is surprising is the next section entitled 'Religious Oppression'. Here we read:

> But the real oppression did not consist in the presence of an alien, pagan power. The real oppression lay in a legalistic interpretation of religion and the will of God. In post-exilic Judaism careful cultivation of the law became the very essence of Jewish life... It degenerated into a terrible and impossible form of bondage proclaimed in God's name. (p. 105)

Jesus sought an end to all such oppression, but unlike those who sought a revolutionary overthrow of the Romans, or those who announced an immediate and sudden end to the world, he proclaimed:

> some ultimate, structural, and all-embracing meaningfulness that goes far above and beyond everything that can be decided or done by human beings. He proclaims some final end that calls into question all immediate interests of a social, political, or religious nature... Instead of proclaiming some particular kind of meaning, be it political, economic, or social, he proclaims

an absolute sense that embraces and supersedes everything... (p. 106)

By using a term, the kingdom of God, whose roots are buried in people's most Utopian yearnings, Jesus revivifies hope for total liberation from all those things that alienate people from their authentic identity. And he announces that the hoped for new and reconciled world is in their very midst (p. 107).

It is interesting to note here the way in which Boff both echoes and recasts Bultmann's — existentialist — biblical theology, which in its own way also sought to draw out those aspects of Jesus' life, preaching and death which transcended his particular historical context. Like Bultmann he stresses the sense in which Jesus' language of the kingdom speaks of men's and women's deepest longings: 'He revivifies hope for total liberation from all those things that alienate people from their authentic identity' (p. 107). But whereas Bultmann sees this hope as being realised in the here and now of the individual's decision of faith, and thus feels able to discard the 'objectivising' language of a final end of the world, Boff wants to hold on to such language as of continuing significance. For the liberation which men and women long for is a liberation not only from their own inauthenticity but from all those structures which hold them in bondage, including, of course, economic and political structures.

Like Bultmann, Boff also wants to stress the distinctiveness of Jesus' message. But whereas Bultmann saw this as the existential call to decision of Jesus' preaching, Boff relates it closely to the practical, social implications of Jesus' preaching and way of life. Whereas many of his contemporaries saw the kingdom as a wholly future event, Jesus 'anticipates the future and brings the utopian element right into the heart of present day life' (p. 107). In his own *praxis* the end had already in some sense come.

That absolute goal and end was mediated through concrete gestures, anticipated in certain surprising behaviour patterns, and made tangible in attitudes that signified that the end was already present somehow in the midst of this life. (p. 109)

Jesus in his preaching encourages people to find their own liberation, calling them to act out their own history, rather than invoking the power of God to 'liberate' them in a paternalistic way. That is to say, Jesus rejects the misuse of power. He tangibly represented the power of God's love to inaugurate an order that does not violate people's freedom nor exempt them from the task of taking charge of their own human project (p. 108). In his subordination of ritual service to the concerns of people, in his creation of new fellowship for those who were outcast or discriminated against, in his respect for the liberty and the differences of other people, he himself inaugurated the process of liberation. Such freedom on Jesus' part however brought him into fatal conflict with the religious authorities of the day who upheld a tightly controlled religious system. Thus Jesus dies because he remains faithful to the openness to God and to others which characterised his whole life. He dies in the faith that this kind of love and openness is indeed that which brings him closest to the Father. His resurrection provides the vindication of this belief in that

> it signifies the full enthronement of human reality (body and soul) in the divine realm; hence it signifies complete hominisation and liberation… Death is overcome, and a new kind of human life begins. Human life is no longer ruled by the mechanisms of death and exhaustion; instead it is invigorated with the divine life itself. (p. 122)

The critical question is of course what light such a reading of Jesus can shed on the issues which primarily exercise the Liberation Theologians. What does the liberation which Jesus offers have to say in a situation where the majority of the human race live under conditions which are inhumane, which are oppressive, from which they long for release? What specifically does it have to offer when we believe that the oppression is the result of *structural* elements in our global situation? Boff argues that once we have understood the sense in which the oppression of the poor world is the result of the existing social structures, then the first thing which has to be done is to 'denounce and thereby to unmask the vaunted progress of modern times'. Beyond that the task is to proclaim and anticipate a whole new meaning for human society and a whole new way of using the rich set of instruments provided by science and technology. Instead of being used to generate some people's domination over others, they must be used to resolve the age-old social problems of hunger, illness, poverty and discrimination. (p. 127)

In this respect Jesus' *praxis* is exemplary.

And because Jesus proclaimed a universal and ultimate meaning, his followers have a deep hope that there will be a radical transformation when the partial meanings of our present world will be taken up into a global meaning which transcends all our anticipations of it. Meanwhile however Boff recognises that in the Latin American situation those who follow are unlikely to see the realisation of such a global meaning but will more likely share the experience of Jesus' cross.

It is not hard to feel that Boff's portrayal of Jesus is achieved almost in spite of what he has learnt from New Testament scholarship. His interest in the socio-political context of Jesus' preaching is hardly furthered by an account which locates the real oppression of Jews, not in their dominance by a foreign power but in the legalism of the Pharisees; which sees the Jewish authorities as primarily responsible for his death. His account of the universal significance of Jesus' preaching of the kingdom draws on Bultmann, but in a way which runs against the grain of Bultmann's existential interpretation. His emphasis on Jesus' *praxis*, as opposed to his sayings and teachings, certainly resonates with discussions in New Testament studies about the significance of Jesus' meals with tax-collectors and sinners, but is interpreted in terms which are not sufficiently earthed in the historical contingencies of the times: relativisation of human self-sufficiency, creation of a new kind of solidarity, freedom from oppression, the subordination of ritual service to people. The latter point however does nothing to explain the importance of ritual concerns to Jews in the first century, why for instance they would give their lives in the attempt to gain control of the Temple, the seat of all 'ritual'.

Boff's difficulty is that he is, rightly in my judgement, pointing to elements in Jesus' life and teaching which he sees as of continuing significance but which the scholarship of Dodd, Bornkamm and others, which he relies on, largely neglected. In consequence he gives a somewhat distorted account of those features. What precisely are they and how might more recent work in New Testament studies complement his own?

What then are the elements of Jesus' life and death which, in Boff's view, transcend the circumstances of his time and can be fruitfully applied to his own situation? They seem to me essentially of two kinds. On the one hand he identifies in Jesus' teaching and actions a commitment to certain values: of love, of openness, of human interdependence and freedom. On the other he derives from Jesus' proclamation of the kingdom certain views about the course of history: (1) that it is tending towards some point where our regionalisation of meaning, the attempts of particular societies to build themselves a world of meaning which excludes, marginalises and therefore oppresses others, will be overcome and (2) a belief that meanwhile it is the task of those faithful to the gospel to 'anticipate' that final global meaning, to mediate it through concrete acts which, while they will not themselves bring in the kingdom, are nevertheless pointers to others, forms of proclamation of the gospel of the kingdom of God.

What I now want is to suggest some ways in which an account of Jesus' life and death which looked more closely at the interrelation between Jesus' beliefs and actions and the social, cultural, economic and political realities of his time might provide further clarification and insight. Just because Bultmann and his school were principally concerned with the existential dimensions of the gospel, they neglected the social and political context of first century Christianity.

Let me give some indications of how such an account might help.

1. Boff's claim that Jesus advocated an openness which transcends any regionalisation of meaning is arrived at by contrasting Jesus' teaching and *praxis* with the narrow legalism of the Pharisees. This kind of portrayal has of course been all too common among biblical scholars. It has been strongly

attacked, notably by E. P. Sanders in *Paul and Palestinian Judaism* (London 1978) and *Jesus and Judaism* (London, SCM 1985), and is certainly misguided. However, not all interest in the Law is legalism. The Pharisees may indeed have delighted in and insisted vigorously on the importance of obedience to the Law. But why? Accounts of Pharisees in terms of works righteousness and legalism owe too much to internal Christian debate. Can recent social historical approaches to the subject assist?

Here the account of purity regulations which was offered by Mary Douglas in *Purity and Danger* (London 1966) may help. Douglas argues there that an important function of such regulations is to reinforce the external and internal boundaries of the group. Communities who live under threat from more powerful neighbours or indeed occupying forces may develop such regulations in order to defend themselves from assimilation and attack. Conversely it is difficult for the leaders of groups under such pressure to abandon a tightly structured set of rules and develop or advocate a more effervescent kind of religion. Seen in this light Pharisaic attention to and cultivation of purity rules may be seen as a quite natural tendency to set tighter lines around the group and to enforce a greater internal discipline within it. If Neusner is right that even before 70 C.E. the Pharisees were engaged in a process of transferring the centre of the cult away from the Temple to the home and the local community, then that transference was in all likelihood related to attempts to set up strong social boundaries around the group, organised now less as a nation state than as an ethnic, religious community.[2]

Such a picture offers some promising ways of understanding features of Jesus' teaching and behaviour which theologians like Boff are attracted to. Jesus' meals with tax-collectors and sinners evince a very surprising openness in a society where there were forces at work attempting to strengthen group boundaries. But the point is that we can now gain a clearer

[2]See my *Jesus and the Transformation of Judaism* (London, DLT 1980), ch. 6 and M. Borg, *Conflict, Holiness and Politics in the Teachings of Jesus* (Mellen 1984) and W. Meeks, *The First Urban Christians* (Yale 1983), p. 97.

understanding of the nature of that openness. It is not simply the rejection of a narrow legalistic vision of God and the social practices which flow from it; it is rather to be seen as a rejection of attempts on the part of religious leaders to forge the people into a more cohesive group in an alien world. Sharing the same table with those who are significantly socially deviant, who live at odds with the group's norms, or who indeed are agents of an alien and threatening power, is clearly very different from keeping oneself apart from such people and associating as far as possible only with members of one's own group.

What such an observation points up is the fact that Jesus' meals are in a way more problematic than traditional interpretations might suggest. He was not simply dismissing a narrow, sectarian view of religion; he was rejecting a strategy which was in many ways a highly responsible one in the difficult times in which Jews lived. It was certainly a strategy which contributed to Judaism's survival through centuries of persecution and discrimination. Opening the doors to one's enemies and failing to exclude deviant members of the group are recipes for trouble, as indeed the story of Jesus' own betrayal by Judas suggests. And yet paradoxically a willingness to engage creatively with the alien and the other, even if the other seems threatening and dangerous, may lead to the birth of new social worlds of great fecundity. In Jesus' case such openness to the alien is theologically rooted in a vision of the fatherhood and mercy of a God who in his dealings with his creatures disregards social and even moral boundaries (Matt. 5.45). This then may provide an understanding of Jesus' actions and preaching which offers both a sociological and a theological grounding for Boff's conviction that it demands the continuing criticism of our own tendencies to absolutise our own social worlds, and with them of course our own group interests.

2. Different problems are raised by Boff's attempt to wrest a doctrine of history from Jesus' preaching of the kingdom. Boff is heavily dependent on Dodd's and Jeremias' notion of realised or inaugurated eschatology, the notion, that is, that Jesus announced that the final goal of history had already in some sense been achieved in and through his coming. The way Boff

puts it is to say that Jesus looked for some final global meaning which he mediated concretely through his own praxis. He appeals to Mark 1.15; Matthew 3.17; Luke 17.21:

> [Jesus] does not say that the Kingdom of God is coming in the future but that it is at hand now, that it is in their very midst. With his own presence the Kingdom, too, is made present: 'But if it is by the finger of God that I cast out devils, then the reign of God is upon you' (Luke 11.20). His presence is the appearance of the stronger who overcomes the strong (Mark 3.27). (p. 107)

The difficulty here is that Boff moves too quickly from talking about Jesus' exorcisms and his announcement of the coming of the kingdom to talk of liberative *praxis* and 'some ultimate, structural, and all-embracing meaningfulness which goes far beyond everything that can be decided or done by human beings' (p. 106). The actual nature of Jesus' behaviour and beliefs is concealed in language which enables us to make the transition to present political concerns too quickly. Exorcisms are associated with belief in demon possession; Jesus proclaimed that the kingdom of God would 'come with power' in the life-time of his hearers (Mark 9.1). Jesus' understanding of liberation involved, that is to say, the breaking of Satan's power over men and women and the inauguration of a new age when sickness and sorrow would be no more.

Underscoring Jesus' specific hopes and expectations in this way has advantages and disadvantages for those who look for the practical corollaries of Christian belief. On the positive side there is a recovery of the quite practical concern in Jesus' ministry with overcoming human suffering and its physical manifestations, which is easily lost in the more abstract language of 'ultimate structural meaningfulness'. But, negatively, it makes it abundantly clear that Jesus' expectations that such suffering would be banished from the earth have not yet been fulfilled and that his belief that such fulfilment was at hand was mistaken.

Such a recognition of Jesus' mistakenness clearly raises very large questions for any interpretation, such as Boff's, which seeks to exploit its contemporary relevance. If Jesus erred in this might he not also have erred in other matters? Can we any more accept his ethical and social teaching which we discussed under (1) above? I can only state here[3] that I do not think that the truth of Jesus' teaching about the fatherhood of God and love of enemies is conditional upon the truth of his sayings about the imminence of the kingdom. However, it is clearly far from easy to derive a compelling doctrine of history from Jesus' preaching of the kingdom, if we regard its predictive aspects as false. This may not be such an unmitigated disaster as it might appear but a number of moves are required before we can reach a more satisfactory position.

Relating Jesus' ethics to his eschatology has long been recognised as one of the principal tasks for evangelical ethics. In this respect one of the major difficulties has been the legacy of Johannes Weiss' account of Jesus' eschatology. According to Weiss (*Jesu Predigt vom Reiche Gottes* 1892), Jesus in his preaching of the Kingdom announced a final, decisive act of God which would put an end to history as we know it and inaugurate a new age. The new age would be the result of God's activity alone; men and women's efforts to improve their world would be judged at the end when the old world order was replaced by the kingdom to be inaugurated by God. This was a quite explicit attack on Ritschl's understanding of the kingdom which saw it as the fruit of men's and women's self-activity, as a community which was to be built up here on earth but which continued into a supernatural kingdom beyond this life.[4] On Weiss' view men and women's role was to repent and to await God's saving action. *Attempts to improve or rebuild the existing order were ultimately faithless.*[5]

Weiss' account of Jesus' teaching was seized upon by those who rejected liberal theology after the First World War. What was now said to be required was not planning and moral effort

---

[3]I have discussed this in 'Apocalyptic Strangely Relevant' in W. Horbury, ed. *Templum Amicitiae, Essays on the Second Temple presented to Ernst Bammel, JSNT* Supplement Series 48, (Sheffield 1991) pp. 237-263.

[4]A. Ritschl, *Instruction in the Christian Religion*, I, A, para. 5.

[5]See J. Weiss's commentary on Mark 4.26, in *De Schriften des Neuen Testaments*, (Göttingen 1907, p. 114), where he comments that the growth of the seed is 'God's work. Only humanity with its willing and doing is excluded.'

directed to building up the kingdom, but rather belief in the future action of God, whether 'future' was understood chronologically or existentially. The most that can be allowed on such a view is that Christians, pending the final decisive divine action, may make 'mediative gestures', post 'signs of the kingdom' by their lives and actions. Determined planning and the attempt to meet the pressing concerns of the world by developing programmes of action through rational analysis and the application of Christian principles were rejected as merely contributing to the work of human history which will be judged at the final coming.

Dodd was himself a representative of the kind of liberalism which Barth had so sharply attacked after the First World War. His doctrine of realised eschatology was in effect an attempt to counter interpretations of Jesus' eschatology which deny that there can be any proper Christian view of history and progress (except to say that it is all under judgement). Dodd argued that the absolute was already present in the sphere of the temporal and that it was present both judging *and enabling* men and women to embark on new lives and create the new world which Jesus 'founded'. It was certainly Dodd's view that Christianity had contributed significantly to the development of modern Europe. But such a view, however comforting it might be to those who wanted to identify Christianity and Western civilisation, failed to attend sufficiently seriously to the mythological elements in Jesus' belief, to make sense of, e.g. the exorcisms or indeed to provide a convincing account of Jesus' expectations of the future. It also failed to offer any account of the dark dissonances between European history and Christian ideals.

The problem then may be formulated as follows. On the one hand, Jesus expected the imminent 'coming of the kingdom with power'. In the life-time of his followers Israel's hopes would be fulfilled, its sovereignty restored, sickness and want overcome. In this he was mistaken. Disaster was to befall Israel in 70 C.E.; sickness and want continue to be a deeply disturbing feature of our world. On the other hand, Jesus was possessed by a new vision of God's will for the world; in his life and actions this new openness was already being expressed and he taught that those who wished to gain life needed to follow this way. In such a vision are contained images and concepts which have indeed helped subsequent generations shape and rebuild their world. The question is: how can we appropriate such a vision, knowing what we do about the persistence of evil in the world.

This issue was raised sharply in a paper by M. Taylor, circulated to the group, which has subsequently formed the basis of his illuminating book, *Good for the Poor*. How can we go on hoping, and encouraging those who work in the field of development, when we know that while there will be 'successes' there will be an equal number of new disasters and scourges which have to be dealt with: that there is a kind of uneasy balance between the overcoming of problems and the emergence of new ones?

Accounts of Jesus' teaching which stress his expectation of an imminent end (Weiss and others) run the risk of discounting those elements in Jesus' teaching which may provide resources for ethical and social action in the present. They also rarely (here Schweitzer is an important exception) take note of the fact that Jesus, in his expectations of the future, was mistaken. On the other hand accounts like Dodd's which do attempt to show the implications of Jesus' beliefs about the kingdom for present courses of social and ethical action, in practice fail to take sufficient account of the future element in Jesus' teaching, of the stern note of judgement on 'the present age' which it contains and, again, of its mistakenness. What is required is an account of Jesus' beliefs in the future which recognises their mistakenness while at the same time *explaining* how they relate to the subsequent history of Christianity.

One way of trying to understand how Jesus' beliefs in the imminent coming of the kingdom, though mistaken, contribute to subsequent historical developments in the community of his followers, is to consider their social *function*. Belief in the coming of a new age provides the context in which new values can be articulated which are both continuous with and transcendent of the traditional values of the group. To announce a new age is also to announce the end of the present age and therefore to arouse expectations of change and renewal. It is also to claim divine sanction for such change and renewal, for it is God who ushers in the new age. That is to say, we may see millenarian beliefs as important means for engineering change in traditional societies. They enable prophetic, liminal figures who anticipate significant cultural shifts to invoke traditional sources of authority for their message of change. They are indeed in themselves mistaken. But they constitute, as it were, the rockets which lift the space craft out of the field of gravity of the old world order and which may then be discarded once it has reached its new environment.

Of course this is not the only way in which such notions function in society, but it is the one which perhaps comes closest to what Jesus effectively did when he pronounced the imminent coming of the kingdom. Subsequently, such beliefs may be appropriated by many groups for different purposes. Even those which have initially been articulated by disadvantaged groups in highly explosive social situations may later be used by dominant social groups to maintain control. Nevertheless if we look to their use in situations of rapid social change, we may venture a broad generalisation. Such beliefs are of powerful effect among groups which are largely denied access to institutional power (the control of military, political and religious and economic institutions) and who long for change, for whatever reason. Such longings may be awakened or sharpened by prophetic figures who offer the hope of a transformation of people's lives which speaks to their deepest needs. The hopes which the prophet offers may in turn articulate new values, which can be worked out in the coming cultural changes. Millenarian movements then are not specifically political. They do not work through the existing institutions. But they may well prepare the way for political action by raising people's expectations and disposing them to revolt or military insurrection. In this sense they are sometimes spoken of as 'pre-political'.[6] The wariness of such groups which modern

---

[6] One might compare and contrast the role of the millenarian prophet with that of theatre or poetry in politics. Both may be marginal or liminal phenomena which contribute sometimes very powerfully to political change. Both may be unaware of the political effects of what they are saying. But equally there are certain forms of theatre which are *self-consciously* political, which may indeed invoke particular theories of social change as justification of their work. Here it is less easy to find an

colonial administrators and Roman governors alike have shown is evidence of their awareness of the political dangers posed by such movements.

Such a reading of Jesus' millenarian beliefs and activity may help to advance our understanding in a number of ways. In the first place Jesus emerges as a millenarian prophet, a liminal figure, anticipating major changes in the cultural history of the world. By raising his people's expectations of change, by freeing his followers from bondage to the past, by articulating a vision of a new world, he opened the way for major cultural changes which have played their part in the history of the last two millenia. How significant or indeed beneficent a part is then of course a matter of debate. But the fact that Jesus was mistaken in his beliefs about the millenium is not material to that debate.

Moreover, on such a view, the fact that Jesus was mistaken in his beliefs about the end is liberating. We no longer need to attempt to make his beliefs about the end our own (as did the dialectical theologians) nor to attempt to paraphrase them (as do variously Dodd and Boff). This means, among other things, that we are released from the constraints on planning and moral effort which Weiss' view of Jesus' preaching of the kingdom had been taken to imply by many theologians. The important thing about Jesus, we can now see, is not that he announced the imminent end of the world, and that therefore all human attempts to work out a better future are at best idle, at worst rebellious and Promethean. It is not that he proclaimed that in face of the coming kingdom his followers were to do nothing but wait and watch (in this respect, as Christopher Rowland has argued, Weiss distorted the picture, anyway). The important thing, in this connection at least, is that he was a significant agent of social and cultural change, that he enabled the poor and the oppressed to find a voice and a purpose and

---

analogy within the sphere of millenarian prophecy. There are certainly figures who have political goals. In so far as they seek justification for this it is in terms of some theological account of the social changes which are envisaged, rather than a strictly political one. Even here, of course, one could argue about the meaning of 'strictly political'.

a vision of a new world to live and die for, as he was prepared to live and die for it himself.

What this means practically is that those who seek to follow him should continue to work to realise his vision of a just and open society *as best they may*. Many, not least those for whom Boff writes, may still have little more political power than those who first heard Jesus. Their task will be to keep alive that vision of openness and justice, as many have indeed done by seeking to embody it in basic ecclesial communities, often with great courage and self-sacrifice. This may indeed mean that from their position they can do little more than post signs for the kingdom, point to a reality beyond the harshness of their present world.

However, in so far as Christians do enjoy some measure of political power, then they must surely use it to embody within their society at large the values which Jesus proclaimed. To opt out of using one's power to work for greater peace and justice would be to connive at present injustice. Christian activism is not, or need not be, a flight from the Gospel; it is the proper response to Jesus' command to seek the kingdom of God and its righteousness by those who have the means of influencing the course of their societies. Even those Christians who do have a measure of power to embody the values of the kingdom in their own societies will have to ask themselves how far they can properly plan and work within the existing constitutional, political and economic arrangements, how far they will wish to use their power to work for fundamental change in those arrangements. In this connection they will need to listen seriously to the voice of those like Boff who accuse the powerful nations of the world of systematically exploiting and impoverishing the 'two thirds world'.

What I have suggested so far is that had Boff been writing his essay at the present he could have found much better allies in the field of New Testament scholarship than he did. The scholars to whom he turned were in important respects both Lutheran and individualists. Since both these terms are very broad let me specify the senses in which I intend them here. They were Lutheran in two respects: first in that they regarded Christian faith and life as fundamentally a liberation from Law and therefore found it difficult to see Jesus as in any way concerned with laying the basis of a new society with new laws and constitutional arrangements; second in that they regarded Christian faith as essentially a private matter which had a bearing on one's political life and responsibilities only in so far as it enabled one to become truly oneself and therefore free to act rationally in the world. This of course relates quite directly to an individualism which regards human acts as only accidentally related to the social context in which they occur. On such a view salvation is ultimately a matter between God and man or woman alone; its societal implications are secondary.

By contrast the approaches to the New Testament which I have been sketching, not least because of their indebtedness to social anthropology and the sociology of knowledge, take seriously the interrelationships between individual human identity and the society in which a particular person is nurtured and receives his or her formation. New Testament historians working in this area are interested in the ways in which ideas contribute to the development of societies and also are shaped by different groups and interests within those societies. They seek to elucidate the social function of ideas and beliefs, and also the way in which ideas may be manipulated by different groups within society. On such a view then Jesus is to be seen as a figure with a particular role in his own society (that of a liminal figure who anticipates change) whose ideas may subsequently receive a variety of treatments which may in part subvert his original intentions.

This in turn opens up the possibility of an understanding of the Law which is quite different from the Lutheran. Jesus differs from the Pharisees not in that he abominates Law as something fundamentally opposed to grace; but in that he resists, in a way which might well seem imprudent, Pharisaic attempts to set tighter boundaries around the group. Such perspectives applied to the study of Christian origins may provide valuable assistance to those who have a vital interest in the interaction between belief and practice and who also need to give a critical account of the diversity of Christian political attitudes and beliefs, conservative and radical.

However, such perspectives, while they may serve some of Boff's goals, also bring problems for Christian thinkers and activists. Some of these problems arise directly from the functionalism of the social historical accounts that are being offered; some are inherent in many if not all truly historical approaches to the subject.

The first question about functionalism can be treated quite quickly. The kind of functionalist account of Jesus' millenarian beliefs that we have just sketched out is useful in directing attention to the ways in which beliefs interact with, are shaped by and shape, society. It directs attention to the actual social function of a belief, e.g. of precipitating social change, which may well be different from the functions intended by the one who uttered it. It is easy to assume that such a treatment of beliefs is indifferent to their sense or content, what they are actually saying about the nature of the world. This is however neither necessary nor desirable. In order to understand how particular beliefs, e.g. in the millenium, function, we must clearly discover as much as we can, not only about what they meant to the prophet himself, but also to those who heard him. In Jesus' case we need to know not only when he thought the kingdom would come, but what kind of kingdom he thought it would be, what kind of a God he proclaimed. Functionalist accounts of theological beliefs, that is to say, need to take the *theological content* of such beliefs seriously if they are to offer as full an explanation as possible of their function.

What is more troubling about such accounts is the way they suggest that Jesus was mistaken in what he believed, for this seems to conflict directly with the biblical presentation of Jesus as teacher and Son of God. This takes us to the second set of questions: how such social historical views of Jesus can be reconciled with the views of him to be found in the biblical texts.

One of the most obvious questions here is this. In what way do our historical reconstructions of Jesus' life and thought provide or contribute to ethical *motives* for Christian believers today? Why should the fact that Jesus of Nazareth thought that it was better to keep open the lines of communication to those outside the group constitute or otherwise generate a reason for our acting one way or another?

Boff's answer to this is threefold. First, he appeals to a prior belief in the resurrection as the divine vindication of all that Jesus stood for and therefore as the ground for Christian belief in an ultimate realisation of Jesus' aims in history (pp. 122f.); second, he offers an historical account of what Jesus stood for; and third, he argues from similarities between Jesus' situation and the situation in Latin America to particular courses of action to be followed by the Churches there.

Thus his approach is by no means a purely historical one: it rests centrally on his claims about the resurrection. Nevertheless, without his historical reconstruction of the social and political intentions of Jesus it would not actually generate any reasons for Christian action. The resurrection signifies that death is overcome and that a new kind of human life begins which will ultimately triumph; the ethical implications of such claims can however be derived only from their conjunction with other claims about what Jesus actually taught and did. And this requires an historical enquiry into the gospel records.

But the question now is: why, if Boff's approach is based on the New Testament belief in the resurrection, does he not also accept the New Testament accounts of Jesus, of his nature, mission, ethical authority for the Church and so on? Paul, when he wants to make an ethical point, appeals not to Jesus as a millenarian prophet (hardly a concept he would have immediately recognised, even if it might be applied, in some respects at least, to him, himself), but, e.g. to the early Christian belief in the incarnation of the pre-existent Lord (2 Cor. 8.7ff.; Phil. 2.5ff.). Some would argue that it would be better to remain within the theological perspectives of the New Testament rather than to attempt what is at best a highly revisable reconstruction of the meaning of Jesus' life from perspectives which are in many ways quite alien to it. Certainly to mix the two approaches, as Boff does, might seem to be having the worst of both worlds. It lacks the coherence and certainty which a simple rendering of the New Testament witness would command once its authority is recognised; and it introduces elements which are not open to rational scrutiny, into an argument which is otherwise so open. Would a thorough-going social anthropological enquiry not require an examination of the Christian belief in the resurrection itself, seeing it in the context of a considerable history stretching back to the second century B.C.E., would a fully fledged biblical theology not need to remain within the perspective of faith (of the resurrection faith) which informed the New Testament authors themselves?

It is I think not to be denied that a thorough-going historical approach to the New Testament would indeed pose questions about the nature of the early Christian belief in the resurrection of Jesus, similar to those which we have been putting about Jesus' belief in the imminent coming of the End. How does such a belief in the resurrection function within the different communities which made up the early Church? In what sense does it serve to create new communities, to integrate divided ones, to order or to legitimate a particular type of social grouping? Questions equally might be asked about the genesis of Jewish belief in the resurrection. It emerges at a time in Jewish history when the Jewish religion has been proscribed by a foreign overlord and when therefore devout observers of the law are suffering for their piety. In such a context belief in rewards for the righteous in this world is severely challenged; the emergence of a belief in rewards in an after-life when the dead shall be raised (Dan. 12.2) becomes intelligible.

To point this out is to show how different and indeed potentially inimical are the various components of Boff's answer. Is this a reason for recommending an abandonment of the project altogether? Should he, and indeed other Liberation Theologians, turn aside from their fascination with the historical Jesus and seek instead to derive ethical injunctions from the (authoritative?) theological concepts of the Bible itself rather than from the *uncertain constructs* of our historical imagination? Or should he indeed, as some might suspect he already does, abandon the theological nature of his enterprise and declare openly his commitment to a particular reading of history?

Such questions come naturally enough to theologians, schooled as they are in a long tradition of searching for certainty in truth. The uncertainty of the historian's findings and the existence of competing views which nonetheless command respect within the scholarly community seem to make it impossible to build such findings into the theologian's palace. The theologian deals in certain and assured truth and such truth is one. As Lessing put it in a famous dictum, expressing a conviction of rational philosophers and theologians alike (though not I suspect his own conviction): 'Accidental truths of history can never become the proof of necessary truths of reason'. On the geometrical (Spinozist) view of truth, theology and history do not mix.

But here, as Janet Soskice has reminded us,[7] we need to pause for more than a moment. When theologians speak of truth as one and certain, they often imply that such truth is God-given (as opposed to 'man-made'), a possession therefore which is beyond criticism and revision. Whether such a possession would be good for one, was called into question by Lessing. Such possession, he said, makes us lazy and arrogant. Whether we can in any way claim that the Bible or the theological, doctrinal tradition contains such truth, has been questioned in a sustained and damaging way by historical critical studies of the Bible and doctrine since at least the time of Spinoza himself. The Bible contains great diversity; it is clearly the work of human communities and writers; the different theological views to be found in the Bible, like the different accounts of the same events which it offers, overlap, complement and contradict each other. Nor is there, unsurprisingly, any unanimity in the many accounts which 'Biblical Theologians' offer of the biblical writings.

This is not to deny that the Bible represents reality in some important and indeed special (even privileged) way. It is rather to assert, as the sheer diversity of views makes evident, that representations of reality in the Bible need to be complemented and revised in the light of each other, and indeed of representations of reality outside the Bible. One has to allow that what is in the Bible is revisable and also that different, themselves revisable, views of the same reality are also interesting and informative. Nor should we be unduly

---

[7]In discussion in the group and more fully in her *Metaphors and Religious Language* (Oxford, 1985).

worried about such emphasis on the revisability of both biblical and extra-biblical views of reality. What we say about things may be true, may tell us something about what is the case, even though we shall find ourselves wanting to revise such accounts at a later date.

What such a view does deny is that the biblical texts are to be seen as the only way in which the reality to which they point could be represented; as it denies that they offer a definitive or exhaustive account of that reality. There should in a way be nothing so very surprising about such denials. The apophatic theology of the Cappadocians and Thomas' discussions of the analogical nature of theological predication both argue that any attempt to represent the divine mystery in human language is limited.

What does this mean in relation to Boff's bringing together of social historical accounts of Jesus' life and teaching with biblical or doctrinal claims about his resurrection? Simply, that once we allow that neither view has a monopoly of the truth then there is in principle no reason why we should not entertain both sets of claims and attempt to see how they may complement, criticise and enrich each other. At the very least, we may say, there is no reason why a social historical view of Jesus' life should not help to fill out our understanding of what it was that Jesus believed and taught and thus to enrich our understanding of claims that God raised him from the dead.

Importantly, too, a readiness to accept that there may be different ways of representing reality, different perspectives on the truth,[8] helps us to appreciate a further feature of Boff's account, namely his claim that the historical reality of Jesus is both illuminated by and also illuminates the historical situation of the poor in South America. Seen from their perspective, the story of Jesus, which comes to us in its by no means harmonisable narratives, comes into sharp relief. To look at it from this perspective is to see something which other perspectives,

---

[8]Here I think of a paper kindly shown me by Janet Soskice entitled, 'The truth looks different from here'.

including a 'universal' biblical theology, might have screened us from. Such 'local theologies', which may be assisted by the methods of social historical criticism, need to be recognised as having a 'voice' among the many voices of the Bible and the tradition.

All this is to do no more than to plead that such social historical accounts should be allowed to interact with the views of Jesus which are to be found in the New Testament writings, including the claim that he was raised from the dead. How they might interact is of course a much larger subject.

Clearly on some views of the two they are wholly incompatible. A social historical account, just because it is historical and therefore based on analogy with human experience, cannot contemplate claims about the raising of the dead. Certainly if one takes the view that such claims represent the whole truth and nothing but the truth, offer, that is to say, an exhaustive and unrevisable account of the matter, then it is hard to see how there could be any complementarity between the two.

Once however we recognise the particularity of the Bible's cultural and historical perspective, the position changes. We can recognise then that the language of resurrection, of final judgement, of the coming of the Son of Man gives expression to a system of beliefs which enabled people to make sense of their world, to offer some representation of its reality, to regulate their lives. It enabled them to see the suffering and oppression in their society as neither ineradicable nor acceptable; it gave them hope in a better world; it expressed a deep faith in an ultimate reality to which such things were inimical. One day all tears would be wiped away, the oppressors cast down, the humble and meek exalted. Such beliefs, as Paul and the Gospels variously testify, provided a powerful way of preaching the Gospel and of narrating the story of Jesus. In him, not least in his cross and resurrection, they saw the beginnings of the fulfilment of such hopes and the expression of the reconciling love of God. His resurrection from the dead was a token that the dark forces of the world could be and would be overcome.

Obviously that is the most inadequate of sketches of how such beliefs were articulated in the early Christian communities.

Nevertheless perhaps it is sufficient to allow us to make some modest suggestions about how such an account of Jesus' resurrection might complement the social historical account of Jesus as millenarian prophet that we have proposed. Put very simply the question is this: how do we relate two stories, one which sees Jesus as an important agent of cultural change, the other which sees him as the agent of the divine purposes whereby the world will be ultimately set to rights?

I want to make three points. Firstly, it follows from what I have said above that we shall not want to reject one account and simply uphold the other. We shall rather try to allow both stories to shape our understanding of the world and to stir us into action. Each story will complement and qualify the other.

Second then, let us consider how the biblical story complements and qualifies the millenarian one. It reminds us most powerfully of the death and suffering of Jesus. If Jesus was the agent of social and cultural change, he was so as the one who was rejected and mocked, condemned to a shameful and tortured death. He was the victim of dark forces of violence and power, betrayed by his friends and handed over to an alien ruler. Social and political change is not just a matter of more and better planning. As many Christians could testify, it is the elusive prize of a long road of sorrows, where each gain seems to be met with fresh set-backs and sorrows. Hope for change and improvement, for freedom and liberation can come not from confidence in one's control over the processes of change, but from a deeper faith in the ultimate vindication of the good. The 'mistakenness' of millenarian beliefs, that is to say, may not be fatal. It may lead us to revise what is being said, in some such way as I have just suggested, as indeed it has been revised constantly throughout the course of human history.

Lastly, what does the story of the millenarian prophet have to add to the biblical stories of Jesus' death and resurrection? It reminds us that it is a story which has its analogue in the concrete struggles of men and women through history. That what is told as a story to end all history is itself a story to make history, which has given sense and direction to those caught up in the struggle for right and dignity, for the values of love and openness. It brings the gospel story into our world, liberating it from its theological captivity and privatisation. For Liberation Theologians to abandon their interest in the 'historical Jesus' would in a sense be for them to abandon precisely those elements in their theology which bring the gospel stories alive. As they indeed insist, it is the reading of the two 'texts' alongside each other, the text of the Gospel with the 'text' of the struggle of the poor of South America, which renews and invigorates the Christian vision of God and the world.

# Index of Names

# Index of Biblical References